Varieties of Capitalism and Europeanization

Varieties of Capitalism and Europeanization

National Response Strategies to the Single European Market

Georg Menz

OXFORD
UNIVERSITY PRESS

OXFORD

UNIVERSITY PRESS

Great Clarendon Street, Oxford OX2 6DP

Oxford University Press is a department of the University of Oxford.
It furthers the University's objective of excellence in research, scholarship,
and education by publishing worldwide in

Oxford New York

Auckland Cape Town Dar es Salaam Hong Kong Karachi
Kuala Lumpur Madrid Melbourne Mexico City Nairobi
New Delhi Shanghai Taipei Toronto

With offices in

Argentina Austria Brazil Chile Czech Republic France Greece
Guatemala Hungary Italy Japan Poland Portugal Singapore
South Korea Switzerland Thailand Turkey Ukraine Vietnam

Oxford is a registered trade mark of Oxford University Press
in the UK and in certain other countries

Published in the United States
by Oxford University Press Inc., New York

British Library Cataloguing in Publication Data

Data available

Library of Congress Cataloging in Publication Data

Data available

Typeset by SPI Publisher Services, Pondicherry, India
Printed in Great Britain
on acid-free paper by
Biddles Ltd., King's Lynn, Norfolk

ISBN 0-19-927386-3

1 3 5 7 9 10 8 6 4 2

Contents

Introduction

The future shape of politico-economic governance in Europe has attracted considerable academic interest and has spawned an often vociferous public debate throughout Europe about how different varieties of capitalism can, should, or indeed must adapt to cope with new demands, new demographic realities, and an increasingly interlinked global economy. While the entire decade was one of epochal changes and transformations, often at breakneck speed, the mid-1990s were a particularly exciting time to have studied in Europe. In France, the austerity measures imposed by the Juppe government led to widespread protests and a strike, which almost paralyzed public life for a few weeks in the fall of 1995, leading some observers to draw parallels between the *refus* and the 1968 protest, which toppled General de Gaulle. Germany, meanwhile, underwent an intensive process of brooding soul-searching (*Nabelschau*), experiencing the challenges involved in reunification and witnessing a heated debate about whether *Modell Deutschland* required a neoliberal overhaul. Meanwhile, the Netherlands implemented sweeping reforms in social and labor policy that attracted considerable attention and interest abroad. Even in Austria, otherwise renowned for its (postwar) consensus-style politics and general stability, the Grand Coalition government collapsed in late 1995 over a disagreement on austerity measures in the budget, introduced to meet the Maastricht criteria.

Aside from these macropolitical developments linked to the process of European integration, in the mid-1990s the phenomenon of posted workers became clearly visible in Germany, and Berlin in particular. While the region was undergoing a spectacular boom in construction activity, linked to the move of the German capital there and substantial efforts to position the city as an economic hub in Central Europe, unemployment among domestic construction workers was soaring. In the heart of the newly unified city, Potsdamer Platz, the gigantic construction of a new office and entertainment center was carried out by Polish and Portuguese workers, toiling away for a fraction of German wages. Was this nineteenth-century Manchester-style capitalism at the heart of the new Berlin Republic? Was this still Rhineland capitalism or perhaps a symbol of a movement towards a new type of *Spree Capitalism*? No such mass wave of posted workers entered Germany's neighboring countries with comparatively high wages, such as Denmark, the Netherlands, Belgium, or Sweden. What could account for these different outcomes? And why was it that in Germany, a country traditionally characterized by a relatively potent labor movement, such substandard wages had become possible? These initial questions led me to pursue an inquiry that culminated in this book. It examines the wage regulation for posted workers under the auspices of the liberalization of service provision in Austria, France, the Netherlands, and Germany, as well as other Northern European high-wage countries. Its central argument is that the internal configuration of domestic actor coalitions is a crucial variable in accounting for these wage differentials.

Having spent a brief stint as a construction worker on a house renovation project in Berlin's Prenzlauer Berg district in the late 1990s, I moved to Pittsburgh shortly thereafter to commence writing my doctoral thesis that formed the basis for this book. Along the way, there have been a number of people and institutions who have gone out of their way to support and advise me and to whom I am greatly indebted. I would like to thank first and foremost my key advisor and mentor Dr. Alberta Sbragia who has encouraged me to start, pursue, and finish this project. She provided excellent feedback, useful suggestions, and constructive criticism and has served as a constant source of motivation. I would also like to thank Dr. B. Guy Peters, co-chair of this dissertation for his insightful comments and his 'just-in-time' letters of recommendation. Dr. Mark Hallerberg provided a thorough and rigorous critique of the various 'first drafts' and encouraged me further to include additional variables, additional countries, and, indeed, additional lines of reasoning. Last but certainly not least, I owe a great debt to Dr. Reinhard Heinisch whose invaluable insights into the intricate details of Austrian politics and neocorporatist theory more generally I have tapped into on numerous occasions.

The United States Department of Education, the French Ministry of Foreign Affairs (*Bourse Chateaubriand*), the European Union Center at the University of Pittsburgh, the Austrian Nationality Room at the University of Pittsburgh and the German Academic Exchange Service (DAAD Scholarship) have all provided financial support towards my doctoral studies at various stages, for which I am also very grateful. A light teaching load during my first year at Goldsmiths College (courtesy of the head of department Dr. Carl Levy) and a position as Visiting Research Associate at the University of Pittsburgh permitted the revision of the dissertation into a book manuscript. I also received the Best Dissertation Award of the European Union Studies Association (of the USA) and would like to express my gratitude for this honor.

Dominic Byatt and Claire Croft at Oxford University Press were very helpful and encouraging in processing the manuscript.

There were a number of individuals with whom I held fruitful discussions about this project. I would like to thank Patrick Le Gales, Guy Groux, and Richard Balme at the Fondation Nationale des Sciences Politiques in Paris, and Jacques Vilrockx and Janine Goetschy in Brussels.

In Germany, I would like to thank Werner Eichhorst, Wolfgang Streeck, and Roswitha Pioch at the Max Planck Institut in Cologne, Georg Worthmann and Klaus Zuehlke-Robinet at the Wissenschaftszentrum Nordrhein-Westfalen in Gelsenkirchen, and Claus Offe at the Humboldt-Universität in Berlin. In Austria, thanks are due to Peter Biegelbauer at the Institut für Höhere Studien in Vienna and Anton Pelinka at the Universität Innsbruck, and in the Netherlands to Marc van der Meer at the Universiteit van Amsterdam.

Over the course of 2000–2, I logged some major mileage and conducted a series of interviews with officials at ministries, unions, and employer association in Paris, Bonn, Frankfurt, Berlin, The Hague, Amsterdam, and Vienna as well as Brussels, Copenhagen, Stockholm, Oslo, and Luxembourg. Their time and efforts are much appreciated as are their insights into the policymaking process I relied upon heavily.

On a more personal note, I would like to thank my parents and siblings for their support and encouragement.

London
September 2004   Georg Menz

European Liberalization, National Varieties of Capitalism, and Re-regulation

With supranationalization of social policy and re-nationalization of economic policy equally unlikely in the internationally liberalized European political economy, it will above all be national industrial relations that will have to deal with the pressures for social re-regulation that arise from the operation of an international market.... Future research ... will have to establish the true potential of national re-regulatory responses to international liberalization. (Streeck 1998)

'Ditte is 'ne heisse Kiste !' [That's a hot-button issue!]
(Representative of Berlin State Senate in an interview with the author on the issue of posted workers, Berlin, 1999)

Workers Across Borders

European integration has tremendously advanced both its pace and scope over the past 25 years. The Single Market project at once revitalized and 'dusted off' the original ambitions and aims contained in the 1957 Treaty of Rome. This resurgence of the European project, itself heavily colored by the renaissance of liberal ideology of the 1980, has captured considerable scholarly interest and public concern. European Union (EU)-led market liberalization, targeted at guaranteeing the four freedoms of capital, goods, service, and labor mobility, has created considerable pressures for change, adaptation, and remodeling of the parameters and institutions that constitute the basis of Europe's diverse systems of politico-economic governance. In short, 'when Europe hits home' (Börzel and Risse 2000) the direct and indirect repercussions of the European project's liberalizing impetus can be considerable.

In the early 1990s, shortly following reunification, the German construction sector experienced a boom. Yet, somewhat perplexingly, unemployment among German construction workers was soaring. Despite the decision to move the capital from Bonn to Berlin, generous tax incentives to renovate and construct buildings in the new *Länder*, and an obvious need for the renovation of the many decrepit apartment blocks of eastern Berlin, this region, along with other eastern cities such as Leipzig and Dresden, was particularly affected by rising numbers of unemployed construction workers. A casual visitor to the myriad construction sites in and around Berlin could have been forgiven for being slightly taken aback by the Babylonian multitude of languages heard there. While it is true that the construction sector had historically attracted a large number of migrant workers from Turkey, Yugoslavia, and Italy, just as elsewhere in Northern Europe, the novelty of Irish, English, and Portuguese voices was remarkable. 20,000 workers from various EU member states were toiling away on German construction sites in 1993. By 1995, that number had risen to 132,000. All of them were 'posted' or temporarily sent to Germany by subcontractors, registered in other European low-wage countries like Portugal, Greece, Britain, and Ireland. In addition, large numbers of workers from Central and Eastern Europe were employed as subcontractors as well, ostensibly within the framework of bilateral labor agreements, but in practice often employed illegally and subject to abusive practices and exploitative wages (Werner 1996; Menz 2001). The fact that the political center of the Berlin Republic was quite literally built by non-Germans who received a fraction of standard German wages, despite a tradition of presumably powerful trade unionism, might be taken as a very powerful symbol of the impact of EU-induced liberalization. Irish and Portuguese employees were paid according to the standards of their home countries, implying in the latter case an hourly wage of one-sixth of what their German colleagues were taking home.

Remarkable to the casual observer, other high-wage countries such as Austria, Sweden, and Denmark did not experience such massive influx of 'posted workers' from elsewhere in Europe, despite major construction projects being undertaken there, too. How was this possible? How was this legal? How could Portuguese workers be constructing and renovating government ministry buildings in central Berlin and receive such pitiful wages? Equally baffling is another question: Why were there no similar developments in Paris, Vienna, or indeed Stockholm?

European Liberalization and National Re-regulation

To Euro-skeptics, critical of the liberal nature of the Single Market, the issue of posted workers seemed to encapsulate their worst fears. The liberalization of service provision, one of Maastricht's 'four freedoms' that was already contained in the 1957 Treaty of Rome, abolishes the national regulation of market access. Higher-wage Northern European countries cannot ban cheaper competitors from southern and western member states. This instance posed a perfect example of 'negative integration' (Scharpf 1991, earlier: Taylor 1983) that abolished and undermined member states' capacity to regulate their labor market and social policy. No 'positive integration' was forthcoming, either, since there was no Europe-wide regulation of (minimum) wages. Henceforth, workers sent to Germany by Portuguese or Irish companies were subject to contracts signed under Portuguese or Irish law. In effect, this created 'islands of foreign law' (Hanau 1996) on the territory of the receiving country. The fact that Germany—and much less so the Netherlands—was the primary target destination of workers posted under the auspices of the EU liberalization of service provision seemed to confound fears that the EU was helping to undermine further the foundations of the bastion of highly organized 'Rhineland capitalism.' Critics on the left feared that by creating a two-tier labor market structure in Germany, the EU's liberalizing impetus was guilty of jeopardizing workers' rights and wages.

However, liberal voices challenged the allegation that European deregulation enabled 'wage dumping.' Instead, it was suggested that the case of Portuguese subcontractors sending their workers to Berlin, Vienna, or Copenhagen should be regarded as an instance of the Single Market at work. Portuguese companies used their key competitive advantage; low wages imply low costs for construction projects. European integration was meant to unleash greater competitive pressure; consumers in high-wage Northern European countries should welcome a downward cost spiral for construction projects. Finally, the dormant and rarely exploited freedom of transnational service provision was having a real impact.

Clearly, the repercussions of this aspect of Europeanization created both winners and losers. It unleashed heated debates on the nature of the Single Market. It also makes for a marvelous case study of the impact of top-down

Europeanization and the potential for re-regulatory response strategies. Is this indeed an instance of social dumping? Is it a case of the downward spiral or the regulatory race to the bottom, fears which lie at the heart of center-left skepticism vis-à-vis the EU? Here, this fear seems to be borne out: Portuguese workers receive substandard wages, putting unionized high-wage German workers out of business. By contrast, economic liberals can claim that legitimate competition over price levels and more pronounced competition are precisely what the Single Market promised to deliver.

This volume examines this case study of the practical and very concrete impact of Europeanization, and the way in which a sample of diverse organized European varieties of capitalism may respond to and cope with top-down EU-led economic liberalization by devising *national response strategies*. It therefore contributes to the unfolding debate on Europeanization, while seeking to challenge and amend some of the insights this strand of literature has generated so far. In analyzing the way in which attempts were made to re-regulate the EU liberalization of service provision, simple predictions of convergence on a deregulated, liberal model of politico-economic governance are questioned. Such fairly pessimistic accounts dominated the 'first wave' in the renaissance of comparative political economy. In providing a more nuanced detailed analysis that draws on the institutional differences between different European varieties of capitalism and highlights their importance in affecting national re-regulatory response strategies, this study shares more in common with 'second wave' efforts in this field that stress continued resilience of distinct institutional configurations of politico-economic governance, notwithstanding the considerable external and internal pressures associated with Europeanization and globalization. Where the analysis parts way with some of the efforts in this vein, however, is in emphasizing that adherence to a pattern of 'divergence within convergence' is not equally shared across Europe. Two points deserve emphasis. The German political and economic system generates a liberal, business-friendly re-regulation that seals in a two-tier wage structure. More generally, employer organizations in a number of European countries prove their ability to imprint their preference on the policy outcome. This book thus makes a contribution to *both* bodies of literature, while demonstrating how a link between them can be established, thus establishing avenues for future research straddling this divide.

How is European integration affecting the national regulatory capacities of politico-economic systems of governance or different varieties of capitalism? EU market-building is said to proceed 'negatively', that is, through the abolition or at least undermining of national regulatory room for maneuver. However, challenging previous accounts of Europeanization, I argue that some potential for national re-regulation does exist. Is the impact of the liberal deregulatory Single Market project somehow filtered? I argue that powerful interest groups, such as trade unions and employer organizations that are a core component of the institutional configuration of the divergent systems of capitalism in Europe do indeed exert significant influence on national attempts of coping with EU-led market liberalization. Can such national re-regulation be consistent with the spirit and letter of the Single Market? Given the relative weakness of EU level labor and social policy, member states are induced to take (re-)regulatory matters into their own hands, producing a complex 'patchwork' pattern of regulation. 'Negative integration' or European deregulation may be countered and partly obscured by national re-regulatory response strategies.

This volume explores the impact of one aspect of the European Single Market, the *liberalization of service provision* (LSP), and its re-regulation at the national level in France, Austria, Germany, and the Netherlands, while also considering developments in other high-wage Northern European countries that are subject to the LSP: Belgium, Luxembourg, Denmark, Sweden, Finland, and Norway. Why is this often neglected core aspect of the Single Market relevant? Companies registered anywhere in the EU now have the right to provide their services anywhere else in the EU. This has profound consequences, which became obvious in the case of the Portuguese construction workers 'posted' to Germany.

In the absence of any EU regulation, contracting companies could refer to the terms of an obscure international multilateral treaty of 1980, permitting them to choose between the labor law and conditions of the sending *or* the receiving country. Obviously, service sector companies preferred to choose Portuguese over German regulations, since it meant paying only Portuguese wages to their workers. The only exception is a hard core of labor laws, constituting what in international law is considered part of the *ordre public* (public order), which applies to *all* workers in a given country, regardless of European deregulation. Thus, paying Portuguese wages is legal, but ignoring laws on working hours, like the French 35-hour week, is not.

Bridging the Gap: 'Europeanization' Affecting National Models of Governance

Scholarly attention has shifted relatively recently from exploring the underlying dynamics of the European integration process (Moravcsik 1998) to a focus on the top-down effects of EU membership on state–society relations, domestic policies and institutions (Héritier et al. 1996; Schmidt 1996b; Knill and Lehmkuhl 1999; Cowles et al. 2001; Knill 2001; Héritier et al. 2001; Börzel 2002, Radaelli and Featherstone 2003). In an early definition, 'Europeanization' is conceptualized as 'a process reorienting the direction and shape of politics to the degree that EU political and economic dynamics become part of the organizational logic of national politics and policymaking' (Ladrech 1994: 69). Unfortunately, the concept has since become overstretched and employed to use varying and often conflicting scenarios. I concentrate on the 'central penetration of national systems of governance' (Olsen 2002) or the top-down impact of 'when Europe hits home' (Börzel and Risse 2000). However, I concur with Helen Wallace's (2000: 370) observation that 'Europeanization is a shaped process, not a passively encountered process'. In analyzing the impact of Europeanization on the policy domain of labor and social policy, I insist that there is room for national response strategies or bottom-up processes of Europeanization. The study therefore responds to Olsen's (2002: 933) query 'what determines the responses, adaptability and robustness of domestic institutions, including their ability to ignore, buffer, redefine or exploit external European-level pressures'. In a useful summary of the state of the art, the same author proposes *experiential learning* and *competitive selection* as two responsive processes, whereas Radaelli (2000, 2003) previously distilled four types of national level responses from the literature (cf. Cowles and Risse 2001): inertia, absorption, transformation and retrenchment. Absorption, defined as 'change as adaptation', consists of accommodating imposed policy changes. If the more fundamental underlying paradigmatic logic of political behavior is being modified, this constitutes transformation.

The problem with these categories of Europeanization is that they may not fit all policy fields equally well. Indeed, many of the empirical studies in this field draw on the field of environmental policy (Knill and Lenschow 1998; Knill 2001; Jordan 2002). However, in policy domains such as economic, labor, and social policy, a conceptual framework that applies to the compliance or lack thereof with EU directives is not necessarily appropriate. In these policy fields, Europeanization has commonly proceeded 'negatively' (Taylor 1983; Scharpf 1996), that is, through the abolition of barriers to transnational flow of labor and services. Even the modest pro-active 'positive' social policy efforts of the 1970s focused predominantly on the promotion of labor mobility (Geyer 2000). Consequently, the basic dilemma in social and labor market policy consists of the inevitable clash between efforts to construct a Single Market and the national regulation of these domains (Rhodes 1991: 252ff.). Here, the threshold for 'absorption' might be too low and inclusive, while the definitional standards for 'transformation' might be rarely reached. Previous scholarly efforts have emphasized that national regulatory environments may or may not be affected by top-down Europeanization (Knill and Lenschow 1998; Cowles et al. 2001; Héritier et al. 2001) depending on the 'goodness of fit', that is, the level of compatibility between existing and EU-induced regulations (Héritier et al. 1996). It is questionable to what extent this concept can be usefully applied to market-making fields such as labor and social policy, given that the deregulatory implications of intra-EU labor mobility and service provision both fundamentally undermine the regulatory environment of member states. In addition, the definition of 'fit' is quite vague anyway (Radaelli 2000), often specifying only poorly and *post hoc* what may or may not be considered as such. The concept is also slightly static, since the EU impact may indeed be defining for fragile or even disintegrating domestic institutions.

National responses to top-down Europeanization in the policy fields of labor and social policy are colored by the internal institutional and organizational characteristics of unions and employers, embedded in national systems of political economy and industrial relations. This argument advances the recently formulated insight that the impact of Europeanization is conditioned by the changes of the strategic position of domestic actors (Dimitrova and Steunenberg 2000; Knill 2001). I argue that the organizational power, including government access, of domestic interest groups in the 'pre-liberalization stage' (Heritier et al. 2001) *combined with these actors' preferences* critically shape the overall policy outcome. In market-related policy fields, European negative integration undermines national regulation. Unlike environmental policy, which is a common empirical field in the Europeanization literature, in social and labor market policy Europeanization is therefore not primarily a matter of implementing EU directives, but of *coping with and responding to* the liberalizing effects of European integration. Given the neocorporatist legacy of continental Europe, 'dominant actor coalitions' (Knill and Lehmkuhl 2002: 26off.) and 'informal veto players' (Heritier et al. 2001) will almost always be present. What is decisive for the regulatory outcome is hence not the presence or absence of such coalitions per se. It is more fruitful to analyze *both* the organizational power of interest groups to assess whether and how they can shape national re-regulation *and* to examine their preference. This point is embraced by analysts suggesting an examination of domestic actors beliefs (Kohler-Koch 1999). Returning to Radaelli's (2000) four categories, we need to assess whether the outcome of Europeanization might be *inertia, accommodation* (Netherlands), *transformation* (Germany), or *retrenchment* (Austria and France). The outcome, I suggest, depends on both the relative strength on relevant interest associations and their attitude versus EU-induced liberalization. There is no 'regulatory competition' at stake here, nor are domestic actors' beliefs decisively shaped by the EU. In contrast to Radaelli (2003:42), I maintain that the way in which national systems respond after the initial domestic equilibrium has been challenged by Europeanization can be predicted *ex ante*.

While national re-regulatory efforts must not collide with the underlying principles of the Single Market, domestic level interest groups may nevertheless become active in the formulation of national response strategies. Knill and Lehmkuhl (2002: 26off.) point out that EU-induced change in the national regulatory environment will most likely occur if there is no domestic dominant actor coalition. Change will occur, however, if such dominant actor coalition embraces the impetus from the EU. Strong actors exist in the field of labor and social policy in most continental European states due to the pervasive neocorporatist heritage. Since there is no prediction as to 'how the new equilibrium must look' (Knill and Lehmkuhl 1999:10) following the impact of EU liberalization, 'the changing distribution of resources (and ultimately power) between domestic actors' (Radaelli 2000) becomes pivotal. The question of Europeanization here thus does not concern 'compatibility' or 'goodness of fit', but rather the distribution of power amongst relevant domestic interest groups, which *can* be predicted, Radaelli's (2000) scepticism notwithstanding. What matters, then, is whether unions or employers are organizationally powerful enough to influence national re-regulation that will either be protectionist, seeking to re-establish national authority, or liberal, enhancing the EU-induced liberalization.

Organizational Power of Unions and Employers Shape National Response Strategies

The organizational and institutional power of relevant interest associations is embedded within different models of politico-economic

governance. This insight has been elaborated in the context of the literature on varieties of capitalism in the (re-)emerging subfield of comparative
political economy (Albert 1991; Crouch and Streeck 1997; Kitschelt et al.
1999; Coates 2000; Scharpf and Schmidt 2001; Hall and Soskice 2001; Sharp
and Schmidt 2002; Yamamura and Streeck 2001, 2003; Watson 2003; Blyth
2003; Hay 2004; earlier: Polanyi 1944; Shonfield 1965; Zysman 1983). While
early efforts have been pessimistic about the prospects for highly organized
and regulated social market economies to avoid succumbing to the pressures of convergence and resembling the Anglo-Saxon liberal variety of
capitalism (Streeck 1996), more recent efforts stress continuing divergence
(Hall and Soskice 2001) and highlight the importance of domestic institutions that filter the external impact and help condition the adaptation
process. Other analysts have pointed out that though some institutions
and mechanisms of organized capitalism might be too useful to discard
(Hall and Soskice 2001), they are radically reoriented in their function and
come to serve the goal of ensuring global competitiveness, a function
termed 'competitive corporatism' (Rhodes 1997).

However, the comparative political economy literature has been
strongly influenced by developments in international political economy,
especially the debate on globalization, and has not previously systematically utilized the insights generated by the Europeanization literature. In
fact, the role of the EU as a catalyst of change in the fields of economic and
labor policy is often underestimated. Critics on the left accuse the EU of
being an agent of globalization, eradicating national room for maneuver
through the Maastricht criteria (Hay 2004). However, far from ringing in
convergence, in designing national re-regulatory responses, different domestic actor coalitions will produce different outcomes. The nature and
power of such actor coalitions will hinge on the organizational and institutional power of relevant interest associations, which depend in turn on
the institutional configuration of the respective model of politico-
economic governance. Thus, different varieties of capitalism generate
different responses to a common EU-led impetus. I argue that national
response strategies to Europeanization in labor and social policy will be
colored by the domestic balance of power between unions and employers.
These labor market interest associations attempt to influence re-regulation
in their favor. Their capacity to do so hinges on their organizational–
institutional characteristics.

Strongly Neocorporatist and Statist Systems Produce Protectionist Response Strategies

While the external impetus of Europeanization was constant, different national models of politico-economic governance in the ten high-wage member states analyzed here thus generated different wage regulations for posted workers and re-regulated EU-induced liberalization in distinct fashions. Both highly neocorporatist Austria and statist France developed the most comprehensive and protectionist response strategies, while intermediate neocorporatist Germany and the Netherlands produced more liberal regulations, which continue to provide some incentives for the provision of services by construction companies from low-wage countries.

Top-down Europeanization triggers national response strategies conditioned by the relevant national model of politico-economic governance. Far from spawning a general trend towards convergence, within the remaining room for maneuver the policy responses of these various models differ substantially. The national level is therefore not rendered obsolete through economic liberalization impetus from the EU, but in fact enhanced in its significance. This insight dovetails to some extent with the 'second image reversed' (Gourevitch 1978). The domestic arena is therefore affected by EU-induced liberalization, but, within this arena, national responses in the form of implementing EU directives or—as described here—re-regulating EU initiatives may emerge. This insight amends some of the more pessimistic assessments of the future of organized 'Rhineland' capitalism (Albert 1991; Crouch and Streeck 1997; Kitschelt et al. 1999). The external impetus of Europeanization does not automatically lead to a general convergence on a 'liberal' deregulated wage level for posted workers. If anything, Europeanization highlights existing structural features of different models. Thus, as will be demonstrated, Austria and France produce protectionist re-regulations based on a combination of organizational power and preferences; a stand-off with superior government access by unions in the former, more powerful yet 'protectionist' employers also enjoying superior government access in the latter.

Intermediate Neocorporatist Systems Produce Liberal Response Strategies

By contrast, in Germany and the Netherlands employers possess superior organizational characteristics and a more liberal attitude. Employers' preferences lie in a more liberal re-regulation, establishing a wage gap between wages for directly employed workers and posted employees of foreign subcontractors. This gap is less pronounced in the Netherlands, and also applies only to postings of less than four weeks.

Contributing to the varieties of capitalism literature, this study underlines the importance of domestic level institutions in responding to Europeanization. However, while the resilience of the German model has been emphasized (Thelen 2001), this study highlights an Achilles heel of *Modell Deutschland* that surfaces in the elaboration of the German response strategy. In strongly neocorporatist systems (Austria), the formulation of labor and social policy is traditionally resigned to the social partners. Relative power parity ensures compromise solutions. Mandatory membership on the part of employers and high unionization rates guarantee support among the clientele and strong enforcement mechanisms. Given overlap between political parties and interest groups, parliament traditionally served merely as a notary.

In statist systems (France), the state formulates labor and social policy in loose but noncommittal coordination with the social partners. Given weak unions and better organized employers with superior access to government, employers enjoy an advantage in shaping the policy outcome. Although governments are not entirely insulated from societal interest groups (Hall 1986), ultimately, they enjoy considerable leeway in molding labor and social policy.

In intermediate neocorporatist Germany, social partners enjoy autonomy (*Tarifautonomie*) in setting wages. However, they have to rely on government intervention for such wages to be declared universally applicable (*erga omnes*), not just binding on (German) businesses that are members of the employer association. Government access therefore proves particularly important. Re-regulating the LSP occurred in two phases: first, legislation was passed; second, wage bargaining over the minimum wage ensued. This process proved very lengthy. The case study of responding to the LSP highlights two potential breaking points of the German model: first, employers may exit out of their obligation to pay standard wages by utilizing foreign subcontractors; second, the organizational principle of sectoral subdivision underlying German industrial relations supports the side that can unify its components. The employers unified behind the rallying cry of keeping down wages, while it proved impossible to interest sectoral unions not immediately affected by the LSP to support joint union efforts. While it may be true that employers do not abandon existing institutions of organized capitalism wholesale (Thelen 2001; Hall and Soskice 2001), outsourcing to foreign subcontractors has enabled them to do so in service sectors. The elaboration of a national response strategy to an external impetus of liberalization demonstrates the employers' advantage within the existing institutional framework given a unified position and wage preference vis-à-vis a much more divergent union position.

National response strategies to top-down Europeanization are by no means unitary. They are conditioned by the institutional configuration of domestic interest associations in relevant policy domains. In labor and social policy, powerful interest associations typically exist. Their organizational characteristics influence the amount of influence they can exact on the nature of national re-regulation of EU policy. Therefore, national models of political economy can be said to respond differently to the common impetus of Europeanization given varying levels of power enjoyed by either organized labor or business there. Strongly neocorporatist and statist systems produce self-preserving protectionist responses. Intermediate neocorporatist systems generate much more liberal responses that create new dynamics resulting from a multi-tier wage level for domestic and foreign employees. In the German case, this response highlights problematic aspects of the German model and underlines challenges the union faces.

Methodological Considerations

In order to maximize variance among national configurations of labor market interest associations, the case selection includes strongly neocorporatist Austria and *etatist* France as 'most different' cases and opposite extremes and intermediately neocorporatist Germany and the Netherlands in between (Table 1.1). Six additional high-wage 'medium'-level and strongly neocorporatist EU/EEA (European Economic Area) members are discussed: Belgium, Luxembourg, Finland, Sweden, Denmark, and Norway. The re-regulation of the LSP focuses on the wage regulation of wages for posted workers. Since transnational posting to high-wage countries is most lucrative, the case selection is limited to this group and can therefore regrettably not include pluralist or liberal member states such as Ireland or the UK. As these are low-wage countries, they serve as source, rather than target countries of transnational service provision, making re-regulation at home irrelevant (Table 1.1).

Different constellations among the actors led to different re-regulatory outputs. The *key hypothesis* is that the overall policy output or *national response strategy* to LSP in terms of the structure of wages for posted workers in a given country will be shaped by the outcome of interaction amongst unions and employers, and possibly government. In other words, *the response strategy reflects the preference of the strongest actor*. Possession of *relational power* cannot be predicted *ex ante*. Rather, it is computed based on a model I develop in Chapter 3, taking into consideration institutional and organizational characteristics of organized labor and business. Organizational strength is conceptualized as a combination of four variables: *degree of organizational centralization, internal coherence*, and *representation among their clientele* (see Table 1.2). A fourth variable is *access to government* because a stronger actor may wish to embed his preferred option into legislation.

A national response strategy consists of some action taken in response to the EU LSP, resulting in a national re-regulation of the wages for posted workers. This strategy will be the outcome of the interplay of actions informed by preferences of government, unions, and employers and filtered through institutional configurations leading to informal agreements or legislative action.

What preferences do actors have? Knill and Lehmkuhl (2002) remind us that the attitude of interest groups vis-à-vis the EU's liberalizing impetus

Table 1.1 Case selection based on an imaginary scale of neocorporatism and a maximization of variety by selecting two *most different* and two intermediary cases, with the ranking of the shadow cases provided in brackets (based on Schmitter and Lehmbruch 1979; Schmidt 1982; Lehmbruch 1984; Przeworski and Teune 1970)

Austria	Germany–Netherlands	France
Highly neocorporatist	Medium level of neocorporatism *Most different* from Austria on some, *most similar* on other dimensions	Low level of neocorporatism
(Norway, Sweden, Denmark, Luxemburg)	(Finland, Belgium)	

Table 1.2 Strength of labor market interest shapes national re-regulation

Representation among clientele + Access to government		
Internal coherence	→	Organizational power
Organizational centralization		

makes a decisive difference. *Preference formation* of the players will be deduced from rational choice and historical institutionalism. Based on the predictions of preferences generated by these bodies of literature, *alternative hypotheses for actors' preferences* can be derived and later juxtaposed with the empirical evidence.

The predictions of the *rational choice institutionalist* approach (Ostrom 1990; Shepsle 1989; Tsebelis 1990) are based on the utility maximization of the aggregated interests of individual members. Such utility maximization I take to mean *in practice* the pursuit of economic rationale. Unions can therefore be expected to push for the maximization of wages for posted workers and employers will attempt to minimize these costs as far as possible. As a second analytical step, a more sophisticated set of preferences is considered: Could it be rational for either side to constrain their demands? Are unions interested in defending the rights of a group of workers beyond their immediate 'turf' and hence their due-paying membership base? Can employers be interested in reaping the benefits of maintaining current price levels on the labor supply side, thus keeping constant the price level of construction projects?

The *historical institutional* approach (Hall 1986, 1989; Skocpol 1979; 1992; Steinmo et al. 1992) is used to deduce preferences not simply based on economic considerations but rather on historical legacy. What kind of preferences are actors likely to possess based on past historical experience? How are decisions taken at past junctures likely to impact upon future decisions and preferences? Such account by necessity has to draw on a brief historical analysis of industrial relations and economic policy formulation in France, Austria, and Germany. The historical institutional approach is also developed enough to generate not just a set of preferences, but also predictions as to the outcome based on past experience.

To sum up, different constellations among interest associations ('national models') with a given distribution of power among them (*independent variable*) cause varying public policy response strategies to liberalization, operationalized as the wage structure for workers posted from other countries within the framework of the LSP (*dependent variable*).

The European Union's Liberalization of Service Provision (LSP)— Origin and Implications

The LSP is very much at the heart of the European project. It is already contained in Articles 59 through 66 of the 1957 Treaty on the European

Community (Treaty of Rome). It came into effect after a transition period on January 1, 1970. Largely neglected by EU scholars and policy analysts alike, it lay largely dormant until the early 1990s, when a series of events and key ECJ decisions coincided to vitalize it. Part of the reason why the LSP had caused relatively little attention until then was linked to national governments' attempts to limit market entry by foreign companies by engaging in discriminatory acts that failed to register on the European Commission's 'radar screen' and were, in any event, difficult to prove, including the insistence to meet national certification criteria. Just as the European Court of Justice (ECJ) landmark case of *Cassis de Dijon* clearly established the principle of mutual recognition for the trade in goods, which until then was still subject to functionally similar regulations that could be construed to be nontariff barriers, so in services, too, did legal uncertainty as to the extent of the exact contours of the Single Market effects limit its practical implications. In particular, the legal status of posting workers transnationally was opaque and unclear until the early 1990s. Was this practice indeed covered within the framework of the liberalization of service provision? Could Portuguese construction workers indeed be sent to France to help construct the new high-speed train tracks? And if so, could the sending company legally continue to pay home country wages to such posted workers, rather than host country wages? Until the two Mediterranean rounds of enlargement of 1981 and 1986, wage discrepancies between existing members remained insignificant in any event, with the partial exception of Italy. When Greece, and later Spain and Portugal joined the EU, its citizens were subject to temporary bans on *labor mobility* of up to seven years. The northern high-wage countries were keen on maintaining a regulatory handle on the access to the labor market then, just as they did in 2004, when similar bans were imposed on the ten newcomers from Central and Eastern Europe (CEE).

Three key events occurred in the early 1990s, which very clearly shed light on the practical implications of the LSP and led to its widespread exploitation by high-wage member state companies 'importing' posted workers from low-wage member states through chains of subcontractors. Since these posted workers were not directly employed by host country companies, they could be reimbursed at the low wage rates of their home countries.

The 1991 Rome Convention

On April 1, 1991 all EU members made an important amendment to international private law, by signing the so-called Rome Convention, an important multilateral legal agreement, officially known as the 'Agreement on the Law applicable to contract-based obligations'. This convention was negotiated outside of the framework of the EU institutions. Articles 6 and 7 specified that two parties signing a contract involving transnational service provision could *choose* which national legislation was to apply to it. For the transnational posting of workers to other member states this could mean taking the presumably less exacting wages and labor conditions of the *home country* as the legal basis of such transnational service provision. Important exceptions to this rule are mandatory codified legal regulations (*lois de police*) of host countries, which are applicable to all labor contracts within these host countries. In terms of international law, such *lois de police* constitute part of a country's public order (*ordre public*) and can therefore not be overridden or ignored by transnational service providers, even if they choose home country regulations as the legal basis for their contracts. Examples for such *lois de police* are mandatory health and safety regulations codified into law. However, in many European countries, wages are very rarely decreed by law, with minor exceptions such as a minimum wage. Wages are commonly the result of collective bargaining agreements between trade unions and employer association. Although such agreements may be declared legally binding or universally applicable, a procedure known as *allgemeinverbindlich* in German and *etendu* in French, this is not necessarily standard procedure. Even where it is, from a legal perspective it was far from clear whether national governments could indeed impose such universal applicability on foreign companies, that is to say, *extraterritorially*. More specifically, to use the French example, it was not established whether the national minimum wage (SMIC) could indeed be considered part of the *ordre public* before the ECJ Rush Portuguesa ruling.[1]

---

[1] Thus, Portuguese company Rush Portuguesa paid the workers posted from Portugal to France Portuguese wages, which are below the French SMIC. The French government's position on this issue can be ascertained from an internal document for French labor inspectors issued by the interministerial delegation against illegal labor (MILUMO) obtained by the author. In it, the anonymous authors insist that ' . . . *leurs travailleurs doivent percevoir un salaire horaire au moins egal au SMIC'* [their workers must receive an hourly wage at least at the level of the SMIC; MILUMO 1993: 10]. This was also the official position of French business (Interview with representative of French employer association, 2000). However, it was not clearly established whether the French SMIC did indeed constitute part of the *ordre public* before the French national re-regulation. In fact, the very fact that such re-regulation was pursued—explicitly making mandatory French wages—suggests that the mandatory character of French wages had previously *not* been established.

The ECJ Rush Portuguesa Decision

On March 27, 1990 the ECJ 'Rush Portuguesa' ruling[2] rendered null and void the decision of the French immigration office OMI to impose work visa requirements on Portuguese workers posted to a construction site near Paris as subcontractors to French conglomerate Bouygues. At the same time, the Court made clear that

... communal law does not forbid that the member states apply their legislation or their collectively agreed wage regulations to all persons performing a paid activity upon their territory... [author's translation from the French].

The Single Market

Finally, on January 1, 1993 the Single Market was completed, establishing the EU. The Maastricht Treaty contained the so-called 'four freedoms', liberalizing the interchange of goods, capital, labor, and services. Although the legal framework of the LSP had been set forth through earlier events, Maastricht had an important symbolical and psychological effect on all actors. The combination of the Rome Convention and the ECJ Rush Portuguesa case highlighted and demonstrated the potential for service sector industries to exploit the LSP by outsourcing projects to subcontractors from low-wage member states. In the service sector, wages typically constitute a substantial proportion of total operating expenditures. In the construction sector this figure approaches 50 percent.

The implications of the LSP for countries with high-wage levels are manifold. Companies from low-wage countries gain access to markets in the service industries of high-wage countries, and do so with a considerable competitive advantage. National regulatory mechanisms, which in the past had been used to control access to the labor market, market entry and thus foreign competition more generally, as well as immigration, were overridden and rendered obsolete by the LSP.

At first glance, an obvious divide emerges between the preferences of the labor market associations regarding a possible re-regulation, though this difference of interests is not actually equally strong in all countries, as will

---

[2] Act C-113/89 Rush Portuguesa Lda against Office national d'immigration. The Court's 'Seco and Desquenne' decision (February 3, 1982) Act 62-63/81, collection 1982, p. 223 had already opened up room for national response strategies, but this decision had largely been ignored by actors throughout Europe.

become apparent in Chapters 4 and 5. Business generally appreciated the potential wage savings to be realized from outsourcing projects to subcontractors, which would be held responsible for paying (substantially lower) home country wages and social security contributions only. By contrast, unions were concerned about job losses arising from such outsourcing, the increased competition from cheaper competitors, and competition over the level of contributions to social security systems. They were worried about possible 'social dumping' and fearful of a 'race to the bottom' in terms of social standards. The governmental positions also differed, depending on the political composition of coalitions and, more generally, attitudes regarding economic liberalization and European integration.

Increasing the Scope of the LSP?

While this study focuses on the impact of the LSP and its re-regulation at the national level throughout the 1990s, the issue at stake is by no means of purely historical interest, since the European Commission intends to push ahead further with the liberalization of service provision, while ongoing negotiations in the framework for the General Agreement on Trades in Services (GATS) similarly aim to add liberalizing impetus.

After several years of protracted negotiations, in 1996 a directive was passed at the EU level (96/71/EC), which sought to address the issue of posted workers within the framework of the LSP. While this directive is mentioned in Chapter 4, the genesis of this directive is not analyzed in great detail[3] because it was passed significantly *after* all affected high-wage member states had passed national re-regulatory response strategies and its effect on these states was minimal. The directive simply institutionalized the right for member states to impose certain rights and obligations on companies posting workers to their territories. In doing so, the directive simply followed the course of the Rome Convention and the ECJ Rush Portuguesa ruling, without imposing conditions that were more exacting than those already included in national re-regulations. A benevolent interpretation of this directive is that it provided legal coverage and support for the already existing national regulations—here, the 'umbrella' metaphor might be apt. A somewhat more critical description would see this directive as congruent with a tendency towards 'lowest common denominator' policy development in EU labor and social policy.

---

[3] Excellent studies of the creation of this EU directive include Eichhorst (1998) and Worthmann (1998).

Recently, the Commission has proposed to broaden the scope of service sector liberalization. Following the March 2000 European Council meeting in Lisbon that established the goal to render the EU economy more competitive, the Commission drew up 'An Internal Market Strategy for Services' (COM (2000) 888 Final) in December 2000, followed by a July 2000 report entitled 'The State of the Internal Market for Services'. Having received the encouragement of both the European Parliament and the member states, the Commission proceeded to produce a draft directive (COM (2004) 2 Final/3). The purpose of this draft directive is to promote further the establishment of a Single Market in service provision and reduce the regulatory capacity of member states over transnational service providers. More specifically, the directive aims to establish a system of 'single point of contact' at which companies can obtain the necessary authorization to provide their services electronically, eliminate any remaining national restrictions or limitations on the use and employment of foreign service providers and, perhaps more significantly, implements the home country principle. However, this draft directive permits an explicit exemption for the provisions of the posted workers directive (96/71/EC), since it seeks to add to the existing *acquis* (as stated in Article 13), rather than override it. Article 38 therefore specifies that the home country principle does not override this previous directive and permits the receiving state to impose labor and social conditions to the extent that they are covered within this directive. Although the directive also exempts financial services (Article 9), the home country principle of regulation and supervision ('Single passport') has in fact been long in place in this part of the service sector.

Outline of the Book

The remainder of the book proceeds in the following fashion. In Chapter 2, the key argument that EU member states do possess room for maneuver in responding to and re-regulating the Single Market is further developed with reference to the emerging literature on the effects of Europeanization on EU member states and (European) comparative political economy. Engaging and challenging the key insights of these two bodies of literature, I demonstrate how an exciting research agenda can be constructed straddling the divide. However, the capacity to generate national response strategies is crucially shaped by the influence and relative power of trade unions and employer association. Therefore, an introduction to the neo-corporatist and statist systems of political economy and industrial relations is provided. The posting of workers concerned chiefly the construction sector. The importance and relevance of this component of the service sector is evident from its position as being the largest employer in the private sector across Europe. In addition, its corporate governance structures and structural composition are highly representative of the private sector more generally. Large, internationally active conglomerates dominate the scene in France. These companies offer 'turnkey' or 'all-round' services to their clients, subcontracting and outsourcing various components of major construction projects. By contrast, small and medium enterprises (*Mittelstand*) are more common in Austria, Germany, and the Netherlands. Traditionally, they were more likely to cooperate and form project-specific working relationships; however, with the partial exception of Austria, the trend in the construction sector is moving towards French-style all-inclusive service providers, which leads to the employment of subcontracting companies, and commonly even several layers or chains of subcontractors.

Chapter 3 presents an organizational power model to assess the relative strength of these interest associations based on characteristics including strong organizational centralization, internal coherence, representation among their clientele, and access to government. This permits a prediction as to what side will be more effective in shaping the national re-regulation and what preferences the two sides will have. In addition, drawing on historical and rational choice institutionalism, I distill hypotheses for the preferences of unions and employers regarding the wage regulation of posted workers.

Chapters 4 and 5 contain the empirical heart of the book. The genesis and implementation of the re-regulation of wages for posted workers is described and analyzed in both the core and the comparative cases, drawing on extensive field research. Particular attention is being paid to the position, interests, and actions of trade unions, employer association, and the ministries of labor in elaborating and designing the response strategies.

The empirical analysis is linked to the book's broader theoretical concerns about Europeanization and comparative political economy. In Chapter 5, the implications of the various responses are closely analyzed. Comparing the responses, three common patterns are identified. First, there is the statist-juridical response found primarily in Francophone countries, but also Finland. It is protectionist and state-led. Second, there is the strongly neocorporatist response of Austria, Norway, Denmark, and Sweden. It is protectionist and based on the consent and input of the social partners. Legislation is passed in Austria and Norway, while in the other two Scandinavian countries an internal compromise among the social partners is found. Both of these response patterns entail the extension of standard wages to posted workers.

Third, there is the intermediate neocorporatist response of Germany and the Netherlands which is liberal and shaped by the employers as the stronger side. This response extends only minimum wages to posted workers. The liberal Dutch and German responses henceforth point to organizational fallacies of the union movement, an Achilles heel of *Modell Deutschland* commonly neglected. By contrast, the more protectionist responses elsewhere underline both resilience to change and the persistence of national differences in responding to closer European integration.

In the concluding chapter, the implications of this study for the debate on Europeanization and comparative political economy are further developed. Nation-states do have room for maneuver in coping with the challenges and demands inherent in the construction of the EU Single Market. They are not mere passive objects of change. However, their response capacity to EU-induced economic liberalization is critically shaped by the power of domestic actors, particularly interest associations such as trade unions and employer association. The exact nature of these various models of politico-economic governance and industrial relations is therefore crucial, especially organizational characteristics of the two 'camps' embedded institutionally in these models. In examining these responses, more general observations can be derived about the relative capacity of West European models of politico-economic governance to cope with external pressures of economic liberalization.

2

Europeanization Meets Organized Capitalism

Die Kapitalmärkte beginnen die politischen Kräfte zu disziplinieren, weil unzureichende politische und strukturelle Rahmenbedingungen dazu führen daß das mobile Kapital renditeträchtigere Investitionsorte sucht. [The financial markets are beginning to discipline the political authority because unacceptable political and structural conditions will encourage mobile capital to search for more profitable locales for investment.] Josef Ackermann, central executive officer of Deutsche Bank (FAZ 4 September 1999)

Die lähmende Aussicht, daß sich die nationale Politik in Zukunft auf das mehr oder weniger intelligente Management einer erzwungenen Anpassung an Imperative der 'Standortsicherung' reduziert, entzieht den politischen Auseinandersetzungen den letzten Rest an Substanz. [The paralyzing vision that future policymaking at the national level will be reduced to the more or less intelligent management of the imposed adaptation process to the dictate of establishing 'acceptable' investment sites completely deprives political conflicts of any remaining substance.] Jürgen Habermas (1998) *Die postnationale Konstellation*, Frankfurt: Suhrkamp: 95

Given the pressures of Europeanization, is there any room for maneuver left for nation-states to design their own macroeconomic policies? What are the contours, limits, and parameters of such policies? How will nation-states re-regulate economic liberalization through national response strategies? Finally, do all European systems of politico-economic governance respond to the external impetus similarly? These highly salient questions will be explored and addressed throughout this volume.

Organized Western European varieties of capitalism are presumably coming under pressure, not only because their statist and neocorporatist institutional character is allegedly ill-suited to cope with the twin pressures of Europeanization and globalization, unlike the presumably more competitive and efficient, but certainly leaner and meaner liberal Anglo-American model. There are also potentially more serious internal challenges, including the prominence of neoliberal ideology among decision-makers both of the political right and the reformed Social Democratic parties of the late 1990s, the evaporation of relative parity in power between organized business and labor, and a tendency for employers to 'exit' from the postwar consensus, either by relocating production abroad, or by retreating from their commitment to consensual neocorporatist decision-making processes. That unique institutionalized continental mélange of social and welfare policies with more liberal and competition-oriented aspects appears to be severely threatened.

The case of workers posted in the context of the liberalization of service provision provides a splendid example to study the clash between national regulatory capacity and deregulating and liberalizing top-down Europeanization, which undermines this very capacity. The Single Market has undermined or outlawed avenues pursued by government to control and limit access to their territories and markets. Whereas governments used to favor domestic companies in their procurement of public works, bar foreign service providers from market entry through a host of discriminatory measurements, and limit labor migration, none of these measures are legally permissible any longer.

The analysis pursued in this volume examines whether the type and character of organized interest associations in the policy domains of labor markets and wages matter when it comes to responding to an external impetus of market liberalization. Do these organized interest associations still make a difference when it comes to the formulation of national response strategies to transnational challenges? Will the responses of a neocorporatist system differ from statist or 'intermediate' neocorporatist systems and if so, how and why? Does the neocorporatist paradigm still usefully contribute to our understanding of policymaking in certain policy areas? Are the responses across countries—presumably most different in the configuration and position of their interest associations according to neocorporatist criteria—indeed distinct? Or is there indeed some convergence and hence an erosion of differences between cases formerly as distinct as France and Austria?

Europeanization: Top-down and Bottom-up

European integration has dramatically accelerated its pace and scope since the mid-1980s. Scholarly attention has recently shifted from the earlier focus on 'bottom-up' Europeanization, involving the shift of decision-making power to the EU, towards the examination of the 'top-down' implications and effects of Europeanization on the member states (Héritier et al. 1996; Schmidt 1996b; Héritier et al. 2001; Knill 2001; Börzel 2002; Featherstone and Radaelli 2003). Earlier theoretical approaches to the EU sought to unearth the dynamics of the integration process from a functionalist (Haas 1958, 1964; Lindberg 1963), liberal intergovernmentalist perspective (Moravcsik 1993, 1998), or institutional approach (Sandholtz and Stone Sweet 1998; Stone Sweet et al. 2001). More recent analytical endeavors, however, have sought to clarify the implications of the 'central penetration of national systems of governance' (Olsen 2002). This study thus contributes to this nascent vivid debate on the dynamics of the top-down effects of closer European integration. The internalization of Europe proceeds not only through implementation and adaptation processes, but also through ways in which the institutional rules of the game are affected at the national level (Knill and Lehmkuhl 1999; Cowles et al. 2001; Knill 2001). One of the novel contributions I make is to assess the room for maneuver left for nation-states in their re-regulatory capacity, that is to say how the formulation of national response strategies to Europeanization proceeds. Given that the EU is characterized as a harbinger of economic change and liberal transformation, both by its supporters and its critics, does the claim hold true that any national re-regulatory capacity has been undermined dramatically or even rendered obsolete, as has been commonly suggested within the early globalization literature (among others: Ohmae 1990; but skeptical: Hirst and Thompson 1995)? What kinds of national re-regulatory response strategies are still possible? How will such measures be affected by the distribution of power amongst relevant interest associations in the policy field of labor market policy? This study provides answers to these pressing questions.

Unfortunately, the debate on Europeanization has given rise to a bewildering array of definitions and has often stalled due to the employment of individual 'custom-fit' definitions that cannot be expanded beyond limited empirical applications. In this study, I concentrate on the top-down impact of Europeanization and its bottom-up re-regulation and hence the interaction of domestic political structures and the EU, using the concrete public policy fields of labor and social policy as the empirical basis. One limitation of concepts developed in the Europeanization literature is that they are often extremely abstract or were developed with particular policy fields in mind, and hence do not fit others equally well. Concepts such as the 'goodness of fit' (Héritier et al. 1996) or 'absorption' (Radaelli 2000) were developed with top-down Europeanization (Knill and Lenschow 1998; Cowles et al. 2001; Héritier et al., 2001) and policy fields in mind, in which proactive EU policy initiation transpires to the national level in the form of EU directives, implying implementation and adaptation pressure. However, while there has been some such EU activity in labor and social policy, notably with the development of trans-European labor migrant social rights (Geyer 2000), much EU activity in this field has taken the form of 'negative integration' (Taylor 1983; Scharpf 1996). The abolition of barriers and the encouragement of the transnational flow of labor and services have profoundly affected ('Europeanized') member states' social and labor policy. In this process, the movement towards the creation of a Single Market undermines national market regulation (Rhodes 1991: 252ff.). Indeed, some of the pessimism pervading in the 'second wave' literature in comparative political economy (Albert 1991; Streeck 1996) stems precisely from the fear that closer European economic integration undermines the regulatory capacity and ultimately the macroeconomic autonomy and sovereignty of member states, without allowing them much room for re-regulatory measures. To capture the second-order effects this deregulatory aspect of the Single Market has, I refer to it as having a 'top-down and horizontal' impact.

However, rather than simply conceptualizing Europeanization as a process of imposed implementation or 'learning to cope with Europe', it is more appropriate to conceive of it as a 'shaped process, not a passively encountered process' (Wallace 2000: 370). Given that this two-way process of top-down *and* bottom-up is played out in an arena of multiple tiers of governance (Marks 1996, 2003), opening up room for multilevel games (Snyder and Diesing 1977; Putnam 1988), it becomes clear that the national arena is far from being rendered obsolete or unimportant. In fact, it is precisely here at the national level where national response strategies to Europeanization are being devised. While the impact of closer economic integration and the drive towards the Single Market is commonly negative, that is, deregulatory in nature, national re-regulatory strategies partly counteract, clout, modify, or, in extreme cases, even hijack the initial impetus. The limits and borders of Europeanization are contested, and it is precisely this struggle over both contours and content that will continue to provide the texture of political conflict in Europe in the twenty-first century. What emerges, therefore, as a result of the Single Market, is a patchwork of EU-induced liberalization and deregulation and partial national re-regulation, as Table 2.1 illuminates.

Europeanization thus may consist of the interplay between a liberal top-down impetus and national bottom-up re-regulatory strategies. Domestic level interest groups will attempt to shape such strategies. In pleading for the importance of the national arena and emphasizing the crucial role of national-level interest groups, I move beyond the recently formulated insight that the impact of top-down Europeanization is conditioned by the changes of the strategic position of domestic actors (Dimitrova and Steunenberg 2000; Knill 2001). I argue that the organizational power, including government access, of domestic interest groups *combined with these actors' preferences* critically shape the overall policy outcome. But, challenging previous work in this vein (Radaelli 2003:40–2), it is

Table 2.1 Conceptualizing top-down and bottom-up Europeanization

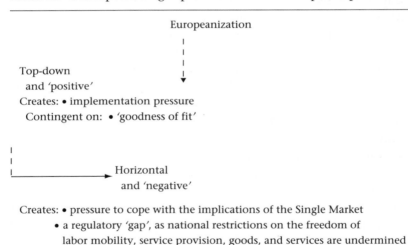

Europeanization

Top-down
  and 'positive'
Creates: • implementation pressure
  Contingent on: • 'goodness of fit'

Horizontal
  and 'negative'

Creates: • pressure to cope with the implications of the Single Market
  • a regulatory 'gap', as national restrictions on the freedom of
    labor mobility, service provision, goods, and services are undermined

Bottom-up

Creates: • 'national response strategies': national re-regulation of European impetus,
    seeking to cope with the regulatory 'gap'
  • possibly attempts to manipulate/'set the agenda' for EU level re-regulation

maintained that these preferences are not necessarily shaped by 'regulatory competition' nor is the outcome of the changing equilibrium decisively shaped by Europeanization. Instead, the *ex ante* preferences and organizational power of domestic actor coalitions matter. To assess both and predict the preferences, I design an organizational power model and distill hypotheses from two neo-institutional approaches in Chapter 3.

While ambitious hopes for a Social Europe may be unlikely to materialize, notwithstanding some recent EU activity in this field (Falkner 2004), European labor and social policymaking may be much more complex than hitherto assumed and not simply consist of deregulatory 'negative' aspects of the Single Market on the one hand and modest 'positive' attempts at constructing truly European social policy on the other. Instead, I argue that as a result of top-down liberalization and bottom-up re-regulation, a pattern of complex patchwork regulation emerges, critically conditioned by the power position of domestic actor groups that are embedded in respective system of politico-economic governance.

The Single Market as a Catalyst of Change

The political and economic impact of the Single Market project has been nothing short of revolutionary, at least for continental Europe. While it is true that Maastricht and the Single European Act coincided with a general paradigmatic shift away from state interventionism and an embrace of neoliberal policy and ideology at the level of the member states, it is no exaggeration to portray the EU as a catalyst of economic change in its own right. Indeed, this market-building mission of the EU, described by a critical analyst as 'embedding' neoliberalism (van Apeldoorn 1999), was already contained in the founding treaty of Rome, and to some extent merely 'dusted off' from having been already effective, but lain dormant. In the run-up to 1992 and thereafter the once substantial public sectors were broken up, and economic liberalization, privatization, and deregulation emerged as the watchwords in the context of the formerly somewhat sheltered political economies of continental Europe.

In ringing in macroeconomic change in Europe, the architects of the Single Market drew on both clearly liberal concepts and more statist-mercantilist notions. Critics note that despite this uneasy compromise, progress towards a Social Europe has been modest. The commitment to revitalize and accelerate the Single Market project in the 1980s has meant the abolition of publicly owned monopolies, particularly in infrastructure provision, such as utilities, and transportation. The requirements of tight monetary and budget policy imposed as a pre-condition of European Monetary Union (EMU) have limited the margins for maneuver in macro-economic policymaking. This drive has contributed to an end of the postwar consensus, described by Shonfield (1965), that still permitted substantial Keynesian-style demand stimulus, state ownership and considerable state interventionism, extensive welfare and social policies, and, in a number of European countries, varying neocorporatist working relationships between organized business and labor.

Europeanization Meets Organized Varieties of Capitalism

A common first assumption in the (re-)emerging literature on comparative political economy in the early 1990s has been a negative and pessimistic assessment of the future and viability of organized varieties of capitalism (Albert 1991; Streeck 1996). Analysts perceived of the twin pressures of EU-induced market liberalization and globalization as undermining statist and neocorporatist systems and highlighted convergence pressures. Pontusson and Swenson (1996: 224) summed up the prevailing sentiment when writing that

It has become a commonplace for students of West European political economy to speak of the decline of corporatism, that is, the decline of institutional arrangements for collaborative or tripartite governance of labor markets by representatives of capital, labor, and the state.

Mutatis mutandis this pessimistic assessment was also extended to statist systems such as France because

globalization discriminates against modes of economic governance that require public intervention associated with a sort of state capacity that is unavailable in the anarchic world of international politics (Streeck 1996: 27).

The comparative political economy literature has been strongly influenced by the debate on globalization and has not previously systematically utilized the insights generated by the Europeanization literature. In fact, given the focus on national developments, combined with an emphasis on the somewhat nebulous 'globalization pressures', there lies a danger of underplaying the role of the EU. Critics on the left accuse the EU of being an agent of globalization, eradicating national room for maneuver through the Maastricht criteria. However, I posit, in line with the more recent strand in comparative political economy (Hall and Soskice 2001), that far from ringing in convergence, in designing national re-regulatory responses, different domestic actor coalitions will produce different outcomes. The nature and power of such actor coalitions will hinge on the organizational and institutional power of relevant interest associations, which depend in turn on the institutional configuration of the respective model of politico-economic governance. Thus, different varieties of capitalism generate different responses to a common EU-led impetus.

I suggest bringing together two distinct bodies of literature: the rapidly unfolding debate on Europeanization and the recent renaissance in the field of comparative political economy. Top-down Europeanization needs to be understood not only in terms of the immediate pressure to implement directives, but also in terms of the 'top-down/horizontal impact' of undermining national regulatory capacity and limiting member states' regulatory autonomy to the extent that it collides with the principles of the Single Market. The institutionalized parameters that EMU imposes could also be considered part of this top-down/horizontal impact, though they will not be of major concern for this study. Member states are not mere passive and hapless objects. In fact, the national arena assumes new significance as bargaining and negotiation processes pertaining to the implementation, adaptation, and response to the EU impetus unfold here. Bottom-up Europeanization is created, negotiated, and shaped at this level. Attempts at creating a European re-regulatory agenda may also be initiated here, though this aspect will also not concern us in this study.

No Future for Organized Varieties of Capitalism?

Although more recent scholarly efforts have challenged earlier predictions of convergence or at least questioned and amended it (Hall and Soskice 2001; Kitschelt et al. 1999; Yamamura and Streeck 2003; Hay 2004), it is worth probing the rationale informing the pessimistic predictions of convergence that permeated debates in comparative political economy in the early 1990s. Such assessment was commonly based on at least two factors. First, 'organized capitalism', particularly the German model, appeared to show its limits, partly due to internal factors, including unification and relentlessly mounting mass unemployment, and partly due to its structural incapacity to adopt to the leaner and meaner Anglo-American model. Both academics and policymakers were impressed by the macroeconomic performance in the 1990s of liberal Anglo-American economies that appeared to outperform the lagging Rhineland countries. Second, 'organized capitalism' appeared as a historical epoch, and the postwar consensus that had already been eroding since the 1970s, seemed to have been superseded by more liberal institutions, ideas, and interests.[1]

I emphasize the resilience of national models in generating response strategies to a common external challenge in this volume, and hypothesize that even relatively similar varieties of capitalism such as highly neocorporatist Austria and intermediate cases Germany and the Netherlands will produce distinct outcomes. In line with the more sophisticated efforts of the early 2000s (Kitschelt et al. 1999; Coates 2000; Scharpf and Schmidt 2000; Weber 2001; Hall and Soskice 2001; Schmidt 2002; Yamamura and Streeck 2002; Amable 2003), I thus reject simplistic assertions of convergence of the organized Rhineland states on Anglo-Saxon-style capitalism. These more recent endeavors stress the continued resilience and divergence of national models of capitalism in Western Europe, arguing that organized capitalist systems enable strategies in corporate planning, wage-setting policy, training and education, and labor market policies that can be very much in the interest of both trade unions *and* business.

Having said that, one must not confuse institutional resilience with overall stability, nor ought one disregard the very different policy output produced by these deceptively stable institutions. The balance of power and with it the rules of the game even within organized varieties of capitalism have fundamentally changed. Therefore, the debate of the early 1990s centering on convergence versus divergence (Albert 1991; Crouch and Streeck 1997; Berger and Dore 1996) appears somewhat misinformed in underestimating the significant ideological change in policy output, despite institutional stability. But even the more recent efforts portraying and characterizing different models of Western European capitalism at times overemphasize institutional stability and resilience and underestimate the much more liberal policy output generated by these purportedly stable institutions. Here, comparative political economy analysts somewhat underplay the role of globalization. Increased economic internationalization implies pressure to accept wage moderation, since technological advancements in transportation and telecommunication technology have endowed business with a credible 'exit' threat (Hirschman 1970), i.e. the

---

[1] Let us consider the example of Austria to examine the previously mentioned charges. We quickly see how a shift towards monetarist policy (and EU membership) undermines the foundation of neocorporatism there. Unger (1999) lays out the five key pillars: autonomous monetary policy, employment policy through a substantial public sector (at one point being larger in proportionate terms than that of presumably state socialist Yugoslavia), budget policy, moderate wage policy.

possibility to shift production to production sites with lower wages, weaker unions, and more permissive environmental, social, and labor law. The resultant new role of the state—which nowadays lies primarily in attracting inward investment, competing for the attention of 'regime shoppers' by offering attractive low wages, and making the national economy 'fit' to compete internationally—has been described of that of a *'competition state'* (Cerny 1997; Hirsch 1998), in line with the theme espoused by Ackermann and criticized by Habermas in the opening quotations.

European Political Economy in the Twenty first Century: A Changing Power Balance

The balance of power between labor and capital has fundamentally shifted in favor of the latter. Unions are grappling with a host of internal and externally imposed challenges: a general decline in membership, the shift from the secondary to the tertiary sector, the fading and privatization of the public sector, a 'competition state mentality', and the dictate of permanent wage moderation. Meanwhile, the increasingly aggressive rhetoric and attitude of business associations in Austria (VÖI), France (CNPF/Medef) and Germany (BDI) since the early 1990s reflect this new self-confidence. The ideological underpinning of the role of the state in Western Europe is changing also, as political parties across the spectrum are embracing this new *'embedded financial orthodoxy'* (Cerny 1993). Both traditional Christian social values informing the Christian Democrats and Social Democratic values of solidarity and redistribution are evaporating. The German *Neue Mitte* Social Democrats are indicative of this trend, as are the staunchly neoliberal and business-friendly Austrian Freedomites who replaced the Social Democrats in the coalition government from 1999 to 2004. The postwar consensus between labor and capital in Austria, the Netherlands, and Germany, established even earlier in Sweden, Denmark, and Norway, was based either on power parity between unions and employers (in the smaller states) or on the insight that a consensus-oriented collective approach to wage-setting would maintain social peace, reduce industrial action, and restrain government intervention (Sweden and West Germany). *Business nowadays has much less of an incentive to play by these rules.* National corporatist arrangements are no longer able to control a wide array of economic policy. Wage moderation and labor acquiescence can be attained solely by threatening to exit.

The postwar consensus, convincingly described by Shonfield (1965) and later Przeworski (1985), has evaporated. In the 1950s, foreign competition and maintaining competitiveness compelled employers to agree to collective bargaining, not least to avoid ruinous internal price competition, downward spirals in wages and education standards, and 'low-trust' environments. Nowadays, employers are more inclined to leave neocorporatist wage settling arrangements. They do so by 'exiting' abroad, abandoning or not even joining the employer association and hence the obligation to pay collectively bargained wages, a common trend particularly in Germany (Mahnkopf 1999; Hassel 1999), or withdrawing from neocorporatist institutions to apply downward pressure on wages as in Sweden (Pontusson and Swenson 1996).

Mutatis mutandis, the preceding analysis can be applied to statism as well. 'Keynesianism in one country' has long since ceded to be possible, as France painfully learned during the first Mitterrand government after 1981. National level attempts at controlling the demand-side and renationalizing substantial components of the economy will meet with the disapproval of international investors and capital withdrawal. Financial and commercial transnationalization increases, the public sector decreases under EU pressure, and many of the state's macroeconomic policy tools transfer to the EU level. This leaves very little room for traditional state-centered economic policymaking.

At the same time, employers in an *étatist* system face new choices. Although the national executive is shedding power to the European level where employers do not dispose of the same close relations with government, three new strategies do emerge: (a) increase the amount of influence commanded at the European level, (b) 'exit' and relocate abroad, and (c) use the remaining power leverage at the national level to push for liberalization and flexibilization of the domestic labor market. The French employers have employed all three strategies in the 1990s. Rhetorical advocacy of domestic liberalization (Hay and Rosamond 2002; Schmidt 2002) commonly mixes the purported need to compete internationally with the use of the accommodation of EU policy as a scapegoat for unpopular measures and a source of legitimacy.

New Forms of Tripartite Concertation Across Europe

Refuting claims of the presumably grim future prospects of neocorporatism (and by extension statism), Europeanization has actually encouraged the formation of tripartite macroeconomic policy decision-making in countries without any history thereof and helped sustain and lend new

meaning to existing neocorporatist institutions.[2] Given external constraints, particularly the EMU criteria, but also general challenges such as
the restructuring of welfare systems (Rhodes 1997), macroeconomic concertation has resurfaced in the form of tripartite policy coordination
mechanisms in traditionally non-neocorporatist countries, such as Italy
(Regini 1997), Spain, Portugal, and even Ireland (Aust 1999). Tripartite
concertation has also been revived in Finland and Norway (Mesch 1995;
Fajertag and Pochet 1997), the Netherlands (Visser and Hemerijck 1998),
and Austria (Heinisch 1999).

However, it must be noted that these latter-day tripartite arrangements
have new goals, new aims, and new priorities. They reflect the underlying
shift in balance of power between business and labor. *Their normative
political and economic ambitions are worlds apart from the neocorporatist
arrangements of the 1970s.* Henceforth, it is questionable whether they
should even be described as neocorporatist and whether the literature of
the 1970s can fruitfully be applied to their analysis. Certainly, this is not
your father's corporatism.[3]

Reflecting the new power balance between weaker unions and stronger
business associations, these tripartite alliances aim to render their
countries more attractive investment locales, a development described
variously as 'supply-side corporatism' (Traxler 1996), 'competitive corporatism' (Rhodes 1997), or a shift towards 'embedded neoliberalism' (van
Apeldoorn 1999) and the emergence of 'competition states' (Cerny 1997;
Hirsch 1998). The assistance of the social partners as 'modernization
brokers' (Heinisch 1999) may be needed in implementing otherwise unpopular broader macroeconomic and political projects, such as austerity
measures and cuts in welfare, social and other public spending.[4]

---

[2] Thus, there is a curious parallel to the 1970s when scholars 'discovered' neocorporatism
just as it was waning in importance. Only this time around, analysts are predicting the demise
of neocorporatism just as it is gaining a new lease on life (Schmitter and Grote 1997), yet in a
markedly different form.

[3] No longer is 'negotiating a secure status for workers and unions, insulating these from
economic fluctuations . . . ' a priority, but instead it is all about 'adjusting the governance of
the employment relationship to the imperatives of joint economic success' (Streeck 1998: 15).
This implies that 'the trade unions . . . accept a policy of wage restraint in return for an undertaking . . . to preserve existing employment levels, *and preferably, whenever possible*, to create
new jobs' (Fajertag and Pochet 1997: 11, my emphasis). This is a *'Konzertierung ohne Tausch'*
[concertation without a trade-off] (Regini 1997). There is no obligation whatsoever for employers and the state to live up to their vague promise.

[4] Indeed, the previous and premature gloomy predictions of impending disintegration of
the Austrian social partnership (Crepaz 1994) have proven wrong precisely because the social
partners there were able to adopt this role (Traxler 1995, 1996; Heinisch 1999).

In sum, rather than insisting on either convergence or divergence, it might be more useful to consider the changing parameters of European political economy as part of a process of *functional convergence*. That is to say that despite institutional resilience of neocorporatist and statist systems, much of the functional output produced in terms of economic, social, and labor policy across Europe is indeed remarkably similar. However, some differences remain and to explore the different policy responses generated and provoked by top-down Europeanization it is most fruitful to analyze the institutional power balance between unions and employers at the national level.

Principles and Ideologies of Politico-Economic Governance in Western Europe

The analysis pursued in this volume examines whether the type and character of organized interest associations in the policy domains of labor markets and wages make a difference when it comes to responding to an external impetus of market liberalization. Do these organized interest associations still matter when it comes to the formulation of national response strategies to transnational challenges? Will the responses of a neocorporatist system differ from statist or 'intermediate' neocorporatist systems and, if so, how and why? Does the neocorporatist paradigm still usefully contribute to our understanding of policymaking in certain policy areas? Are the responses across countries—presumably most different in the configuration and position of their interest associations according to neocorporatist criteria—indeed distinct enough? Or is there indeed some convergence and hence an erosion of differences between cases formerly as distinct in the formulation of their wage policy as France and Austria?

To proceed, the key structures of the political economy within various national 'models' of politico-economic governance in Austria, France, Germany, and the Netherlands will be sketched, followed by an introduction to the corporate structure of the construction sector, as a pivotal and highly representative component of the private sector. The key structures of the political economy in the other Low Countries and the Nordic states or the industrial relations structures are summarized in text boxes (Tables 2.2–2.8). Readers interested in the details are referred to the appendix.

Institutions of Economic Governance

Austria: The Tradition of the Social Partnership

Austria has been commonly considered in the literature a near paradigmatic case of neocorporatism. Academic observers began to note in the 1970s that some Rhineland states in particular were decidedly non-pluralist, unlike their Anglo-Saxon counterparts, and that organized interest associations, 'organized into a limited number of singular, compulsory, noncompetitive, hierarchically ordered and functionally differentiated categories, recognized or licensed (if not created) by the state (Schmitter 1974), played a significant or dominant role in the formulation of policy in certain fields, especially labor market policy and wage setting (von Beyme 1977; Schmitter 1974, 1981, 1989; Schmitter and Lehmbruch 1979; Lehmbruch and Schmitter 1982; Schmidt 1982; Goldthorpe 1984; Katzenstein 1985; Marin 1985; Grant 1985; Williamson 1989; Grote 1997; Rhodes 1997).

'Neocorporatism' or societal corporatism was seen as a useful analytical tool in understanding macroeconomic policymaking in a number of Western European countries. It was used especially to characterize the Netherlands, Switzerland, Germany, the Scandinavian countries, and the 'paradigmatic' case of Austria. Katzenstein (1984, 1985) suggested a further distinction between social corporatism in protectionist oriented countries with strong social democratic parties and trade unions in countries such as Norway, Austria, and Denmark and liberal corporatism correlated with highly export dependent economies such as Sweden, Switzerland, and the Netherlands. West Germany was portrayed as displaying traits of both types, thereby presenting a curious combination of both. Indeed, while the Scandinavian countries were commonly described as strongly neocorporatist, Germany and the Netherlands were regarded as more mixed or 'intermediate' types.[5]

The existence of such organized interest associations in the field of labor market policy and their entitlement to determine wages through

---

[5] As has been remarked upon by Lehmbruch (1982) among others, postwar West Germany never actually represented the ideal type of neocorporatist interest mediation. This fact is also pointed out by Scharpf (1991). Scharpf adds that Keynesian policy was never particularly popular in West Germany. For this point see also Allen (1989).

In fact, perhaps surprisingly, throughout the literature Germany is quite commonly only considered a second-tier or 'sub-optimal' neocorporatist society. Schmidt (1982) proposes a scale on which he ranks all OECD member states in regards to their degree of corporatism, based on Gerhard Lehmbruch and Philippe Schmitter's epochal work. Germany is ranked only in a 'medium' position. The same applies to the Netherlands.

collective bargaining in a more or less autonomous fashion enabled certain governments to finetune their macroeconomic policies to the demands of international constraints and pressures and thus appeared to be a perfect mechanism to cope with the 'hard times' (Gourevitch 1986) and oil shocks of the 1970s. Indeed, such systems of *Akkordierung* (coordination) fostered the pursuit of flexible macroeconomic policy, reach compromises between labor and business demands, and facilitate labor acquiescence. This flexibility seemed to correspond perfectly with the needs particularly of small European states (Katzenstein 1985), notably Austria and Sweden (Scharpf 1991).

It is equally important to understand that certain conditions are not absolutely necessary for neocorporatist interest intermediation to occur. Neocorporatism does not necessarily imply tripartism. Although governments in strongly neocorporatist societies generally respect the autonomy of the social partners to negotiate wages (*Tarifautonomie*), they do at least make their preferences known. Neocorporatist theory does not specify that wage negotiations occur at the central level, though this has traditionally been the case in Scandinavia. Shifts to sectoral level negotiations therefore do not necessarily imply the end of Swedish neocorporatism per se (Dølvik and Martin 1997) since negotiations have always been conducted at this level in Austria, the Netherlands, and (West) Germany (Karlhofer and Sickinger 1999: 245).

Although the influence of the Austrian *Sozialpartner* has been waning, well into the 1980s the Economic Chamber (*Wirtschaftskammer*) on the business side, the Austrian Federation of Unions (*Österreichischer Gewerkschaftsbund*) on the labor side, supported by the 'think tank' Federal Worker's Chamber (*Bundesarbeitskammer*), and finally the Agricultural Chamber (*Präsidentenkonferenz der Landwirtschaftskammern*), were being consulted and asked for approval of macroeconomic decision-making in the broadest sense, including, for example, education policy. This powerful 'secondary' or 'shadow' government grew out of a series of five bipartite Wage-Price Agreements between 1947 and 1951, nourished by the need to invest and distribute Marshall Plan aid while securing political and economic stability in this frontline state of the Cold War. These joint agreements culminated into the more formalized 1957 Council on Prices and Wages (*Paritätischer Preis-und Lohnausschuß*), an institution composed of an equal number of representatives from both camps setting prices and wages. The Social Partnership proved extraordinarily stable and even popular despite its fallacies and pervasive criticism both from the right and left (*Der Standard*, 9 November 1997; *Financial Times*, 1 December 1997;

Karlhofer and Talos 1999; Falkner 2000). The term is often used liberally, conflating the political culture underlying its blossoming with the institutions. A more serious threat to the Social Partnership is the tendency of the Black-Blue coalition of the late 1990s and early 2000s to ignore and outmaneuver these hitherto established channels of consultation. While the Austrian economy has benefited greatly from its newly recovered position in the geographic heart of Europe, and the country has managed to attract the Central and European regional headquarter operations of several multinational corporations, the question emerges to what extent the Austrian political economy will remain distinct in the new millennium.

A formal, but relatively unimportant consultation and exchange forum is the Council on Social and Economic Affairs (*Beirat für Wirtschafts-und Sozialfragen*). By contrast, an informal and much more pivotal channel of influence is the social partners' consultation on all legislative drafts even before their submission to parliament. Given the strong linkages, ideological proximity, and the widespread practice of individuals holding offices in both organizations (*Personalunion*) between the Social Democratic Party SPÖ (*Sozialdemokratische Partei Österreichs*) and the trade unions on the one hand and the Conservative Peoples' Party ÖVP (*Österreichische Volkspartei*) and business and farmers on the other, parliament often merely 'rubber-stamped' (Tálos et al. 1993) bills. The fact that Austria was governed by a Grand Coalition between 1945 and 1966 and again between 1986 and 1999 further aided compromise-oriented consensus-style decision-making and division of power and offices. This practice is known as *Proporz* (Lehmbruch 1967).

These institutions of macroeconomic governance have emerged out of the relatively chaotic postwar years and the shared historical experience of civil war, subsequent domestic fascism, and foreign occupation, commonly attributed to internal disunity and violent clashes between the 'black' and 'red' camps. In 1945, a universal, comprehensive central union association was created (*ÖGB*), avoiding the competition between Christian, Socialist, and Nationalist unions, which had scarred the First Republic. At the same time, the Chamber of Labor (*Arbeiterkammer*), which had not been a very important political institution in the First Republic, emerged as labor's 'think tank' for the development of economic, social and monetary policy. The Economic Chamber (*Wirtschaftskammer*) succeeded similar predecessors emerging at the end of the nineteenth century.

The Social Partnership worked on the basis of voluntarism. Not only was its informal role in policymaking in no way legitimized or even mentioned

Table 2.2 Principles of the Austrian political economy

Ideology, interests, and ideas
- Social Partnership—neocorporatist, consensual, bipartite decision-making
- Postwar consensus on a social market economy between the Social Democratic working class 'red' and the conservative Catholic 'black' camp, tendency towards Grand Coalitions

Institutions
- Strong, hierarchical labor market interest associations
- Traditionally substantial public sector, important role of state intervention through state ownership

Challenges
- Embrace of more liberal ideology among employers and major political parties
- Privatization reduces state capacity to steer and manage the economy
- Freedomite Party is particularly hostile to the institution and ideology of the Social Partnership

Questions for future
- Can the Social Partnership assume the role of 'competitve corporatism'?
- Will Austria's embrace of more liberal policy positions lead to 'convergence within divergence'?

in the Constitution of 1955; in addition, its recommendations were not legally binding for either the government or its constituent members. The power of persuasion and *compromise* was thus crucial. The Social Partnership, which for decades lay at the heart of the Austrian political economy, was therefore based on a mutually reinforcing combination of political culture variables and institutions. Table 2.2 summarizes the preceding discussion.

Germany: The Social Market Economy

Germany's political economy is informed by a slightly different combination of ideological strands. The postwar West German 'social market economy' is an organized variety of capitalism that blends three distinct ideologies into a very unique mélange: liberalism, Christian social values, and social democracy. Postwar Minister of Economic Affairs Ludwig Erhard is commonly credited as having been its architect, yet the ideological tenets of the Freiburg School's 'ordeo-liberalism' powerfully influenced the concept of the state as an enabling entity, conducting *Ordnungspolitik*. The country's political economy is colored by the power of large conglomerates in some fields, but also the influential medium-sized companies (*Mittelstand*), and a traditionally very strong organized labor movement. Although major corporations in fields such as banking, automobile, steel, and chemicals survived the war relatively unscathed, and were neither broken up nor nationalized as in France, concessions had to be made to the Social Democratic Party and the trade union movement in the design of the postwar political economy, given their organizational strength and initial labor militancy. As a frontline state of the Cold War, West German capitalism was in immediate competition with state socialist East Germany and could ill afford completely to ignore concerns of the Social Democrats. Direct state intervention into the economy through state aids, private–public associations, and loans by public regional or local savings associations (*Landesbanken, Sparkassen*) existed, though they were not part of systematic economic development plans like in France. Institutionally, the federal government was deliberately weakened in the interest of strong federal *Länder*. The West German central bank *Bundesbank* was independent and fervently dedicated to curbing inflation through monetarist policy as early as 1975.[6]

A major role in economic development and indeed economic governance was reserved for the banks, which commonly act not just as providers of loans, but as financial and managerial consultants and were represented on the boards of directors of major German businesses. This system of *Hausbanken*, described favorably by Albert (1991) and Hutton (1995), allowed the country's three largest banks Commerzbank, Dresdner Bank, and Deutsche Bank to play a key role in managerial decisions, based on their diversified stockholdings. Shareholders with 25 percent of total stock hold veto power. However, a 1999 change in the tax code, encourages banks to sell off their various stockholdings, since they may do so tax free. Also, a 1999 merger created HypoVereinsbank, a fourth major player, while Dresdner has since been purchased by insurance giant Allianz. The early twenty-first century may very well witness an additional consolida-

---

[6] Decentralization of political power and the independent position of the central bank can both be accounted for by the legacy of the past: Germany had never had a strong central government—and, in fact, had only been unified in 1871—except for the extremely centralized regime of the Third Reich. The Nazi regime had not only abolished the states and replaced them with weak *Gaue*, it had also used the central bank as a willful tool to finance its rearmament efforts of the 1930s. The strong tradition of regional powers dating back to the Middle Ages, the fear of a centralized regime and a free reign over the central bank, the almost traumatic memory of the 1917 inflation, and last but not least, the strong shadow of the US model on both the constitution and the political system of the Federal Republic all helped to produce a strongly federal system with an independent central bank.

tion of the industry, after failed merger efforts between Dresdner and Deutsche in 1999.

Keynesianism was never enthusiastically applied in West Germany (Allen 1989; Boyer 1997), perhaps unsurprisingly given the negative historical legacy of state interventionism during the Third Reich. This legacy led to institutionalized power dispersal and dissemination as leitmotifs of the German polity, as is evident in the independent central bank, and the government's reticence to involve itself into wage-setting, generally respecting the autonomy of the social partners in the sphere of collective bargaining. This so-called *Tarifautonomie* dates back to the 1920s, but was abolished by the Nazis and reinstated after 1945. From 1967 to 1977 the Concerted Action (*Konzertierte Aktion*) brought together the peak-level union (German Federation of Unions—*Deutscher Gewerkschaftsbund—DGB*) and employers (umbrella association, Federation of German Employers—*Bundesverband Deutscher Arbeitgeber—BDA*) and large business representatives (including the employers' think tank and policy advocacy association, Federation of German Industry—*Bundesverband der Deutschen Industrie—BDI*) with officials from the Economics Ministry and the Chancellery for informal and legally nonbinding discussions of macroeconomic policy. But this never reached the degree of concertation as in Austria. Consequently, Germany has always been considered an 'intermediate' level neocorporatist state, as mentioned previously. Both Kohl and Schröder have attempted to revive peak-level tripartite concertation in the so-called Alliance for Jobs. However, to date, these discussion rounds have produced scant tangible outcome, as labor has been hesitant to make the concessions that business has been hoping for (Hassel and Streeck 2004). Another important economic institution is an advisory council (*Sachverständigenrat*), composed of economists, academic experts, and representatives from various economic research institutes. It was founded in 1963 as part of a turn towards a more Keynesian direction, but has since turned into a more neoliberal direction.

The social democratic component conducive to the success of Model Germany and social peace were substantial workers rights in managerial co-determination discussed below (Streeck 1992, 1997; Jacobi et al. 1998). However, the German system of work and welfare betrays its deeply conservative Bismarckian roots and relies on the male breadwinner model (Esping-Andersen 1990). Not even in its heydays did Model Germany compare favorably to much more egalitarian Scandinavia on this account. Table 2.3 summarizes the points missed thus far.

Table 2.3 Principles of the German political economy

Ideology, interests, and ideas
- 'Intermediate neocorporatist' case
- Social market economy consists of mix of Social Democratic positions, liberal ideology, and the notion of the state as setting the rules (*Ordnungspolitik*)

Institutions
- Decentralized, sectoral labor market interest associations
- Traditionally substantial public sector, though less pronounced than in Austria

Challenges
- Embrace of more liberal ideology among employers and major political parties, employers can relocate production abroad or threaten to do so as a bargaining chip
- Unions and employers are losing members, especially in the East
- Attempts to relaunch German corporatism seem unsuccessful
- Increasing competitive challenge to high-quality, high-wage production

Questions for future
- Can and should the German model be reformed?
- Does Germany's shift towards more liberal policy positions mean the end of the Rhineland model or indeed convergence within divergence?

France: Statism No More?

The rules of the game of the French political economy and industrial relations are distinctly different from those in Austria and Germany (see Table 2.4). The government has traditionally played a highly pronounced role in intervening, structuring, pruning, building and 'governing' (Hall 1986) the economy, without relying much on the support of interest associations. This tradition dates back to the mercantilist policies of seventeenth and eighteenth-century absolutism. Mercantilism, as practiced by Minister Colbert under Louis XIV, aimed at autarchy through the general promotion of domestic production and the improvement of domestic infrastructure to foster domestic trade and transportation of domestically produced goods. *Statism* or *etatisme* are terms commonly applied to describe the presumably unique character of the French political economy (*l'exceptionalisme française*) (Hall 1986; Levy 1999; Boyer 1997).[7] The

---

[7] See also for industrial relations: Keeler (1987), Wilson (1987), Rojot (1988), Crouch and Streeck (1996); and for economic policy in general: Zysman (1977), Hayward (1973), Keeler (1985).

French state has played a dominant steering role in developing, controlling, and implementing economic policy, a tradition dating back historically at least to the mercantilist policies of the highly centralized absolutist system of Louis XIV. The highly centralized *jacobiniste* French state sought to stamp out the influence of the regional aristocracy as veto players to central decision-making. Industrial and economic policymaking was state-centric and state-led, relying on government expertise, a substantial public sector, further increased after 1945 and again in 1981, and 'expertocracy'. Hall (1986: 164ff.) underlines four dimensions of *étatisme*: (a) cohesiveness and close internal coordination of administrative agencies, (b) the state's insulation from demands of other social actors and societal pressure, (c) *l'état actif*, that is the 'capacity to implement policy, if necessary over the objections of key social groups', (d) political authority of the state and a 'monopoly on political virtue'.

We might add that the particular French form of *étatisme* also implied a particular close link between government and business, especially with the genesis of the 'national champion' policy in the 1960s after which the *plannification* often turned *l'impérativ industriel* into *l'impératif des industriels,* turning it into 'a cooperative endeavor between civil servants and industrialists' (Hall 1986: 168), which conversely implies that unions were being left out of the decision-making process.

The belated French industrialization and the shift from the primary to the secondary sector, which commenced in the late nineteenth century, but only took on significant proportions after 1945, was also state-led. In 1946, a series of five-year plans for modernization and economic development was launched, designed by Modernization Committees and the *Commissariat Général du Plan* (Hall 1986).[8] That same year, a training academy for the future government and business elite was conceived, the *Ecole Nationale d'Administration*, along with other regional *Grandes Ecoles* and *Ecoles Polytechniques*. The pronounced central role of the state (*étatisme*) and the state involvement in economic planning and directing (*dirigisme*) are presumably what makes France exceptional even by continental European standards (Zysman 1977; Boyer 1997; Levy 1999; Hancke 2002). Central planning heavily favored Paris over other regions initially,

---

[8] The same author highlights four developments in the postwar *planification*: (1) a shift from the limited industrial plans of the 1940s and 1950s to global resource allocation in the plans of the 1960s; (2) extension in the early 1960s to the provision of social infrastructure; (3) in the late 1960s and early 1970s a shift in focus from economic growth as such to the provision of social infrastructure, such as universities, hospitals, cultural centers, technological centers; and (4) increasing politization and direct intervention by the prime minister.

though in the 1970s economic planning was influenced by attempts to promote the economic development of the regions. This led to the dispersion of car industry plants in the north and the aeronautics in the southwest (Levy 1999). It is important to note that the control over finance played a key role in statist economic planning and development. The three largest banks (Crédit Lyonnais, Banque Nationale de Paris, Société Générale) were state-owned until the 1970s and again after 1981. Subsidized loans were delivered by semi-public financial funds (*Fonds de développement économique et social*), heavily favoring larger companies and the Paris region (Le Gales and Aniello 2001: 150ff.). Within the government, the Ministry of Finance played a pivotal role, controlling the financial allocation for the various plans as well as for individual ministries (Hayward 1973; Estrin and Holmes 1983: 96; Hall 1986: 173ff.). State-driven industrialization favored *grandes projets* and building gigantic 'national champions' as a means to promote development. Major industry, notably in the automobile sector, was included in the public sector.

Dirigisme was based on close cooperation with business. While labor acquiescence was useful, it was considered less essential. Labor was never admitted to the inner circle of economic decision-making, while the rapport between government and capital was very close.[9] Organized labor remained a weak player, regarded with suspicion by the patriarchal French state and the business elite. While trade unions had to resort to industrial action and demonstrations to make their voices heard, liaisons between state and capital grew even closer in the 1960s, partially due to the rise of an elite (*enarchisme*) that was trained and socialized together in the *Grandes Ecoles* and *Polytechniques*. That lines between business and government elite should become increasingly blurry was certainly promoted by the practice of government officials to 'parachute' into the private sector after some years of government service. In recent years this has meant a joint embrace of 'more market' and the ability of French employers to influence the agenda in the reform of social and labor market policies (Schmidt 1996a,b; Hancké 1999). In particular, the conservative Raffarin–Chirac government, in office since 2002, has attempted to revive social concertation (*réfondation sociale*) to implement cuts to welfare policy and labor market deregulation.

---

[9] Hall (1986: 158) quotes a trade union representative recalling a meeting of the Modernization Committee: 'It seems that everything happens as if the procedure was arranged beforehand in such a way that a certain number of decisions are taken by direct agreement between the employers' representations and the civil servants.'

Table 2.4 Principles of the French political economy

Ideology, interests, and ideas
- Statism—state-centric economic development and industrial planning, some cooperation between state and business
- Uneasy shift between embrace of socialist ideas, authoritarian statism, and liberal notions

Institutions
- Relatively weak labor market interest associations
- Traditionally substantial public sector, important role of state intervention through state ownership

Challenges
- Embrace of more liberal ideology among employers and political parties of the Right
- Privatization reduces state capacity to steer and manage the economy
- Government attempts to build tripartite structure to implement social and labor market reforms, but popular resistance is sustained

Questions for future
- Is statism doomed for disintegration or can it be reinvented and salvaged?

The Netherlands: A Liberal Variant of the Rhineland Model

A small and open economy home to a number of internationally active major conglomerates, the Netherlands possesses a political economy that marries Rhineland-style aspects of neocorporatism and tripartite consultation with more Anglo-American oriented economic liberalism (see Table 2.5). Consensual decision-making has generally assumed an important role in a country historically divided along ideological, religious, and social lines. The more or less institutionalized efforts to overcome these divisions that have led observers to refer to the country as a consociational democracy that brought together (*verzuiling*) the distinct pillars of Dutch society and have importantly informed the process of political party formation and coalition building in the Netherlands (Lijphart 1968), have also had significant implications for macroeconomic policymaking.

Given that the representation of the different ideological currents and societal groups in government have played such a central role in Dutch politics, the role of the bipartite Foundation of Labor (*Stichting van de Arbeid*) and the tripartite Social and Economic Council (*Sociaal en Economische Raad*, known as *Hoge Raad van Arbeid* before 1940) in policy consultation and deliberation is perhaps unsurprising. However, the institutions of Dutch corporatism have significantly increased in importance only since the early 1980s, when the government moved away from French or Belgian-style state interventionism that was predominant in the form of wage decrees in the 1970s.

Faced with inflationary wage increases, slow economics growth, and a generous social policy that permitted the receipt of sickness and invalidity benefits as a way to avoid unemployment, the Netherlands acquired the title of 'the sick man of Europe'. The 1982 bipartite Wassenaar Agreement on wage restraint and annual wage increases below the inflation rate leaves the social partners with more room for maneuver and helped to avoid continued state interventionism into collective bargaining. With the post-Wassenaar rise in central-level bargaining on broad macrolevel issues, centralization in labor market interest associations has increased, most collective bargaining occurs at the bargaining level while umbrella level associations offer policy recommendations and general coordination of efforts (Visser and Hemerijck 1998; interviews FNV 2000, VNO-NCW 2000). Indeed, continuous economic growth, low unemployment rates and collectively negotiated welfare and macroeconomic policy reform

Table 2.5 Principles of Dutch political economy

Ideology, interests, and ideas
- 'Intermediate neocorporatist' case—shift from from state-centric economic policy development towards more consensual neocorporatism in the early 1980s
- Postwar consensus presents a mixture of Social Democratic, liberal, and conservative Calvinist elements that reflect the traditionally highly divided Dutch society, tendency towards Grand Coalitions

Institutions
- Traditionally ideologically divided labor market interest associations, but more consolidation and unity since the 1980s, then growing importance of tripatite and bipartite consultation arenas
- Traditionally substantial public sector, but limited state intervention

Challenges
- Implementation of more liberal ideology and social and labor market policy through tripartite consultative fora seems to have reached its limits

Questions for future
- If the Dutch 'polder model' was more hype than reality, how can the challenge of low-cost competition be met and how can a re-emergence of the dreaded 'Dutch disease' be avoided?

Table 2.6 Key Principles of industrial relations in France, Austria, and Germany

	Austria	France	Germany
Legalistic?	Yes	Strongly	Yes
Role of State?	Provides legal framework, but does not intervene into wage negotiations (*de facto Tarifautonomie*)	Highly interventionist; sets minimum wage; advances social and labor legislation; paternalistic attitude means State often acts as *ersatz* union	Provides legal framework, does not intervene into wage negotiations (*de jure Tarifautonomie*)
Role of unions?	Unitary actor, highly centralized	Ideologically fragmented, often divided, low unionization rates, but militant, especially in public sector	Sectoral unions are most important actors; low degree of centralization
Role of employers?	Unitary actor, highly centralized	Relatively well organized, well connected to government	Sectoral employers are most important actors, employer association face problems of member retention

attracted much attention to the Dutch 'polder model' in the 1990s (Visser and Hemerijck 1998), though critics note that much of the miracle in terms of the employment record might be linked to the skillful use of invalidity benefits, while the economic record is inflated by the real estate boom (Becker 2001; Delsen 2002).

The European Construction Industry

The construction industry is commonly the largest single employer within the private sector in Europe. It contributes a significant proportion of the

Table 2.7 Key Principles of Industrial Relations in the Netherlands, Belgium, and Luxembourg

	The Netherlands	Belgium	Luxembourg
Legalistic?	Yes, framework-setting	Strongly	Strongly
Role of State?	Provides legal framework, has receded from traditionally highly interventionist role	Highly interventionist; state sets framework, minimum wage, and often also intervenes into wage bargaining	Provides legal framework, but state does not not intervene into wage negotiations
Role of unions?	Have overcome traditional ideological division, sectoral level most important	Divided along linguistic cleavages, sectoral level most important	Unitary actor
Role of employers?	Have overcome traditional ideological division, sectoral level most important	Divided along linguistic cleavages, Sectoral level most important	Unitary actor

overall gross domestic product (GDP). In 1999, it accounted for 5.4 of the percent of value added to the GDP of the EU as a whole, 9.1 percent of the Austrian GDP, 5.5 percent of the German GDP, and 5.7 percent in France in 1995 (OECD Economic Surveys Austria 2003; OECD 1997:162). In 1997, it accounted for 8.1 percent of all employment in Germany (OECD 1998:163), 12.9 in Austria in 1996 (OECD 1999:134), and 6.6 percent in France in 1995 (OECD 1997:162) and a total of 1,600,000 employees in France in 2001.

But the sector not only constitutes a crucial component of the European economy; it also makes for an interesting and important case study to use in the analysis of broader trends for three reasons. First, the structures of corporate governance, ownership, size, and behavior found in this sector in various Western European countries are highly representative of the

Table 2.8 Key principles of industrial relations in the Norway, Sweden, Denmark, Finland

	Norway	Sweden	Denmark	Finland
Legalistic?	Yes, framework-setting in all three Scandinavian countries, but more strongly in FIN			
Role of State?	Provides legal framework, long history of state interventionism into industrial relations	Traditionally reticent, but more interventionist since 1980s	Reticent, de facto Tarifautonomie	Provides legal framework
Role of unions?	High degree of unionization, strong, unified actors in all Nordic countries			
Role of employers?	Unitary actors—in Norway, Denmark, and Sweden periods during which employers considered or actually did leave, voluntarist spirit of 'gentlemen's agreements', withdrawal from central bargaining and/or solidaristic wage-bargaining tradition, most pronounced, long-lasting and serious in Sweden			

'bigger picture', that is to say, of the economic modalities in that country. Therefore, the country-specific politico-economic 'rules of the game' were very thoroughly imprinted on this sector. As will become apparent in the following introduction to the actors, institutions, and interests at play in various European countries, whether it is the specific mode of state interventionism and regulation, the details of industrial relations, or the structure, size, and nature of interaction among market players, in all these respects the construction sector provides a highly representative and fascinating case study of broader particularities of various European models of capitalism. Second, the construction sector was traditionally relatively sheltered from foreign competition. Although there was no monopolistic state ownership typical of other service sector industries in Europe, such as utility provision and transportation, this relative absence of pronounced transnationalization implied that the impact of the EU-induced LSP was quite profound. Just as with other traditionally sheltered service sector industries, then, economic liberalization brought upon by the EU would necessarily imply powerful transformation pressures. While the construction sector is thus comparable to other relatively sheltered and highly regulated economic sectors, the liberalizing impact can be expected to be similarly significant. The third point is related to the first two issues. Since this is a sector that is so typical and representative of the economic structure at large and since we would expect European liberalization to play a significant role, it would appear particularly fruitful to examine the role of interest groups in coping with, responding to, and filtering the impact of the LSP here. In the neocorporatist countries at least, organized labor market associations were and are traditionally well represented in this sector. Both trade union membership and membership in employer organization were generally quite high. In statist France, organized labor in this sector is less well-entrenched, but, as is typical of patterns found elsewhere, employers certainly managed to maintain a relatively close *rapport* with decision-makers in government.

Just as other European service sector providers are experiencing major transformations imposed by more (foreign) competition, easier market access for outsiders, market liberalization and the (often partial) privatization of formerly monopolistic state-owned enterprises, so the construction sector, too, is undergoing significant changes. In many ways, the patterns of corporate reorganization seem to point towards a shift in the direction of the French all-round 'turnkey' service providers. The metamorphosis of major construction companies implies that they are offering the complete planning, development, construction, and often even maintenance, management, and security of building projects (see Table 2.9). This has significant implications for the structure of the sector, since these companies typically act as general contractors and then outsource specialized tasks to individual smaller subcontractors. The resultant pattern is one of a few internationally active major players facing a plethora of small and often minute companies. The substantial use of subcontracting, often in several layers, means that accountability is often defused and irregular patterns and practices of employment may emerge. Given the highly precarious short-term nature of such contract work, combined with the general difficulties faced by trade unions in organizing employees in small and medium-sized enterprises (SMEs), the resultant new corporate patterns can significantly undermine the unions' position.

Construction work is often hazardous, dirty, dangerous, tedious, and unpleasant. While skilled workers and tradesmen are required for specific jobs, building projects also involve low-skilled workers. In marked and obvious contrast to manufacturing, this service provision cannot be delocated geographically, but has to be performed on the spot. Henceforth, rather than exporting work to low-cost locales, one possible corporate strategy in lowering wage costs is to import workers. As becomes clear the LSP has rendered possible this import of workers from within the EU. At first glance, such strategy would appear attractive to business, while unions

Table 2.9 Trends in the European construction industry

- Market consolidation
- Dominance of market by a small number of large, dominant, internationally active players
- Emergence of all-round service providers, especially for large scale projects, including ports, harbors, train lines, train stations, airports, shopping centers, and tunnels
- Services include not only construction, planning, and execution, but also maintenance, security, management
- Growth of small and minute companies that act as subcontractors
- Emergence of chains of subcontractors—problem: loss of accountability, irregular forms of employment, especially at the bottom of the pyramid

→ Trend most/least pronounced in descending order

France
Netherlands—Sweden
Germany
Austria
Norway—Belgium—Denmark— Luxembourg—Finland

face a serious challenge to maintain the relatively high wages of Northern Europe. Table 2.10 summarizes the following discussion.

The Structure of the Austrian Construction Sector

The Austrian economy has traditionally been dominated by small and medium sized companies in the private sector and a substantial public sector. As recent as 1991, 21 percent of all employees still worked in the public sector (Traxler 1999, 245ff.). The structure of the Austrian construction industry reflects this and is thus representative of the economy as a whole. SMEs make up the lion's share, while only few larger players exist. According to government statistics, in 1993, 59 percent of all companies had fewer than 20 employees, and 81 percent fewer than 50. These figures have changed since: in 2001, almost 90 percent of all companies had less than 20 employees, and 95 percent fewer than 50, while only seven companies have 1,000 or more employees (Statistik Austria, Statistisches Jahrbuch 2004: 357).

The few major construction companies are commonly owned and financially backed by banks. Before the privatization of the banking sector that commenced in the 1980s, many major Austrian construction companies were hence indirectly owned by the state. This pattern of corporate governance can be described as a statist Austrian version of the German *Hausbanken* system, where the state plays the role of allocating and administering finance. Traditionally, the three major Austrian banking groups each owned at least one construction company: thus, Bank Austria controlled Porr AG and Stuag, while Creditanstalt owned Universale-Bau, and Raffaisen managed Era-Bau. The acquisition of Creditanstalt by Bank Austria meant that the latter was obliged to reduce some of its construction portfolio under pressure from EU competition authorities and decided to sell some of its Stuag holdings. However, since the mid-1990s, a significant wave of mergers and acquisitions has consolidated the structure of the Austrian construction industry. Henceforth, Strabag Österreich, which took over competitor Stuag together with Bank Austria partially in 1995 and completely in 1999, and merged with Bau Holding AG in 2001, is the biggest player, holding roughly one-third of the domestic market share. The new company Bau Holding Strabag AG now also controls the German Strabag, as well as Austrian Era-Bau. Raffaisen now controls about 25 percent of the shares of this group, while Bank Austria now owns Porr AG and Universale-Bau. By contrast, the privately owned Maculan group, which used to control 14.5 percent of the market in the mid-1990s, has declared bankruptcy since (*Die Presse*, 6 August 1996; *Der Standard*, 10 February 1997). Consolidation has thus reduced the already low numbers of major players in Austria and has further improved the position of Bau Holding Strabag AG (interview Austrian construction company 2001).

In 1996, the construction sector made up 8.2 percent of Austrian GDP. In 1996, the Austrian construction sector employed 12.1 percent of Austrian employees or 200,000 individuals (OECD 1999: 140–50). *The construction sector is thus the largest single employer in the private sector of the Austrian economy.* Roughly 50 percent of employees are organized in the sectoral union *Bau-Holz* (*Der Standard*, 30 October 1996). In 2001, there were 19,359 construction companies in Austria, but only 231 employed more than 100 workers. The small companies are organized by the *Bundesinnung Bau*, while the larger companies are organized by the *Fachverband der Bauindustrie*, both of which are sectoral divisions of the WK (Unger and Waarden 1993: 20). In the 1990s there has been a consolidation trend in the sector. In order to compete successfully for public bids, middle-sized companies form joint ventures (*Arbeitsgemeinschaften*). More recently, larger companies have commenced to bid for jobs on their own and then outsource individual projects to subcontractors (interview Austrian construction company 2001; interview Bau-Holz 2001).

By international standards, the major Austrian construction companies are very modest in size and the sector is characterized by surplus capacity (*Handelsblatt*, 16 July 1996; *Der Standard*, 10 February 1997). Given the saturation of domestic markets, Austrian companies were quick to profit from the opportunities afforded to them by the need for massive renovation and construction in Central and Eastern Europe. However, not all companies actually profited from this eastward expansion in the long term. The Maculan group expanded into Slovakia, Hungary and the new eastern German Länder by taking over entire companies or the majority of shares. Maculan took full advantage of outsourcing to cheaper EU subcontractors in Germany and was negatively affected by deteriorating quality and fines resulting from missed deadlines. Due to financial difficulties it eventually was forced to declare bankruptcy in 1996 (*Die Presse*, 27 February 1996).

Generally speaking, the construction sector profited from the broadly positive economic development in the early 1990s, growing at an annual rate of 11.7 percent between 1990 and 1995 (*Der Standard*, 10 February 1997), due to orders from the expanding corporate private sector. From 1992 onwards immigration from the East coupled with demographic developments (increasing divorce rates, trend towards living single) led to a boom in the construction of apartments and private homes, with total construction in this subsector experiencing a threefold increase between 1986 and 1994 (*Der Standard*, 25 September 1995). The sector's surplus capacities began to surface again in 1995 and thereafter (*Die Presse*, 19 September 1995; *Der Kurier*, 23 August 1995; *Der Standard*, 28–29 October 1995; *Der Standard*, 27 February 1999). Once this demand had been met, the volume of public jobs began to decrease due to budget buts and austerity measures dictated by the need to comply with the Maastricht criteria. This went along with a slight slowdown in economic activity and a slower GDP growth in the mid-1990s (OECD 1999: 24ff.). By the early 2000s, the situation of the Austrian construction sector seemed to have improved somewhat, though the larger companies increasingly relied on securing major projects in Central and Eastern Europe.

Structure of the French Construction Sector

The structure of the French construction industry is representative of the private sector as a whole: a small number of extremely dominant, internationally active players face a plethora of SMEs and very small, often family-owned businesses. Only recently has the French government sought to support such SMEs, after years of nurturing 'national champions' as its preferred strategy of economic development (Hancké 1999; Le Galès 2001). Larger companies in France have exerted pressure on smaller subcontractors to cut costs, following the wave of privatizations in the 1980s, resulting in substandard wages and labor conditions among these subcontractors. Although this trend commenced in automobile manufacturing, it quickly spread to the service sector (*Le Monde*, 16 May 1990, 4 July 1990; *Syndicalisme*, 13 February 1992). As elsewhere, the construction sector is the most important component of the private sector. Its significance has even increased in terms of contribution to the GNP since 1985 (Berthier 1992). In 1998, the French construction sector employed 1,139,800 people (FFB 1999), in 2001 even 1,600,000 (INSEE 2002, Marie-Anne le Garrec, La construction resiste en 2001 et au debut de 2002, July 2002, No. 862).

There are currently 285,000 French construction companies. Of these, 268,000 employed 10 or fewer workers, while only 15,300 had 11–50 employees, and 1,700 more than 51 employees (FFB 2004). Compared to figures from 1998, the pattern is relatively stable. In congruence with efforts to strengthen SMEs, since 1982 larger companies have lost their importance as direct employers, while small companies have become more important. Again, this generalization also holds for the economy as a whole (OECD Country Reports France 1997: 164).

Despite the numerical importance of SMEs for the domestic market, France is home to four of the ten largest European construction companies that dominate 40 percent of domestic turnover (Knechtel 1992: 47). Among those, Bouygues S.A. is by far the largest company both within France and Europe in terms of gross turnover. Somewhat akin to Vivendi, this conglomerate is also a major player in mobile telephony and media through its holdings of TV stations TF1 and TPS. Other major companies include the conglomerate Vinci, created in 2000 out of a merger of SGE-Générale, Dumez, and GTE. Eiffage was formed in 1993 around major player SAE. Bigger French companies are particularly active in the Maghreb and sub-Saharan Africa, but also in the Mideast and Asia (Bouygues 2000, 2004). More recently, they have become active in acquisitions in other European countries, notably the new German *Länder* and Central and Eastern Europe.

France is at the forefront of a major pan-European metamorphosis in the construction sector that consists in the transformation to all-round service provider, including the active management and maintenance of major infrastructure programs, such as toll roads, airports, and tunnels. However, the increasing consolidation at the level of the major internationally active companies in turn leads to an expansion of construction sector SMEs, which enter as subcontractors for specialized tasks (*Le Monde*, 24 April 1991). As mentioned before, such chains of subcontractors (*sous-traitance en cascade*) provide major companies with considerable leverage to apply downward price pressure on elements further down the chain. This is one of the factors accounting for substandard wages and irregular forms of employment at the end of the chain, which constitute frequent occurrences in France (*Le Monde*, 6 August 1987, 16 May 1990a,b, 4 July 1990, 14 June 1991). This development was clearly visible during major construction projects in France in the 1980s and 1990s, such as the construction of the Halles complex in central Paris, the La Défense complex, Eurodisney in 1993–5, the Stade de France for the Soccer World Cup in 1996–8, and major high-speed train TGV lines. Although the sectoral employer association itself suggests eliminating this trend towards subcontracting and reforming the public procurement process so as to exclude abnormally low offers (FNB 1996), the construction sector accounted for one-third of all labor law infractions throughout the 1990s, an unusually high share, indicating that illegal forms of employment of French citizens (*travail dissimulé*) prevail there. While illegal forms of temporary labor and lending of workforce occur, as does the employment of foreigners without a work permit, other illegal aspects of employment are more crucial in the construction sector, especially the payment of substandard wages or social security contributions, and tax fraud. While most forms of illegal employment involve French citizens, among those foreigners found in violation of labor laws, the Portuguese traditionally have held a particularly prominent position (DILTI 1999: 9ff.; Yerochewski 1997; *Le Monde*, 25 November 1992, 24 September 1996). As is typical of the construction sector where work is often unpleasant, dangerous, and physically demanding, immigrants make up a substantial portion of the legal workforce, though this rate has decreased from 28.8 percent of the total workforce in 1970 down to 15.5 percent in 1998. Among the legal foreign workers, Portuguese citizens were strongly represented both in 1970 (8.5 percent) and in 1998 (6.8 percent), while other traditional countries of French labor recruitment such as Italy, Spain, Algeria, Tunisia, and Morocco all play less important roles (Mekachera 1993; FFB 1999: 21).

All five central French unions have sectoral subdivisions for construction. The three employer association are the *Fédération Française du Bâtiment* (FFB), comprising 55,000 companies in the construction sector proper; the *Confédération de l'Artisanat et des Petites Entreprises du Bâtiment* (CAPEB), which organizes companies with less than 10 employees; and finally, the *Fédération Nationale des Travaux Publics* (FNTP), which organizes the 5,500 companies in civil engineering. They are all very important and powerful members of the umbrella employer association Medef (FNCB-CFDT no date; FNCB-CFDT interview 2000; CGT interview 2000; Medef interview 2000; FNTP interview 2001).

The French construction industry is thus both further advanced in the trans-European trend among construction companies towards becoming all-round building-related service providers and simultaneously more split between a small number of globally active construction magnates and a numerical predominance of small enterprises often acting as subcontractors. Medium-sized companies in the French construction sector are disappearing. This is a notable difference to the two German-speaking countries, the Netherlands, and some of the Scandinavian countries, where the *Mittelstand* still plays an important role.

The Structure of the German Construction Sector

Regionalism remains strong in Germany, as does the importance of the SMEs (*Mittelstand*). The skilled artisans (*Handwerk*), having established their chambers and guilds as far back as the Middle Ages, likewise continue to play an important role. The *Mittelstand*, defined as companies employing between 50 and 199 employees, accounts for about one-third of employment both in manufacturing and services.

The SMEs, especially skilled artisans, are organized and represented by the Central Association of German Construction Industry (ZDB—*Zentralverband der Deutschen Bauindustrie*), while larger and medium-sized companies belong to the Central Association of the German construction industry (HDB—*Hauptverband der Deutschen Bauindustrie*). In wage negotiations they both act as employers associations; both are members of the BDA. Their union equivalent is the Industrial Union Construction-Agriculture-Environment (IG BAU—*Industriegewerkschaft Bauen-Agrar-Umwelt*). The potent *IG Metall* plays a small role in the construction sector, as they organize certain professions within the construction-related sector, notably the electricians. Both IG BAU and IG Metall are members of the DGB.

The structure of the construction sector reflects the importance of the *Mittelstand*. Approximately 60 percent of all employees work for companies with less than 100 employees, while only 8 percent were employed by large companies employing 500 or more. This proportional distribution has remained stable over the past fifteen years. In 1995, 84,847 German construction companies employed 1,542,189 employees in the central construction sector. By 1999, this figure had declined to 80,560 companies and 1,229,049 employees respectively (Pahl et al. 1995: 13ff.; Russig et al. 1996; IG BAU 1997; HDB 1999: 10; ZDB 1999: 60; HDB 2004: 4), not least due to the massive arrival of foreign workers posted to Germany under the auspices of the EU LSP. By 2003, the number of employees had further declined to only 605,309 and 76,612 companies (ZDB 2004; destatis 2004). The shrinking of the sector has been particularly dramatic in the East, where employment has fallen from 443,300 to 209,000 between 1995 and 2003 (ZDB 2004). As in France, the construction sector has traditionally attracted first-wave labor migrants from countries like Turkey, (former) Yugoslavia, Italy, Spain, and Portugal. Approximately 9 percent of all employees of German construction companies are non-German citizens (ZDB 1999: 63).

Smaller companies sometimes grow out of the bankruptcy of *Mittelstand* companies. Those made redundant through bankruptcy sometimes manage to secure equipment and tools from their former employer. The initial capital needed to set up a construction company is relatively low (interview HDB 1999). However, the lack of capital is precisely the reason for a relatively high rate of business collapses and bankruptcies if there are delays in receiving payment.

In line with the pan-European trend described earlier, larger companies are increasingly beginning to act as general contractors for major construction jobs and subsequently outsource more specialized tasks to subcontractors (Russig 1996). This development has commenced in earnest in 1991. Between 1991 and 1997 the rate of subcontractor contribution to overall production has grown from roughly one-third to roughly one half for larger companies (interview HDB 1999, HDB 1999, 13)! In the early to mid-1990s, German construction companies were still very much national or even regional players, though the biggest companies had profited modestly from the petrodollar construction boom in the Mideast and Nigeria in the early 1980s (Knechtel 1998).

Typical of the German model of capitalism, construction companies are owned by consortiums, often backed or owned outright by banks or other major conglomerates. The largest German construction companies in terms of gross turnover in the 1990s were Strabag AG (eventually merged with the Austrian consortium Bau Holding Strabag AG and thus intertwined with Bank Austria, itself consequently acquired by German bank HVB), Hochtief AG (majority owned by energy conglomerate RWE since 1990) and the notorious Philip Holzmann AG, owned by Deutsche Bank, Hochtief, and the BfG Bank (interview German construction company 2001). The Schröder government's reactions to Holzmann's spectacular 'double collapse' in 1999 and 2002, intervening the first time to rescue it, but not the second time around, can be interpreted as paradigmatic of its change of heart towards a more liberal policy direction. Holzmann's problems were a result both of ill-conceived acquisitions in France and Thailand and of declining prices in the domestic market, as German companies used foreign subcontractors, thus setting in motion a downward price spiral. Ironically, Holzmann itself had employed, if not initiated this practice of using EU subcontractors (*FAZ*, 19 May 1999, 6 April 2000; interview German construction company 2001). Since Holzmann's demise, other actors have gained market share, particularly Walter Bau AG and Bilfinger+Berger AG (IG BAU 1997), the latter of which is partially owned by the finance and insurance company Allianz.

In 1990, German business journal *Wirtschaftswoche* predicted *das grosse Baggern* (a big wave of construction) for the following decade and recommended the shares of construction giant Holzmann to its readers. In light of reunification and the impending completion of the Single Market, investing in construction sector shares seemed like a safe bet. However, the sector underwent a boom only until 1995, enjoying a substantial stimulus from unification, related major renovation and construction projects in the East, and the decision to move the capital to Berlin. Construction of apartments in the East was promoted through tax incentives until the mid-1990s (Knechtel 1998), while business development and expansion in the East provided added impetus. A favorable economic trend was sustained even in the West despite the 1992–3 recession.

By the mid-1990s, however, the construction sector experienced a substantial and structural crisis, which emerged out of the confluence of at least four major trends. First, the government's tax incentive program for construction in the East expired. Second, given the Maastricht criteria concerning the public deficit, public spending was dramatically reduced. Third, a slump in demand in the East clearly demonstrated that during the boom of the early 1990s companies had accrued surplus capacities, for which there was no longer any demand. Fourth, massive posting of workers from low-wage EU countries such as Ireland, Britain, Portugal, and Greece caused a downward price spiral in bidding first for public and subsequently for private jobs. SMEs experienced increasing difficulties to compete with prices set by the larger companies which were exploiting this newly discovered corporate strategy of outsourcing to lower wage subcontractors. They thus either sought to compete within an environment of deteriorating prices by resorting to the employment of imported labor in a legal or illegal fashion or else found themselves priced out of the market. The severe difficulties experienced by German SMEs were soon to be reflected in the unemployment figures of domestic employees, strongly indicating a partial *replacement effect* notwithstanding relatively strong demand for construction in some regions, most pronounced in Berlin where strong demand for construction services notwithstanding unemployment among domestic workers soared in the mid-1990s. Similar trends were discernible around Leipzig and Dresden.

Table 2.10 Main actors in Austria, France, Germany, and the Netherlands

Main Actors
Austria
Umbrella Union Association ÖGB
Sectoral Union Association Bau-Holz

Umbrella Employers Association Wirtschaftskammer (WK)
Sectoral Employers Association Fachinnung Bau

Ministry of Labor and Social Affairs
Major construction companies: Bau Holding, Porr

France
Umbrella Union Associations CGT, CFDT, CGT-FO, CFTC, CGC (white collar)
 Sectoral Union Associations:
CFDT-FNCB (*Fédération Nationale des Salariés de la Construction et du Bois*)
CGT-FNTC (*Fédération Nationale des Travailleurs de la Construction*)
CGT-FO-FGFOBTP (*Fédération Générale Force Ouvrière du Bâtiment et des Travaux
 Publics*)
CFTC-FBTP (*Fédération Bâtiment-Travaux Publics*)
CGC (*Syndicat National des Cadres, Techniciens, Agent de Maitrise et Assimiles des
 Industries du Batiment et des Travaux Publics*)

Umbrella Employers Association CNPF (renamed Medef)
Sectoral Employers Association in construction FNB (recently renamed FFB)
Sectoral Employers Association in civil engineering (FNTP)
Sectoral Employers Association for SMEs in construction (CAPEB)

Ministry of Labor, Employment, and Solidarity

Major construction companies: Bouygues S.A., Vinci

Germany
Umbrella Union Association DGB
Sectoral Union Association in Construction IG BAU
Sectoral Union Association in Engineering and Processing of Metal IG METALL

Umbrella Employers Association BDA
Sectoral Employers Association in Construction for Small Companies and Artisans
 ZDB
Sectoral Employers Association in Construction for Medium and Larger Companies
 HDB
Sectoral Employers Association in Engineering and Processing of Metal
 GESAMTMETALL
Sectoral Employers Association in the Textile Industry GESAMTTEXTIL

Ministry of Labor and Social Affairs
Ministry of Economic Affairs

Major construction companies: Hochtief AG, Bilfinger+Berger AG

Netherlands
Umbrella Union Associations CNV, FNV
Sectoral Union Associations in Construction FMV Bouw, Hout-en Bouwbond CNV

Umbrella Employers Association VNO-NCW
Sectoral Employers Association in Construction AVBB

Ministry of Social and Labor Affairs

Major construction companies: Koninklijke Bam Groep NV, Ballast Nedam NV

The Structure of the Construction Sector in the Netherlands

For the Netherlands and the other two Low Countries, it is equally fair to say that the construction sector is representative of the economy as a whole. Henceforth, SMEs are predominant, though a few internationally active players exist (van der Meer 2000; AVBB 2000: 14). More recently, consolidation has begun here, too, with the major conglomerates offering all-round services in the construction of major projects, including tunnels, ports, airports, shopping centers, and major public housing complexes. The flipside of this development is the rapid growth of small and minute companies related to an increased use of subcontractors, often consisting only of one employee. In the Netherlands, there were 43,940 construction companies in 2000, but 72,000 companies and 450,000 employees in 2004, according to industry figures (AVBB 2000: 14; AVBB 2004). Of these, nearly 80 percent have less than 10 employees, while only 1 percent had more than 100. These proportions have remained stable over the years (van der Meer and Roosblad 2004: 27ff.). This composition of the market structure also applies to Belgium and Luxembourg.

The two largest Dutch construction companies are Koninklijke BAM Groep NV, formed out of the former Hollandsche Beton Groep in 2002, and Ballast Nedam NV. Another large company, NBM-Amstelland NV, was broken up in 2000, and parts of this company have since merged with real estate company MDC to form AM NV, a construction service provider in the broadest sense. The ownership patterns indicate some similarity with the Rhineland model of bank ownership. Thus, the Dutch banks ING, Rabobank, and Fortis own 30.7, 8.8 and 5.2 percent of the Bam group respectively (BAM 2004). ING also holds 5 percent of Ballast Nedam. However, concurrently with the consolidation process, the bank involvement in the construction sector has decreased somewhat.

The Dutch construction sector profited from a generally favorable economic environment in the Netherlands throughout the 1990s. With stable economic growth and low unemployment throughout this decade, accompanied by relatively high levels of inward migration, the private housing market experienced a boom. Major infrastructure projects such as the enlargement of Schiphol airport helped sustain a constant high demand for construction services. With the beginning of the new millennium, the end of the Dutch economic boom also affected the construction sector. The serious difficulties experienced by Hollandsche Beton Groep led to its corporate restructuring and were symptomatic for the wider difficulties experienced by other major companies that had accumulated surplus capacity. In 2001, a major corruption scandal rocked the Dutch construction sector, with allegations being made that a cartel-like structure of eight major companies had secretly divided up the market for public bids and fixed prices at artificially inflated prices (Brouwer 2002).

The labor market in the Dutch construction sector has been traditionally characterized by the relative absence of ethnic minorities, unlike other European countries. One of the reasons for migrant workers and Dutch citizens of non-European extraction being underrepresented is the legacy of informal recruitment networks that favor 'insiders' over newcomers and therefore discriminates against migrant workers (van der Meer and Rosenblad 2004). This tradition stems from the guild-like structures protecting highly skilled artisans that have generated relatively demanding qualification standards and procedures for those seeking skilled jobs in the Dutch construction sector.

The Structure of the Construction Sector in the Nordic Countries

The Swedish construction sector mirrors the structure of the general economy. Thus, large companies control 60 percent of the total market share, and these major companies (notably Skanska and NCC) have recently become internationally active as well, prompted not least by the almost decade-long domestic recession the country experienced in the 1990s (Lubanski 1999; FAZ, 21 February 2000). This expansion, mainly into the markets of neighboring Nordic countries, particularly Denmark, has been pursued mainly by mergers and acquisitions of local companies, but also by expansion, especially in the case of NCC.

The Danish construction sector is dominated by SMEs that employ 85 percent of all employees in the construction sector. Few of those are active abroad (Lubanski 1999). A number of recent major construction projects, including the Great Belt Bridge between Sweden and Denmark, and the Copenhagen Metro, have increased the attractiveness of the Danish market, leading to the market entry of foreign, predominantly Swedish companies and the takeover of some domestic firms (Lubanski 1999). This has not fundamentally altered the general picture of the domination of SMEs in the sector.

The Norwegian construction sector resembles that of Denmark more than that of Sweden. Thus, SMEs predominate and there are few major or internationally active companies in this sector.

In the Finnish construction sector, we find some major companies which have recently become active internationally, thus the sectoral structure bears some similarities with the Swedish case.

Conclusion

This chapter has explored the dynamics of Europeanization and its implications for various systems of organized politico-economic governance throughout Europe. It has also provided a sketch of these systems in the key countries of this study. Finally, a brief overview of developments and parameters in the European construction industry has been offered, a fascinating, and highly representative segment of the changing European private sector.

3

The Institutional Power of Unions and Employers

The *varieties of capitalism* approach to the political economy is actor-centered, which is to say we see the political economy as a terrain populated by multiple actors, each of whom seeks to advance his interests in a rational way in interaction with others.

[Peter A. Hall and David Soskice, 'Introduction', in Peter A. Hall and David Soskice (eds.), *Varieties of Capitalism: The Institutional Foundations of Comparative Advantage*, Oxford: Oxford University Press, 2001, p. 6]

National systems of embedded institutional politico-economic governance filter the effects of closer European economic integration. In fact, they also help condition the creation of national response strategies. It is clear that different institutions produce different outcomes, that is, different re-regulatory responses to the common EU liberalizing impetus. It is therefore vitally important to examine just how it is that such response strategies are being created, enunciated, and implemented. This is a protracted, complex, and often lengthy process, involving the interplay of trade unions and employer association and, in some cases, government ministries and parliaments. This chapter analyzes the institutional power of the two camps, based on a number of relevant organizational and relational variables, which seek to assess just how much power labor market interest associations can command based on internal coherence, and also how well apt they are in applying and using this power to influence the government. Four characteristics form the basis of this organizational power model: degree of centralization, internal cohesion, control over constituents, and access to government.

Assuming that interest associations are rational actors and assessing their relative strength provides us with a prediction as to which side will be most successful in imprinting its preference on the overall policy outcome. However, what is also required is an analysis of the content of such preference. To that end, this chapter engages the new institutionalist turn in political science and distils hypotheses from the historical and rational choice institutionalist approach regarding the preferences for the *wage structure of wages for posted workers* by both camps: unions and employers.

The Organizational Power Model

The key assertion is that *organizational power will transfer into relational power*. A superior level of relational power helps secure critical influence on the policy outcome, that is, the re-regulation of wages for posted workers. In this fashion, a policy outcome is shaped according to the preferences of the more powerful actor. The model is only applied to the key countries Austria, France, the Netherlands, and Germany. *Ex ante*, it is assumed that government intervention in the form of a legislative initiative will underpin a national response strategy. This model generates a prediction about the superiority of one actor over the other, but does not assess the policy preferences themselves, which shall be derived by distilling hypotheses from the two neo-institutionalist approaches. We need to know which actor will leave his imprint on the outcome, and then we find out what that actor wants.

The analysis proceeds as follows. First, the power of the relevant actors in terms of their internal configuration is assessed. The combined assessments of rankings on relevant characteristics will compose a relative power index.[1] These characteristics include:

1. *Degree of centralization* and hierarchy, measured by the number of actors—a large number of actors representing one 'camp' (labor or business) will be considered an indicator of a low degree of centralization.

---

[1] These assessments are made based on (a) the available literature on unions and employer association in Austria, France, the Netherlands, and Germany and (b) empirical field research carried out. The characteristics of internal power are somewhat similar to what van Waarden (1995) refers to as the 'organizational power' of unions and employer association.

2. *Internal cohesion*, based on the nature of internal command structures: Can the core control its sectoral members? Do the sectoral members have input into decision-making? How does the flow between umbrella organization and components look like?

3. *Representation among clientele*, measured in percentage of total potential constituents (i.e. either workforce or companies), which are members of the interest associations.

4. *Access/linkage to government*: Does the association meet or consult with representatives of the government (both executive and legislative branch) regularly? Is it being consulted in the process of the deliberation of relevant legislation? Note that an *ideological bonus* will be awarded if the ideological position of the government in power at the time resembles that of the interest association: for business this means a center-right, for labor a center-left government.

Second, this allows us to make a prediction about which actor possesses a higher score on the power index. We would expect this actor to be able to imprint his preferences on the policy outcome. Based on the assumption that the internal power index will translate into relational power, it is then possible to generate a prediction about the ideological coloring of government intervention. Drawing on the hypotheses generated by rational choice institutionalism (RCI) and historical institutionalism (HI), each actor can be expected to have two sets of preferences at the outset.

Third, the hypotheses of the two approaches are briefly stated.

Finally, in comparing the empirical evidence with the predictions generated by the power index and the hypotheses of (RCI) and (HI), we are able to evaluate the predictive potential of these two approaches in Chapter 5. The key question here is whose preferences are most clearly reflected in the outcome. Does the new wage structure reflect labor's or business' interests? Based on this assessment, it can be ascertained whether the initial prediction was correct or not. If not, what accounts for this divergence? Have the model's predictions been partially or totally falsified?

We next turn to determining the power index for labor market interest associations in all key countries. The following discussion and assessments are based on the power and organizational characteristics at the period this study concentrates on primarily, that is 1993 through 1996.

The Organizational Power of Austrian Actors

In Austria the trade union movement is highly centralized and hierarchical (Pelinka 1981; van Waarden 1995; Tálos 1993; Traxler 1996, 1998;

interview ÖGB 2001). The central union association maintains tight control over both wage bargaining and more general policy questions. It does not encourage autonomous decision-making by its constituent members. Therefore, a high 'strong' mark is warranted on the two factors of *centralization* and *internal cohesion*. Given a membership basis of 60 percent of the active labor force (Traxler 1998; Greif 1998), a 'strong' is also awarded on the *representation among clientele* indicator. Because of the close ties between the union movement and the social democratic party with numerous cases of individuals holding multiple offices (*Personalunion*) and considering the consultation of both social partners even before bills are presented to parliament, *access to government* for the Austrian unions is very considerable and is ranked as 'strong'.

The Austrian employer association, WK, is also marked by a very high degree of *centralization* and *internal cohesion*. The central umbrella association presides over its sectoral and regional subdivisions and steers and coordinates wage bargaining and develops other policy initiatives (van Waarden 1995; Tálos 1993; Traxler 1998; interview WK 2001). In discussing the coherence of Austrian employers we need to take into account the 'one-member–one-vote principle' which causes a dominance of SMEs over policymaking decisions to the detriment of the larger companies. Smaller companies are overrepresented; they have more input than their size or financial contribution would justify. Thus, while on the former factor a score of 'strong' is appropriate, on the latter a mark of 'medium' is more adequate. *Representation among clientele* is most highly developed, given that membership in the WK is obligatory. Membership can therefore be considered to come close to 100 percent, which is why a score of 'strong' on this factor is justified. The WK maintains close ties to the conservative Peoples' Party ÖVP and, just like its union counterpart, is being consulted extensively formally and informally by government before legislative initiatives are presented to parliament. *Access to government* is therefore very well developed and can be ranked as 'strong'.

Since the government in power in Austria in 1993 was a Red-Black Grand Coalition, no bonus can be awarded to either side based on the ideological preference of the government.

The Organizational Power of German Actors

The German trade union movement is not particularly centralized, since autonomy over wage bargaining rests with the individual sectoral and regional members (Markovits 1986; Swenson 1989; Thelen 1991; Streeck 1992). In fact, decentralization, the avoidance of power concentration, and the federal principle of strong constituents lay at the basis of the foundation of the DGB. The DGB acts in consultation with its sectoral members, usually based on their initiative and never impedes their autonomy over wage bargaining. Therefore, the degree of *centralization* stands at a 'medium', just like *internal cohesion*, given the low amount of restraint and control over its constituents. We recall the pivotal role of sectoral unions, such as the metal sector IG Metall or the service sector ver.di, in policy formulation and wage bargaining initiatives. With a level of unionization of 30 percent, on *representation among clientele* a score of 'medium' is being awarded. *Access to government* occurs through informal hearings of union representatives by the relevant ministries and in the parliamentary committees, yet none of these consultations are binding on the government in any form. Ties to the Social Democratic Party are not strongly developed because the union is officially bipartisan and not ideologically aligned. Thus, a score of 'medium' is awarded.

The German employer association BDA leaves wage bargaining to its sectoral and regional members and seldom applies pressure on individual sectoral members. Indeed, sectoral members are mighty actors in their own right. This is particularly true for the metal sector association Gesamtmetall which contributes the lion's share of dues to the BDA and from whose ranks the president has traditionally been recruited. Internal flow is highly developed, since regional and sectoral members are regularly consulted by the national umbrella organization (interview BDA 2001). On degree of *centralization* and *internal cohesion* a score of 'medium' is awarded. The employer association unites employers employing 80 percent of the total workforce (van Waarden 1995) and is thus fairly representative of the demands of its constituents. This substantial level of *representation among clientele* can be rewarded by a ranking of 'strong'. *Access to government* occurs through very loosely developed ties with the conservative Christian Democrats or the FDP and through informal hearings and contacts to relevant government ministries and formal hearings in parliamentary committees. Thus, a score of 'medium' is awarded on this measure.

Since the government in power in Germany in 1996 was a center-right coalition of the CDU/FDP, an ideological bonus is being awarded to the camp of the employers.

The Organizational Power of French Actors

The French labor union movement is fragmented and even atomized in organizational terms. It exhibits an odd combination of institutional strength at the national level given its presence in advisory councils and very weak representation at the enterprise level, with severe problems in controlling the intermediary sectoral level from the top. The union movement is handicapped by its ideological fragmentation. Although internal consultation and contacts exist amongst them, a common position can hardly ever be reached because of these ideological divisions between the more compromise-prone CFDT and CFTC and the more radical CGT and FO-CGT. Given its activist history, the union movement is not well equipped to control its rank and file; by the same token the umbrella organization is usually slow and cumbersome in taking up the demands formulated by its basis (Mouriaux 1993, 1994; Goetschy 1998; interview CFDT 2000; CGT 2000). For these reasons, *centralization* and *internal cohesion* attains a ranking of 'weak'. The rate of unionization in France is estimated between 7 and 10 percent of the total workforce and has decreased dramatically over the past 20 years (Mouriaux 1993). Given this low degree of *representation among clientele* a ranking of 'weak' is justified. Union representatives are usually consulted informally by the relevant government ministries (interview CFDT 2000; CGT 2000; interview FRMEmpSocAff 2001) or they can make their voices heard on major policy issues through their representation on the Economic and Social Council (interview *Conseil Economique et Sociale* 2000). Recommendations of this body are not binding in nature, however. Government intervention into wage bargaining occurs as does sweeping social legislation surpassing the union movement, the state acting as an ersatz union. Therefore, access to government is ranked as 'weak'.

The French employers Medef (formerly known as CNPF) are a relatively highly centralized association in organizational terms. However, wage bargaining, as in Germany, is left to the regional and sectoral affiliates and the center does not intervene into its constituents' bargaining efforts (interview Medef 2000). The umbrella organization thus acts as a mouthpiece of the sectoral associations, develops policy, and lobbies on behalf of the members' interests. A score of 'medium' is therefore awarded on the dimensions of *centralization* and *internal cohesion*. *Representation among clientele* covers 50 percent of French companies (Ebbinghaus and Visser 1994; Goetschy 1998) which justifies a score of 'medium'. Access to government takes place in a fashion similar to that of the unions, namely through informal hearings at relevant ministries and representation in the Economic and Social Council. Because of the similar social and educational background of business and government elites (Schmidt 1996a), informal access is often facilitated, leading to an overall ranking of 'medium'.

The government in power in France in 1993 was a center-right coalition of the RPR/UDF. Therefore, a bonus is being awarded to the employers' side.

The Organizational Power of Dutch Actors

In the Netherlands, the union movement is characterized by a moderate degree of coverage, an internal ideological division between a social democratic FNV and the Christian CNV, yet constitutes an overall hierarchical organization (Visser 1998). Within these two trade unions relatively tight control over wage bargaining and more general issues is maintained (Keizer 2001). Therefore, a 'medium' is awarded on *centralization* and *internal cohesion*. With a membership of 28 percent, a 'medium' is also allotted for *representation among clientele*. Given the consultation of unions within the framework of macrolevel institutions such as the *Stichting van de Arbeid* and the *Social-Economische Raad*, a 'medium' is granted for government access.

The Dutch employer association *Vereniging van Nederlandse Ondernemingen* (VNO-NCW) has gained organizational centralization, following the unification of VNO and NCW. It is characterized therefore by a 'strong' degree of *centralization* and relatively high coverage (Visser 1998). Developments among the sectoral members are quite closely monitored, but sectoral members are allotted a significant amount of leeway, henceforth a 'medium' for *internal cohesion* is awarded. Access to government is secured through participation in the institutions mentioned earlier and through formal and informal lobbying. The employers are very well apt at organizing their potential clientele, drawing in around 65 percent of Dutch businesses, hence a 'strong' mark is awarded on this count.

The government from 1989 to 1993 was a Grand Coalition of Social Democrats and Christian Democrats, followed by a 'violet coalition' of Social Democrats, and the two right-wing and left-wing liberal parties after 1994. We cannot therefore award a bonus to either side.

As we can ascertain from Table 3.1, both camps receive a very high score in Austria, the stand-off in terms of organizational power suggesting a compromise solution. By contrast, in France, the Netherlands, and Germany there is a gap between the two sides, implying an advantage in terms of organizational power by business over labor. In the French case, employers enjoy a very comfortable advantage. The conservative coloring of government coalitions in France and Germany further augment the position of the employers.

Table 3.1 Comparing the relative power of labor market interest associations

Internal Power Index		Employers		
Unions	Austria	Germany	France	Netherlands
Centralization	Strong–strong	Medium–medium	Weak–medium	Medium–medium
Internal cohesion	Strong–strong	Medium–medium	Medium–medium	Medium–strong
Representation among clientele	Strong–strong	Medium–strong	Weak–medium	Medium–strong
Access to government	Strong–strong	Medium–medium	Weak–medium	Medium–medium
Bonus for ideological proximity:	No	Employers	Employers	No
Comparison of power index	Strong–strong	Medium–strong	Weak–medium	Medium–strong

Actor Preferences

Having established the relative power of the two camps, their preferences shall now be briefly considered. In order to do so, preferences will be deducted both from RCI and HI.

These preferences for all actors will only be outlined very briefly, a more detailed discussion can be found in Appendix B.

Following RCI we would expect employers to pursue utility maximization. This can take two forms: either maximize the wage differential and minimize the radius of internationally applicable *lois de police*. An alternative prediction is that utility maximization might consist in favoring a more protectionist response strategy, ensuring status quo levels of wages and hence prices. This seems particularly likely in countries in which SMEs view foreign subcontractors more as a threat than an opportunity, and influence the employer association to take appropriate action. Given the predominance of SMEs in the Austrian employer association WK, this point is of particular pertinence for Austria and, by extension, for the Netherlands, Finland, Norway, Luxembourg, Belgium, and Denmark. In France, larger companies have great clout in the Medef and the sectoral FNB, while in Germany's BDA both larger (HDB) and smaller (ZDB) construction companies are represented. The prediction for France is hence that a protectionist approach is unlikely to find the endorsement of the employers since it is in the predominantly larger companies' interest not to pursue such solution. For Germany, the prediction is somewhat less clear, ultimately depending on which employer association manages to secure more influence on the BDA. In addition, a rift might occur between the sectoral and the overall employer association since what is in the interest of the one (higher product prices) might not be in the interest in the other (lower wages in general). This issue pertains to the characteristic of 'internal cohesion'. In Austria and the Netherlands, with high internal cohesion we can expect this demand to be either considered and incorporated or completely oppressed. In France and Germany where internal cohesion is lower, a conflict might erupt more easily. Obviously, internal dissent weakens the overall position.

Labor's strategies are obviously different. The unions attempt to minimize the wage differential and render the array of the *lois de police* as inclusive as possible. Alternatively, they concentrate their efforts on their key clientele and disregard posted workers. This prediction is the same for all countries included in this study. Within the trade unions a division might occur if some sectoral divisions but not all support the sectoral union most concerned in the construction sector. Again, this is unlikely to cause any problems in Austria (and the Nordic countries) where 'internal cohesion' is high, but may do so in Germany, the Netherlands and France (as well as the other Low Countries).

Following the HI approach, the agenda of trade unions and employers is by definition much more dependent upon time, place, and concrete circumstances. Hypotheses about strategies and objectives cannot be deducted from abstract exogenous incentive structures, but have to be derived from detailed historical reasoning, taking into account the specific historical legacy of union and employers' positions in all countries of this study, paying particular attention to signs of 'critical junctures' and 'path dependency' as well as the role of ideas where relevant. This discussion is included in Appendix B, while Tables 3.2–3.6 provide summaries of the preferences for actors in Austria, France, Germany, and the Netherlands.

Some of the employer association might be content to settle on compromise solutions with trade unions, or even endorse a somewhat

Table 3.2 Objectives and strategies for actors from a rational choice institutionalist perspective

Business

Objective: Utility maximization, thus profit maximization

Strategy 1: Push for maximization of wage differential, deregulation, minimize coverage of *lois de police*

Strategy 2: Accept small wage differential to avoid downward wage-price spiral

Labor

Objective: Utility maximization, thus maximization of wages for clientele

Strategy 1: Push for minimization of wage differential and maintenance of high wages, extend *lois de police* as much as possible

Strategy 2: Unwillingness to represent posted workers which are not immediate constituents, thus focus on wages of immediate members

Government

Objective: Utility maximization, but definition thereof hinges on ideological position of government (coalition): Conservative/liberal government will favor liberalization and wage differential, leftist government will favor re-regulation and minimization of wage differential

Strategy: Limited to sideline position in countries with *de facto* or *de jure* *Tarifautonomie*, but can apply pressure on interest groups to accept its strategy or else push its own strategy in consultation with social partners

Table 3.3 Objectives and strategies for French actors from a historical institutionalist perspective

French Business

Objective: Apply constant downward pressure on wages, but uniformly so and based on equal conditions for everyone at the outset, not necessarily interested in launching downward spiral on prices and wages

Strategy: Re-regulation is preferable option, best ensured by national response strategy shaped in favor of business, secured through formal and informal contacts to government

Role of ideas? Commitment to equal conditions at the outset (*concurrence loyale*), often somewhat protectionist and wary towards foreign competition entering the French market; neoliberal ideas traditionally of negligible importance

French Labor

Objective: Ensure payment of standard French wages to posted workers, though more militant FO and CGT are less likely to compromise than CFDT and CFTC in achieving this goal

Strategy: Achieve implementation of national response strategy through use of contacts to government (hearings at Ministry of Labor, etc.), apply pressure from below (industrial action, etc.) if necessary

Role of ideas? Commitment towards high wages for all workers, unwilling to accept substandard wages

French Government

Objective: Find legalistic regulation of this issue colored by center-right (neo-Gaullist) government, thus influenced by close ties to business, but also Euroskeptic and protectionist orientation

Strategy: Implement national response strategy

Role of ideas? State intervenes as *ersatz* union at critical junctures, yet this instance cannot be characterized as such; among the neo-Gaullist right a certain Euroskepticism especially towards market liberalization, neoliberalism plays little role; state plays central role of regulator of the framework conditions of industrial relations and intervenes into wage-setting occasionally, state sets minimum wage rate (SMIC)

Other Factors? Government still plays central and dominant role in regulating and 'governing' the economy, yet its policies are often either shaped directly or later interpreted to its advantage by business; commitment of government to curb illegal immigration and illegal labor, two different issues often confounded in public discussion, limit electoral appeal and success of radical right (*Front Nationale*) by addressing some of its demands; government may use quid pro quo strategy by granting unions some favors and business others

Table 3.4 Objectives and strategies for Austrian actors from a historical institutionalist perspective

Austrian Business

Objective: Keep wages low, find compromise solution with labor

Strategy: Attempt to shape national response strategy in its own favor, secured through formal and informal contacts to government (hearings and contacts to Ministry of Labor, etc.) and formal and informal consultation with labor (Social Partnership)

Role of ideas? Before entry into the EU relatively sheltered from competition; neoliberal ideas traditionally of negligible importance

Austrian Labor

Objective: Ensure payment of standard Austrian wages to posted workers; avoid undercutting of wages and wage gap

Strategy: Achieve implementation of national response strategy through use of formal and informal contacts to government (hearings and contacts to Ministry of Labor, etc.) and formal and informal consultation with business (Social Partnership)

Role of ideas? Commitment towards high wages for all workers, including foreign migrant workers (*Gastarbeiter*), unwilling to accept substandard wages even though wage moderation and inter-sectoral wage differentials are tolerated

Austrian Government

Objective: Leave impetus for re-regulation of this issue up to social partners as it is their domain, but respond to initiatives proposed by them; Grand Coalition government generally pursues moderate centrist line based on compromise between the two 'black' and 'red' camps

Strategy: Implement national response strategy based on proposition (usually compromise-based) from social partners

Role of ideas? State generally leaves regulation of certain domains to social partners and then presides over the legalistic implementation or compliance with the outcome of negotiations by the two social partners; neoliberalism plays small role; state sets legalistic framework of industrial relations, yet does not intervene directly into wage-setting

Other Factors? Accession to EU creates need for re-regulation of certain issues; commitment of government to curb illegal immigration and illegal labor in light of mass wave of immigration in the early 1990s from Central and Eastern Europe, two different issues often confounded in public discussion, popular fear of Eastern Europeans taking away jobs and/or undercutting high Austrian wages, limit electoral appeal and success of very successful radical right (FPÖ) by addressing some of its demands

Table 3.5 Objectives and strategies for German actors from a historical institutionalist perspective

German Business

Objective: Keep wages low, attempt to reduce or circumvent system of non-wage labor related costs (*Lohnnebenkosten*), interested in deregulation and a national response strategy to that end

Strategy: Attempt to obstruct national response strategy or else, if passage is unavoidable, color it in its favor, secured through formal and informal contacts to government

Role of ideas? In the early 1990s neoliberal rhetoric and ideas appear within the BDI, strong ideological belief in competition and *Ordnungspolitik*; positive attitude towards EU-induced liberalization

German Labor

Objective: Ensure payment of standard German wages to posted workers, avoid undercutting and wage gap

Strategy: Achieve implementation of national response strategy through use of formal and informal contacts to government (hearings and contacts to Ministry of Labor, etc.)

Role of ideas? Commitment towards high wages for all workers, including foreign migrant workers (*Gastarbeiter*), unwilling to accept substandard wages even though inter-sectoral wage differentials are tolerated

German Government

Objective: National response strategy will be colored by center-right government's ideological commitment towards moderate market liberalization and support for European integration, yet on social policy questions government is open to propositions by social partners with a certain bias towards business; thus we would expect an outcome which is in compliance with any European directive and in favor of market liberalization and business interests given the ideological *couleur* of the government

Strategy: Implement national response strategy based on proposition by social partners, while not intervening directly into wage regulation per se

Role of ideas? State generally leaves regulation of certain domain to social partners and then guards over the legalistic implementation or compliance with the outcome of negotiations by the two social partners; this autonomy over the domain (*Tarifautonomie*) is jealously guarded by the social partners; neoliberalism and market liberalization emerge as ideas in the late 1980s, though they are pursued moderately, liberalization may be pursued through European arena to avoid and circumvent domestic coalition; state sets legalistic framework of industrial relations, yet does not intervene directly into wage-setting

Other factors? Generally compliant attitude towards EU ('model European') means going through European channels for re-regulation first; center-right coalition government is committed towards moderate market liberalization and is a staunch advocate of European integration, government is interested in quick progress in the renovation of East and the new capital Berlin in particular; some commitment of government to curb numbers of applicants for political asylum culminates in 1993 reform to law on asylum; weak and divided radical right

Table 3.6 Objectives and strategies for Dutch actors from a historical institutionalist perspective

Dutch Business

Objective: Keep wages low, further reduce of non-wage labor related costs, aim for consensual bipartite solution, avoiding government intervention

Strategy: Seek consensual bipartite solution that will be business-friendly and minimize government intervention

Role of ideas? Some embrace of neoliberal ideas in the early 1990s; positive attitude towards EU-induced liberalization

Dutch Labor

Objective: Ensure payment of standard Dutch wages to posted workers; avoid undercutting and emergence of two-tier structure

Strategy: Achieve implementation of national response strategy either through bipartite solution with employers or through use of formal and informal contacts to government (hearings and contacts to Ministry of Labor, etc.)

Role of ideas? Commitment towards high wages for all workers, including foreign migrant workers, but some willingness to tolerate income inequality

Dutch Government

Objective: National response strategy will be colored by centrist government's ideological commitment towards market liberalization, welfare state reform, active labor market policy, and support for European integration, yet on social and labor policy questions government is open to propositions by social partners with a certain bias towards business; thus, we would expect an outcome which is in compliance with any European directive and in favor of economic liberalization

Strategy: Implement national response strategy based on proposition by social partners, but do not act unless no bipartite solution is forthcoming

Role of ideas? Government has retreated from more interventionist tradition since the early 1980s; neoliberalism, welfare state reform, labor market deregulation, and market liberalization more generally emerge as ideas in the late 1980s

Other factors? Government will be reluctant to act unless social partners seem not to succeed in finding a solution; in a small, open, transnationalized economy a protectionist policy will unlikely be favored by a centrist government; migration does not emerge as heavily politicized issue until the late 1990s and early 2000s

protectionist position based on historical precedent. This is notably the case in France (and in Belgium, Norway, and Luxembourg). The Austrian (Finnish and Norwegian) association is likely to settle on a compromise middle-of-the-road solution. By contrast, the appearance of neoliberal rhetoric among the employers' camp in Germany (and Sweden and the Netherlands) might lead to a relatively aggressive position.

Conclusion

In sum, this chapter has introduced an organizational power model pertaining to characteristics of the two labor market interest associations. A power index has been presented for associations in Austria, France, the Netherlands, and Germany. Subsequently, hypotheses from the rational choice and historical neo-institutionalism approaches have been distilled for the preferences of the trade unions, employer association, and government.

4

National Response Strategies to Transnational Challenges: Developments in France, Germany, and Austria

The LSP as a Challenge for National System of Politico-Economic Governance

The EU LSP undermines existing national regulatory regimes, previously used to control market access by foreign companies and workers. As part of the Single Market, it is now possible for Portuguese companies to help construct railway lines in suburban Paris or for Greek workers to be posted to Germany to renovate government buildings in central Berlin. In the absence of any specific EU level legislation, the bilateral Rome Convention applied to such transnational service provision agreements, implying home country wages and social and labor provisions for these so-called posted workers.

The prospect of Portuguese workers toiling away on the construction sites of high-wage Northern Europe, all the while receiving Portuguese wages at one-sixth the level of standard German wages, delighted ardent proponents of a liberal European Single Market and infuriated its Social Democratic critics. This is 'Europe at work', proponents of a deregulatory, liberal Single Market argued, while critics on the left saw their worst fears of social dumping and a downward spiral of social and labor regulations materialize in front of their eyes.

The 'Europeanizing' impact of the LSP seemed to open up an exciting new corporate strategy for service sector industries where the physical relocation of production sites for obvious reasons is impossible. Rather than exporting jobs, employers could now 'import workers', remunerate them at substandard wages, offer them the commonly inferior benefits, working time regulations, and social conditions of Southern and North-western Europe, and do all of this perfectly legally. As such, the LSP presents an excellent case study with which to examine the deregulatory, liberal impact of closer European integration that is often alluded to in the literature on comparative political economy (Albert 1991; Berger and Dore 1996; Hollingsworth and Boyer 1997; Crouch and Streeck 1997; Kitschelt et al. 1999; Scharpf and Schmidt 2000; Hall and Soskice 2001; Yamamura and Streeck 2001, 2003), though sometimes slightly conflated with the analytically distinct phenomenon of globalization. This is a story of the architects of the Single Market opening up new possibilities for trans-national service provision, without providing any re-regulatory social legislation that would reflect the significant gap in wage and income levels between the different EU member states.

At first glance, the LSP promotes a new class of posted workers who find themselves in an odd transnational deregulated space, outside of the neocorporatist or statist system of labor market regulation of the host country, while physically very much on the territory of this receiving country. No longer subject to the regulatory capacity of established insti-tutions and mechanisms of national systems of politico-economic gov-ernance, this group of individuals therefore very concretely experiences the retreat of the state (Strange 1996) or rather the neutering of the state's regulatory capacity faced with the unleashed market forces, commonly invoked in the globalization literature.

Room for Re-regulation

How can states cope with this deregulatory impetus of the EU? How do national systems of politico-economic governance respond to a common external impetus? While stressing that the transnational posting of work-ers was perfectly legal within the remit of the LSP, the ECJ in its Rush Portuguesa decision also made clear that the insistence on prevalent wages and labor conditions for such foreign posted workers by the authorities of receiving states was acceptable. However, under the terms of EU law, the discriminatory treatment of foreign service providers is not tolerated. National response strategies that would have imposed wages and labor conditions above and beyond the prevalent national level would un-doubtedly not withstand the critical scrutiny by the ECJ.

How did such *national response strategies* come about? Their contours and content were shaped by the interplay between government ministries, trade unions, and employers. Depending on the national system of polit-ico-economic governance, sketched previously, these actors assumed different positions, played varyingly important roles, and pursued divergent interests.

The argument that different national varieties of capitalism respond differently and may even perpetuate and augment existing differences, rather than simply accept convergence when faced with a common external challenge dovetails with the more recently formulated insights of the comparative political economy literature (skeptical: Goodin 2003; Blyth 2003; Watson 2003). Analysts stress 'convergence within divergence' (Deeg and Lütz 2000; cf. Schmidt 2002). Hall and Soskice (2001: 60) argue that 'nations often prosper, not by becoming more similar, but by building on their institutional differences'. Invoking classic Ricardian notions, they continue to posit that 'the institutional recreation of comparative advantage' (p.63) will occupy policy and indeed corporate planning in choosing how to adapt to pressures of internationalization.

Hall and Soskice reintroduce a focus on the firm. This study does not analyze firm behavior per se, but rather the amalgamated preferences of business in the form of employer association. National institutions filter the external impetus of Europeanization (Schmidt 2002). While it is argued that this impetus will affect preferences, incentives, and strategies of domestic actors, a theme previously highlighted by the 'second image reversed' approach (Gourevitch 1978; Katzenstein 1978), I do not argue that this impetus upsets the internal power balance between these actors *in their response capacity*. It is, however, conceivable that response strategies that favor one side over the other will produce suboptimal outcomes for the respective other side: a protectionist outcome will presumably advance labor's standing, while a more liberal resolution might better incorporate employers' interests.

Europeanization is therefore a truly two-way process. While the regulatory capacity of the state is undermined through Scharpf's 'negative integration', or 'horizontal' and 'top-down' Europeanization, bottom-up re-regulatory responses are also formulated at the national level.

Fear of Mass Migration

The regulatory capacity of the state is challenged by transnationally posted workers, not only in terms of regulating market access, but also in regard to limiting territorial access. Fears of mass migration led the EU members to impose lengthy transition periods on the freedom of labor mobility for the Mediterranean newcomers of the 1980s. History repeated itself in the early 2000s, when Austria and Germany promoted a similar ban on labor mobility *and* the provision of services from the ten CEE newcomers. Not only where the Austrian and German governments successful in securing approval for implementing such national bans from the European Commission, most other current EU member states have followed suit and have imposed temporary bans, varying from two to seven years.

EU eastward enlargement in May 2004 generated significant fear of mass migration from the newcomer states. The relatively high unemployment rates in CEE, combined with a significant wage gap between the regions, would appear to create powerful 'push-pull' migration pressures (Ehrenberg and Smith 1997). However, most recent studies of the phenomenon of East-West migration question earlier predictions of annual emigration rates of 350,000–500,000 individuals annually or up to 3 percent of the toal population of CEE by 2012. They point to the negative demographic development in CEE, implying that by the time the temporary ban on migration and service provision expires, the demographic bracket containing individuals most likely to emigrate will be small (Fassmann and Münz 2002). The considerable wage gap between Central and Eastern Europe generated considerable excitement among union and employer representatives in France, Austria, and Germany (interviews FTP 2001; IG BAU 2001; HDB 1999, 2000; ZDB 2000; Bau-Holz 2001). On September 28, 2000 the German sectoral employers and the union even issued a joint declaration, demanding a ten-year ban on transnational service provision in the construction sector.

Figures 4.1 and 4.2 illustrate that there is indeed a significant wage gap not only within the existing EU, but even more so between the pre-2004 EU and the newcomers. While the average hourly wage for a CEE construction worker is € 2.95, it is € 19.09 in the current EU. A significant wage gap exists between Germany (€ 21.19) and Poland (€ 4.01) or the Czech Republic (€ 3.60). Similarly, the differences between average Austrian hourly wages (€ 22.71) and Slovakia (€ 2.95) and even Slovenia (€ 7.58) are profound. This wage gap of 1 to 7 dwarfs the 1 to 4 gap within the existing EU between Portugal (€ 6.94) and Denmark (€ 26.00).

This chapter analyzes the genesis and implementation of national response strategies in France, Germany, and Austria, while Chapter 5 will provide an additional discussion of developments in the Netherlands, the other two Low Countries and the Nordic countries. The Austrian, French, and German response strategies are summarized in Table 4.2; for comparative purposes I also include developments in the Netherlands in Table 4.3.

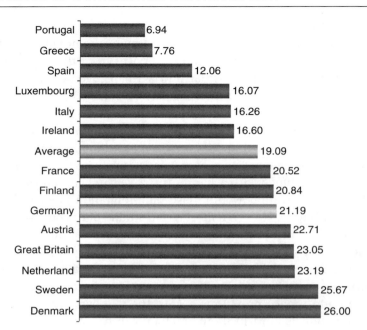

Figure 4.1 Hourly wage costs in the European construction sector in 2000 (in euros)
Source: Eurostat (2003)

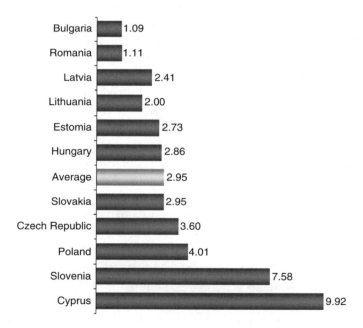

Figure 4.2 Hourly wage costs in the other European Construction sector in 2000 (in euros)
Source: Eurostat (2003)

Table 4.2 National response strategies in Austria, France, and Germany

Austria

Regulation: Arbeitsvertragsrechts-Anpassungsgesetz (AVRAG) 1993, revised 1995, 1999, 2002

Content: Protectionist Re-regulation extending standard Austrian wages and labor conditions to posted workers

Implementation: Legislation, based on union approaching Ministry of Labor. Little employer resistance because SMEs dominate WK and make up bulk of Austrian economy

Dominant Actor: Union, though employers did not resist much

Institutionalist Approach most valuable: Historical institutionalism in general, but RCI draws attention to right-wing challenge of government during revision, role of SMEs influencing employer position

France

Regulation: Loi Quinquennale relative au travail, à l'emploi et à la formation 1993, amended by minor changes to the Labor Law in 2000

Content: Protectionist Re-regulation extending standard French wages and labor conditions to posted workers

Implementation: Legislation, based on government initiative, actively supported by one sectoral union CFDT-FNCB and sectoral employers FTP, endorsed by other unions, tolerated by CNPF/Medef. Relatively protectionist employers sought to avoid downward wage-price spiral

Dominant Actor: Government, but sectoral union and employers lobbied and neither other unions nor employers were opposed

Institutionalist Approach most valuable: Historical institutionalism in general, but RCI draws attention to right-wing challenge of government

Germany

Regulation: Arbeitnehmerentsendegesetz (ArbEntsG) 1996. amended in 1999, 2003

Content: Re-regulation extending new minimum wage to posted workers *in the construction sector only.*

Implementation: Legislation, based on active Minister of Labor and sectoral lobbying efforts by HDB, ZDB and IG BAU on the one hand and liberal Minister of Economic Affairs on the other. Implementation long delayed because umbrella employers BDA, sectoral employers *Gesamtmetall* and *Gesamttextil* blocked it. Sectoral employers were more conceding to union demands. Finally, a low minimum wage was found and declared universally applicable.

Dominant Actor: Employers

Institutionalist Approach most valuable: RCI in general, but historical institutionalism draws attention to neoliberal ideas among employers and tradition of covering all foreign workers within the union

Table 4.3 National response strategy in the Netherlands

Regulation: Modified Sectoral Wage Contract for Construction Sector CAO Bouw
   1996–1999 Wet arbeidsvoorwaarden grensoverschrijdende arbeid provided
   legislative framework, but few changes
Content: Re-regulation extending standard Dutch wages to posted workers *only in*
   the construction sector and only to postings for more than four weeks
Implementation: Collective wage agreement, based on sectoral union pressure from
   FNV Bouw. Sectoral employers AVBB agreed because four week 'window'
   permitted them enough flexibility, umbrella employers VNO-NCW permitted
   regulation because it was liberal enough and no spillover effects were feared.
Dominant Actor: Employers
Institutionalist Approach most valuable: RCI in general, but historical
   institutionalism draws attention to consensus-oriented decision-making geared
   towards wage moderation in the Netherlands

The National Response Strategies: Interplay between Employers, Unions, and Government

The national arena is not rendered obsolete by the pressures of European-ization. In fact, it is precisely at this level, where the bargaining contest over the nature of the wage regulation for posted workers unfolds. Trade unions and employer association attempted to influence, alter, and modify this regulation. As will become apparent, actors in some countries preferred the status quo of home country regulation, and therefore obstructed, delayed, or attempted to impede the formulation of a national re-regulation.

The role of government varied across the national cases. Generally speaking, the governments of highly neocorporatist countries such as Norway, Sweden, Austria, Finland, and Denmark were at least initially somewhat hesitant to become involved in the regulation of this policy domain, preferring to leave regulation to the social partners. In intermedi-ate neocorporatist countries, such as Germany and the Netherlands, the government was much less hesitant to become involved in the regulation process. However, governments in both countries were careful not to impinge on the autonomy of wage-setting that the social partners enjoy (*Tarifautonomie*). By contrast, statist systems such as France, Belgium, and Luxembourg saw the government play a central role in the formulation of national re-regulation. Within government, the Ministry of Labor was charged with developing a legislative draft which formed the basis of such re-regulation.

As Tables 4.2 and 4.3 demonstrate, Austria and France responded quicker and in a more protectionist fashion than either the Netherlands or Germany. In the former three countries, there was also significantly less conflict over the nature of re-regulation between the two camps than in Germany, where multiple cleavages emerged. In general, the strongly statist and strongly neocorporatist countries responded more quickly, more swiftly, more comprehensively, and in a more 'protectionist' fashion. By contrast, responses in the two intermediate corporatist countries Germany and the Netherlands came about notably slower, created considerably more conflict, especially in Germany, and were significantly more 'liberal' in nature.

Despite the stronger organizational position that French business enjoys with respect to the divided feeble trade union movement and notwithstanding the good contacts to a conservative government, the French employers were not keen to promote a truly liberal deregulatory solution. Instead, they preferred clear rules of the game and 'equal starting conditions', even if this meant foregoing the cost advantages offered by non-French service providers. Austrian employers, matched with a very powerful union, were unwilling to challenge the union on this issue, particularly because the apparent advantages of outsourcing and subcontracting appeared more as a menace than as an opportunity in an economy predominantly composed of SMEs. The position of Dutch and German employers proved to be markedly different. Dutch employers preferred the 'flexibility' afforded to them by the LSP. Only due to strong pressure from the union were employers willing to accept the application of Dutch wages for workers posted for more than four weeks. German employers proved particularly bellicose. While the sectoral employers might have been willing to make some concessions to the union, the umbrella employer association, under pressure from other sectoral employers, decided not to cede an inch to the unions. The battle over the German national response strategy therefore turned out to be messy, protracted, fought on several fronts, and hence particularly bloody.

Another major difference in the response strategy between strongly neocorporatist Austria and statist France on the one hand and intermediately neocorporatist Germany and the Netherlands is the remit of regulation. While the Austrian and French re-regulation applies to the entire economy, the German and Dutch re-regulation is limited to the construction sector.

Access to government proved particularly important. In Austria, the Minister of Labor at the time was a former construction worker and former head of the sectoral union Bau-Holz. This eased access to government and helped the Austrian umbrella union ÖGB gain strong influence on the draft legislation. In France, the president of sectoral employers FNTP was an old school friend of the Minister of Labor, helping employers to influence the regulation. In Germany, the Minister of Labor, while a union member and considered part of the left-wing of the Christian Democrats, was unwilling to create legislation which would have set wages by decree. This meant that the ultimate core of the German response strategy, the wage level for posted workers, would be set through negotiations between the particularly aggressive employers and unions. In the Netherlands, a bipartite solution was found that avoided government intervention.

EU Level Re-regulation: A Belated Non-intrusive Lowest Common Denominator Solution

The main objects of study in this volume are the national responses to the EU-induced liberalization, however, it would be unfair to charge that the European Commission had been oblivious to the effects of deregulation implicit in the LSP. An EU directive was generated and passed in 1996. However, its effects were minimal and it did not intervene into already existing national regimes and national response strategies. The adjustment pressures for the high-wage member states were negligible.

Member states' interests diverged considerably on this issue. The result was thus a least common denominator regulation, which stood at the end of a long and protracted attempt at arriving at a mutually agreeable solution. In the process of bottom-up Europeanization, various member states attempted to shape and create such EU directive, using their own national response strategy as a template, which would both advance their interests and minimize transaction costs in the adaptation process, a strategy referred to as agenda-setting in the EU literature (Heritier 1996; Pollack 2003). However, the final result of this directive was based on an Italian initiative that satisfied most countries involved, but ultimately changed very little.

Low Against High-Wage Europe: The Battle over an EU Directive

On August 1, 1991 the Commission had first prepared a draft council directive which would have imposed on member states the duty to 'see to it that, whatever the law applicable to the employment relationship, the undertaking does not deprive the worker of the terms and conditions of employment which apply for work of the same character at the place where the work is temporarily carried out . . . ' and proceeded to define a number of minimal rights, including working time, minimum wage, and health and safety standards (COM (91) 230 final, Article 3: p. 21).[1]

This initiative was then debated by the European Parliament. The Economic and Social Council was consulted as well. Based on their suggestions, the Commission presented a second and revised proposal on June 16, 1993 (COM (593) 225 final). The discussion about the exact coverage and the hard core of applicable labor conditions continued, as did the debate about temporary exceptions for postings of less than three or one month. Yet essentially the draft was blocked in the Council of Ministers for Labor and Social Affairs. During the deliberation a clear front of countries emerged, which were explicitly against any such regulation, namely Great Britain and Portugal. France, Denmark, and the Benelux countries were clearly in favor, while Germany oscillated between the liberal position of its Ministry of Economics and its labor-friendly Ministry of Labor until it assumed the presidency in late 1994. Ireland, Greece, Spain, and Italy though less categorical in their refusal were not to be convinced of the benefits of such European directive for the longest time. The German presidency failed to deliver a concrete regulation as well, despite the activist role of Minister of Labor Blüm who attempted to find a compromise solution and scheduled meeting of the Council on July 8, September 22, and December 6 and 21 in 1994 (interview DEMLabSocAff 2000).

During the French Presidency in the first half of 1995, French Minister of Labor Michel Giraud who had initiated the *Loi Quinquennale* (see later) took up the ball from the Germans and presented a new and revised version of the directive. This directive was already limited to the construction sector, and left a large number of items up to the discretion of the member states, including the hard core of labor conditions applicable. Yet it included no transition period, during which home country wages would

---

[1] In this draft, the authors also pointed out that 'a particular problem arises, however, where a Member State places obligations, notably with regard to pay, on firms based in and working on its territory, and these firms are faced with competition . . . from a firm based elsewhere and not subject to the same obligations. Legitimate competition between firms is the overlaid by potentially distortive [sic] effects between national requirements' (COM (91) 230 final, *9bis*, p. 4). The wording seems very indicative indeed: The problem of unfair competition is thus certainly acknowledged, but from a business point of view and not from the perspective of workers and in consideration of social dumping.

prevail, unlike previous versions. Even so, Britain, Portugal, Spain, Italy, and Ireland were opposed to the French initiative (Eichhorst 1998: 243). The 1995 accession of Finland, Sweden, and Austria, all of which supported the French proposal therefore did not suffice to turn the table and result in a qualified majority.

In early 1996, the Italian presidency finally managed to spindoctor a compromise solution, which was able to garner the support of both the high-wage Northern European countries, which had already expressed their sympathy for the French, and to some extent the German proposal, and the low-wage Southern and Western European countries. In essence, the Italian version modified the French proposition by limiting a transition period, during which home country wages and labor conditions would continue to apply, to four weeks and simultaneously making the introduction of this very period optional. The skeptical group of low-wage Southern and Western European countries could be convinced, not least because Italy, Ireland, and Greece could secure minor concessions.[2] Portugal and Britain continued to block and veto even this proposal.

The EU directive 96/71/EC 'concerning the posting of workers in the framework of the provision of services' (COM 96/71/EC final) was finally passed on December 16, 1996 and was to be implemented by the member states by December 16, 1999 (EIRO 1999). Upon closer inspection, the impact of this directive is very limited indeed and amounts to *little more than a safety net* for the existing national response strategies:

- It defines a hard core of labor conditions such as working time, paid annual holidays, minimum wages, and health and safety standards which now have to be applied to posted workers if they are part of the legal code or the collective agreements declared universally applicable in the target countries of posting (Article 3, Section 1).
- This essentially changes very little, since such standards–to the extent that they were part of the *ordre public*–could (and theoretically had to) be applied already. To the extent that they were part of the collective agreements they were applied to posted workers anyway in practice, if this solution was agreeable to both labor market interest associations, as the Austrian regulation demonstrates.

---

[2] For Italy and Ireland, exceptions were made for short-term installation projects of less than eight days (Article 3, Section 2), which were explicitly not covered by this directive. The concession made for Greece was that the merchant navy was not included, either (Article 2, Section 1).

- It leaves the question of the transition period up to the member states, though it limits such period, if it is indeed chosen, to a maximum of four weeks. Again, this is lowest common denominator solution, which is not intrusive into member state arrangements at all. Thus, member states can find either relatively restrictive regulations with no such period as in France or a relatively liberal solution with a period of four weeks as in the Netherlands (see later).[3]
- Although it is true that both high-wage Northern European countries and low-wage Southern European countries are now forced to implement this directive, the practical effect of this requirement is minimal. The high-wage members already disposed of either legalistic solutions or response strategies based on agreements between the social partners. Low-wage countries without such regulations, such as Greece, Italy, Spain, Portugal, Ireland, Britain, and Italy, do have to find such response strategies, but since they are de facto not affected by the posting of workers and 'wage dumping', the impact will be minimal. Even so, these countries are under no obligation to modify their own régime of social and labor conditions or to modify their minimum wages.

The French National Response Strategy

Developments in the French Construction Sector—The Fear of Mediterranean Migration

In France, the posting of workers from other European member states did not assume significant proportions until the late 1980s. Corporate restructuring and the increased use of subcontractors coincided during this period with the entry of low-wage states Spain and Portugal into the EC. Free mobility of labor from Greece and the two Iberian countries was restricted until 1988 and 1993 respectively.[4] The LSP was not explicitly re-regulated at the national level in France (Desmazières de Séchelles 1993: 473ff.). To prevent the feared uncontrolled labor market access of workers

---

[3] The original four week transition period embedded in the first Austrian legislation was later abolished in the 1996 modification of the legislation (see later).

[4] (Art. 45(1) of the Act of Accession of Greece and Articles 55–56 for Spain and 215–218 for Portugal, later shortened to December 31, 1991 in Council Regulation 2194/91). The transition period was also upheld by an ECJ ruling of March 27, 1983 (Case 77/82 *Peskeloglou vs. Bundesanstalt für Arbeit* ECR 1085), which made clear that (Greek) workers were barred from labor mobility during the transition period.

from these countries and to safeguard the monopoly on labor recruitment held by the National Office of Immigration (*Office Nationale d'Immigration—ONI*), the French government passed a decree on December 8, 1986.[5] This decree explicitly stated that citizens of these three countries needed to obtain a work permit issued on an individual basis by the ONI until the end of the transition period on January 1, 1993. Immigration from Portugal was feared since there is a sizable Portuguese immigrant community already in France (*Le Monde*, December 17, 1992a; Mekachera 1993), which could have served to provide the ethnic network through which chain migration flourishes. The Portuguese are among the leading three immigrant groups represented in France, along with Algerians and Moroccans (Mekachera 1993). As immigration was slowly emerging on the political agenda as a 'hot' item, promoted by the rise in the electoral fortunes of the right-wing xenophobe *Front national*, the government sought to avoid being perceived as tolerating inward migration.

Increasing Illegal Employment in the French Construction Sector

Larger companies exert considerable downward pressure on French SME subcontractors. In response, SMEs often resort to illegal forms of employment[6] to meet tight deadlines and even tighter calculated costs in the construction sector. This may involve substandard wages, no overtime and vacation pay, illegal forms of employment ('payment under the table') or the employment of undocumented migrants (*Le Monde*, May 16, 1990a, b, April 24, 1991; *Action juridique* 1994). Trade unions are relatively weak in the

---

[5] The directive concerning work permits for Greek, Spanish, and Portuguese citizens states that 'Article 48 of the Treaty of Rome which grants nationals of a member state the right to take up employment on the territory of another member state can only be applied to Portuguese citizens after the transition period of seven years, that is to say after 1 January 1993' ('L'article 48 du traité du Rome, qui reconnaît aux travailleurs rassortisants d'un Etat membre le droit d'accès à l'emploi sur le territoire des autres Etats membres, ne pourra être appliqué aux rassortisants portugais qu'à l'expiration d'une période transitoire de sept ans, c'est-à-dire le 1er janvier 1993') ('Décret 86-1267 du 8 décembre 1986 relatif aux autorisations de travails délivrées aux ressortisants grecs, espagnols et portugais' (quoted in Journal Officiel de la Republique Française of December 12, 1986: 14917)).

[6] While illegal forms of employment does not always take the form of the employment of illegal foreign residents, illegal forms of employment of foreigners was and is concentrated in the construction sector, according to the interministerial coordination office for the fight against illegal labor (Délégation interministérielle à la lutte contre le travail illégal—DILTI). Regionally, it is concentrated in the Île-de-France (greater Paris) and the southeastern region of Provence-Alpes-Côte-d'Azur (French Riviera) (*Le Monde*, May 16, 1990a, b; DILTI 1999).

private sector in general, and among small companies in particular. This renders illegal and exploitative behavior easier for employers. Subcontracting became increasingly popular in the service sector in the late 1980s. Between 1987 and 1991, the total number of infractions involving illegal forms of employment increased from 328 to 5,883 annual cases! Simultaneously, illegal forms of employment of foreigners increased from 1,716 registered cases to 3,808 (*Le Monde*, November 20, 1992, November 25, 1992, December 17, 1992b; *Syndicalisme*, October 12, 2000). Behind the backdrop of the increase use of 'subcontracting in several layers' (*sous-traitance en cascade*), the posting of workers commenced, especially in the construction sector and involving predominantly Portuguese workers and companies (*Le Monde*, August, 5 1987, December 18, 1987, September 24, 1996; Ministère de la Justice 1999; DILTI 1999).

In 1987, a government study found 160,000 construction companies without any actual employees! This attests to the growing role of subcontracting through convoluted chains (*Le Monde*, December 1, 1988). In the late 1980s, several major construction projects including Mitterrand's *grandes projets* were underway in France: the La Défense office and apartment annex to western Paris, the Bibliotheque Nationale, the Musée d'Orsay converted from being a train station, the major high speed rail TGV links between Paris and the hinterland, the amusement park Eurodisney on the outskirts of Paris, the Eurotunnel between France and Britain, and the Montblanc tunnel to Italy. The construction titan Bouygues SA was involved in all of these projects (Bouygues 2000).

Going to Court over a Subcontractor: The Rush Portuguesa *Case*

In the early fall of 1986, French labor inspectors apprehended Portuguese workers employed on the site of a TGV Atlantic line in suburban Paris near Villebon-sur-Yvette. Hired by a company registered in Porto (Portugal) by the name of Rush Portuguesa and engaged as a subcontractor by Bouygues SA, none of the workers possessed a valid work visa. They had entered France as tourists. The departmental labor inspector of Evry thus initiated legal action (*procès-verbal*) against Rush Portuguesa on October 27, 1986, accusing it of the illegal employment of workers without work permits (*Le Monde*, December 18, 1987; Bonnechere 1995: 335). Rush Portuguesa itself was set up and chartered in March 1986 by the former boss of the construction sector of the Bouygues group, a French citizen originally from Portugal by the name of Albert Bernardo. Although the company only maintained 5 permanent employees in Portugal, it posted approximately 200 workers to France (*Le Monde*, December 18, 1987). There is thus strong evidence to suggest that Rush Portuguesa was little more than a creation of Bouygues, set up explicitly to cut down on wage expenditures. While this had been the chief rationale for posting workers from Portugal, Rush Portuguesa was not actually being held accountable for paying its workers Portuguese wages only. In fact, it had not been firmly established yet that any French wage regulation, including the minimum wage SMIC, possessed the character of an internationally binding *loi de police* (Taquet 1993: D8).

The crucial question that the court deliberated involved the issue of the coverage of the LSP. Was the posting of workers under the *auspices of the liberalization of service provision* indeed permissible, even if it involved countries that were still subject to restrictions on *labor mobility*? The case was transferred from a tribunal in Nanterre to an administrative court in Versailles, and finally to the ECJ in Luxembourg, seeing that it involved a conflict between national labor law and Community legislation on the freedom of service provision and labor mobility (Articles 5, 58, 66 of the Treaty of Rome). The French authorities argued that the company was violating the ban on labor mobility. By contrast, the company held that posting workers from Portugal to French construction sites constituted an instance of a *service provision* rather than a case of *labor mobility*, and hence the French authorities had no right to demand work permits. The ECJ decision *Rush Portuguesa vs. ONI* of March 27, 1990 permitted member states to impose their national labor law and wage regulations upon posted workers in a nondiscriminatory fashion, without, however, granting them permission to restrict access to the labor markets for posted workers, as the French authorities had attempted to do (Desmazières de Séchelles 1993: 481ff.; Robin 1994; *Liaisons Sociales*, February 6, 1997). Thus, the ECJ accepted the line of argument of the company's lawyers that this case constituted an instance of service provision (*Le Monde*, March 29, 1990, January 30, 1991):[7] '...communal law does not impede the member states from applying their legislation or their collectively agreed wage regulations to all persons performing a paid activity upon their territory...'[8][author's translation from the French].

---

[7] Act C-113/89 Rush Portuguesa Lda against Office national d'immigration. The Court's 'Seco and Desquenne' decision (February 3, 1982) Act 62–63/81, collection 1982, p. 223 had already opened up room for national response strategies, but this decision had largely been ignored by actors throughout Europe.

[8] The relevant passage from the ECJ ruling in French reads: '...le droit communautaire ne s'oppose pas à ce que les Etats membres étendent leur législation, ou les conventions collect-

The ruling stated that it was permissible for the member states to 'impose respect for these rules by appropriate means' (*imposer le respect de ces règles par les moyens appropriés*).

Responding to Rush Portuguesa: L'Etat *intervenes*

The French national response strategy is very much a response to the case of Rush Portuguesa. The French government interpreted this ECJ decision as an invitation to create a national regulation of the wages and labor conditions applicable to posted workers (Moreau 1995: 3; interview FRMEmpSocAff 2001). Seeking to seize upon the room for maneuver afforded by the ECJ ruling, the Ministry of Labor first issued a directive (*circulaire*) on May 2, 1991 (interview FRMEmpSocAff 2001). This *circulaire* issued to all departmental labor inspectors intended in its own words to 'specify the rules to be applied to companies from European Economic Area countries coming to exercise a temporary provision of service in France in the construction and civil engineering sector'. It was aimed at ensuring that posted workers would benefit from French wages, social and labor law, and that French companies would be protected from unfair competition, 'especially if the foreign companies come from low-wage countries' (Ministère du Travail 1991: 2; *Liaisons sociales*, May 21, 1991; Robin 1994).

This document foreshadows the official response strategy implemented two years later. While it is not a law and possesses only administrative character, its analysis reveals the official stance of the French Ministry of Labor. Even though it was as yet unclear as to whether the national minimum wage SMIC did indeed constitute a *loi de police*, the ministry insists that hourly wages paid to posted workers must meet or exceed the SMIC (Ministère du Travail 1991: 10). The *circulaire* further demands that the 'normal and usual salary in this category of qualification and this region' is being paid to posted workers—even though this specification was not covered by a *loi de police* and might have conflicted with EU regulations on the nondiscriminatory treatment of foreign companies. The decree enforces regulations pertaining to health and safety, overtime, and working time regulations. Its intention is quite clear. It seeks to keep shady subcontractors and

ives de travail conclues par les partenaires sociaux, à toute personne effectuant un travail salairé ... sur leur territoire ... '

temporary labor agencies from posting workers to France (interview FRMEmpSocAff 2001).

Creating a Protectionist Response Strategy: The Politics of Moving Towards Implementation in France

The key component of the response strategy was contained in Article 36 of the Five Year Law pertaining to employment, labor, and educational training (*Loi Quinquennale relative à l'emploi, au travail et à la formation professionnelle*), initiated by the Ministry of Labor under the stewardship of neo-Gaullist Minister Michel Giraud in April 1993. This Article extended all French social and labor regulations along with French wage levels to posted workers. Despite the somewhat Socialist wording of its title, the intention of this comprehensive legislative package was to liberalize the labor market, by liberalizing working time regulations, reducing employer charges for low income groups, and reducing employee representation rights. In light of an unemployment rate of 12 percent, the underlying rationale was that reducing employer charges and reducing the costs for employee representation would encourage job creation (*Syndicalisme*, December 23, 1993; Conseil Economique et Sociale 1993; EIRR 239, 1993: EIRR 1994a). The liberal character of this law introduced by the center-right RPR/UDF coalition under Prime Minister Edouard Balladur might have been reinforced by a certain thirst for revenge after the dominance of the Left in the early 1980s and early 1990s, which had partly reversed the Right's brief flirt with neoliberal policy in the mid-1980s. The Balladur government had also vowed to cut down on illegal forms of employment (*Financial Times*, October 6, 1993; *Le Monde*, June 23, 1993, August 24, 1993, September 29, 1993; interview CFDT 2000; CGT 2000). Tellingly, Article 36 of the *Loi Quinquennale* was presented along with measures designated to combat illegal forms of employment (Hennion-Moreau 1994).

Aside from wanting to fight unemployment to win the competition for nomination as the neo-Gaullist presidential candidate in the 1995 elections against then-President Chirac, Balladur was concerned about the electoral rise of the radical right. He sought to profit from anti-immigration sentiments by having included Charles Pasqua in his cabinet, a right-wing conservative who coined the phrase *immigration zéro* (later revised to 'zero illegal immigration') as a policy goal and took a restrictive stance on extending citizenship to second generation 'immigrants'. Just like other European countries, France witnessed a prolonged and fierce debate on immigration in the early 1990s. The relatively generous bestowal of citizenship to any individual born on French territory (*ius solis*) and the very basis of French identity, presumably based on adhesion to political republican ideals, rather than ethnicity (Brubaker 1992), came under attack from the far right, especially Jean-Marie Le Pen's *Front Nationale* (Le Pen 1984; Schain 1987). The Right criticized the bestowal of French citizenship upon young descendants of migrants from the Maghreb countries, particularly the practice of dual citizenship (Hollifield 1994). Balladur responded to pressure from the far right by limiting the rights to asylum and deporting illegal migrants, following passage of the August 24, 1993 law on entry and exit of foreigners (*'relative aux entrées et sorties des étrangers'*, *Syndicalisme*, November 4, 1993). Both the *Front* and the right wing of the RPR were also voicing increasing Euroskepticism (*FAZ*, June 18, 1993), profiting from the hesitancy among the populace that had found its expression in a bare minority for the Maastricht Treaty in 1992. Meanwhile, leftist populist nationalism (and Euroskepticism) found its voice in Chèvenement's newly founded *Mouvement des Citoyens* (Citizens' Movement), a party that split from the Socialists.

Notwithstanding Balladur seeking to 'push the right buttons' of immigration, labor market deregulation and fighting illegal employment, this ambitious legislative package was greeted with lukewarm support, even from within his coalition government. It encountered harsh criticism among the opposition Socialists, Greens, and Communists (*Le Monde*, September 29, 1993). The opposition parties disliked its liberal and deregulatory agenda. Within the two government parties, Giraud's measures were criticized for being too incoherent, piecemeal and overly cautious (*Le Monde*, June 23, 1993, September 29, 1993). Meanwhile, the employer association CNPF and the association of small enterprises CGPME were generally supportive of the overall goal of liberalization as their official reactions reflect. They were especially enthusiastic about reduced employer charges. The reaction on the part of the unions was unilaterally and entirely negative with a few exceptions, notably concerning the efforts to curb illegal employment (*Le Monde*, September 7, 1993; *Syndicalisme*, August 26, 1993).

The Position of Actors in France: Employers and Unions Face the Loi Quinquennale

Concerning the question of wages for posted workers the differences between the two camps were not substantial. In its *avis*, the social partners, united in the *Conseil Economique et Sociale* (*Conseil Economique* 1993: 14), criticized the government for conflating illegal employment (*travail clandestin*), illegal forms of supplying workers (*prêt de main-d'oeuvre*), and illegal trafficking in workers (*marchandage*) in the measures proposed. However, in their individual reactions, all of the unions and the employer association were supportive of the French national response strategy. The following section examines the attitude, opinions, and actions of the individual associations in more detail.

The French Employers: Preferring National Protectionism to European Liberalization

On the employers' side, the CNPF (since renamed Medef) and the two construction sector employer association FNTP and FNB (the latter since renamed FFB) approved of the regulation, without becoming particularly active. The employer camp was prepared to accept the obligation to pay standard French wages to all employees active on French territory. This may appear somewhat surprising, given that it had been a French company that had been caught in the act of employing dodgy 'post office box firms' as subcontractors, which led to the ECJ ruling.

What accounts for this attitude? The French *patronat* viewed the liberalization of service provision more as a threat than as an opportunity (interviews Medef 2000; FNTP 2001; FFB 2001). The ECJ decision had dispelled any remaining doubts about whether or not restrictions on market access by companies from low-wage EU member states were viable. Thus, the employers feared unfair competition (*concurrence déloyale*) by foreign companies not required to pay standard French wages.[9] They favored equal rules of the game for everybody (interview Medef 2000). In that way, a downward spiral of wages-prices and all-out competition could be avoided, which would have pitched those companies taking advantage of subcontracting against those that did not. The employers did not support deregulation, citing *le dumping social* induced by bad players (*mauvaises joueurs*) as a concern (interview Medef 2000; FFB 2001).

The construction sector employers proved most vocal. The FNTP supported re-regulation. There was no internal divergence on this issue.

---

[9] During that same year, the CNPF demanded that the EU employ 'effective means of protection' against imports from companies paying exploitative wages and thus constituting unfair competition (*FAZ*, June 18, 1993).

Members favored a regulation that would stamp out unfair competition, and do so without any transition period. As early as 1990, then-President Philippe Levaux had publicly criticized the use of Portuguese subcontractors as 'warping the competition' (*faussant la concurrence*) (*Le Monde*, April 19, 1990). The organization's representatives maintained friendly personal relations both with Socialist Minister of Labor Martine Aubry and her conservative successor in the Balladur cabinet Michel Giraud. The latter had attended the same preparatory school for university (*collége*) as the federation's president and the two were thus close personal friends. The LSP was viewed as a potential social danger, destabilizing prices and work conditions in the sector. For this reason, the association actively used its good contacts to the administration to lobby for a re-regulation. It also alerted the CNPF to the problem and informed it of its position. The FNTP coordinated its actions with the FNB (interview FNTP 2001).

The second construction employer association FNB shared the concerns of the FNTP. It perceived foreign competitors entering the domestic market on unequal terms as a danger, jeopardizing the level of prices and social conditions. In order to avoid *concurrence déloyale* and European competitors outbidding French companies on their own turf, the association favored equal starting conditions for all players and thus equal wages for all workers on French territory. Although larger companies were somewhat more agnostic about the issue than the SMEs, even they accepted the implications of the *Loi Quinquennale*—including Bouygues! The FNB coordinated its position with the FTP, without engaging in any active lobbying efforts itself (interview FFB 2001). The official commitment of the federation to join forces with labor authorities in the fight against illegal forms of employment is reflected in a position paper. This paper proposes that subcontracting ought to be limited to less than 50 percent of the total sum of a given project and that 'abnormally low bids' for public jobs should be eliminated from the competition, unless it can be proven by the company in question that this offer is based on legally acceptable means of cost reduction (FNB 1996). This paper underlines the position of the federation, and presumably its members, to stabilize and maintain the level of prices in the construction sector rather than engage in fierce competition.

A few months after the ECJ Rush Portuguesa case, in December 1991, both sectoral employer association had signed a joint declaration with the sectoral unions addressed to the Ministry of Labor, in which they requested an application of the entire régime of French wages and labor regulations to foreign enterprises from the first day onwards of the commencement of their activities on French territory (interview FNTP 2001; FFB 2001). However, even before the *Loi Quinqennale*, both sectoral associations and the CNPF were convinced that the French minimum wage SMIC was applicable in any case, since it formed part of the *ordre public*, though this was far from being established legally (interview Medef 2000; FNTP 2001; FFB 2001).

The CNPF was consulted formally and informally by the Ministry of Labor during the process of the elaboration of the *Loi Quinquennale*. These consultations are not in any form legally binding on the government, however. The CNPF liaison officers did not dispose of close contacts to the Ministry of Labor, nor the Balladur government in general, despite its ideological color (interview Medef 2000). The association was generally supportive of the regulation developed at the Ministry of Labor, but did not engage in active lobbying itself. The sectoral associations FNTP and FFB, strong and financially potent members of the CNPF, had both expressed their approval to the CNPF. Other sectoral associations did not voice any resistance to it. The *leitmotif* of protection against unfair competition was accepted as legitimate. In order to avoid a downward spiral of prices set in motion by *mauvaises joueurs*, French construction companies therefore supported the government's efforts to introduce regulation, ensuring a level playing field and equal wages. The CNPF did not stand in the way of these sectoral demands (interview Medef 2000; personal communication to author 2000).

'Same Work—Same Wage': French Unions Passively Embrace the National Response Strategy

On the union side, it was commonly accepted that maintaining the principle 'same work-same wage' for all workers on French territory ought to be defended (interviews CFDT 2000; CGT 2000). The unions therefore univocally supported the national response strategy as proposed by the Ministry of Labor. Fighting illegal labor and exploitation of illegally employed workers were among the few issues addressed in the *Loi Quinquennale*, which even the most critical unions, the FO and the CGT, approved of. However, despite its generally favorable stance, there was relatively little activity on the part of the trade unions, with the exception of the sectoral construction union CFDT-FNCB. All the unions are being consulted during a number of formal and informal sessions with the Minister of Labor Michel Giraud over the course of the summer of 1993 (*Syndicalisme*, August 26, 1993; *Le Monde*, August 24, 1993).

The CFTC had repeatedly insisted on the principle of equal rights and equal wages for workers employed on French territory and was therefore strongly opposed to any social dumping and increased competition through the presence of companies not bound to standard wages. Despite its generally high level of activities during the period of the elaboration of the *Loi Quinquennale*, when it expressed its opinions in informal consultation sessions and through written statements addressed to the Ministry of Labor, it did not take any concrete steps concerning the regulation of wages for posted workers, since it was content with the regulation proposed by the Ministry (personal communication to the author CFTC, October 2000).

The CGT had been similarly active over the years in protecting the right of foreign workers in France. Although it was extremely critical of the *Loi Quinquennale*, it did support the regulation of the wages for posted workers in the form proposed in principle. The CGT did not engage in any active lobbying efforts on this issue, however, since it was satisfied with the regulation proposed by the Ministry (interview CGT 2000).

The FO's position resembled that of the CGT. Although it was highly critical of the *Loi Quinquennale* in general, it supported the intent to crack down on illegal forms of employment, though with certain reservations. A detailed internal position paper questions the political will to apply already existing sanctions to employers and expresses concerns about the government using its new legal repertoire to infringe upon the rights of immigrants and their organizations, rather than the employers (*Force Ouvrière* 1993: 30–1). These caveats aside, however, the organization supported the regulation of wages for posted workers, without actively becoming involved in this issue.

The CFDT, and specifically its sectoral construction organization, the CFDT-FNCB (*Confédération Française du Travail—Fédération Nationale des Salaries de la Construction et du Bois*), became very active. During the collective bargaining rounds of December 1991, it had initiated a joint declaration of the social partners addressed to the Ministry of Labor, demanding which the payment of standard French wages to all employees on French territory from the first day of their posting onwards. It also repeatedly lobbied in favor of foreign workers and against illegal employment. On March 10, 1993, the union signed a joint declaration on the combined fight against illegal forms of employment in the construction sector with the Ministry of Labor (*Syndicalisme*, May 20, 1993) and launched an informational campaign against illegal forms of employment in the construction sector. The CFDT-FNCB urged the umbrella federation CFDT to support a national regulation, which would enforce and write into law the regulation it had favored previously. As is true of the other unions, the umbrella association CFDT accepted the government's proposal since it met its own objectives, without having taken much action (CFDT-FNCB, May 23, 1995; interviews CFDT 2000; CFDT-FNCB 2000).

Passive Approval of Government Action: Summing up Union and Employer Positions

In sum, the nascence of the French national response strategy can be described as the product of a government initiative accepted by both sides. In both camps the level of activity remained relatively low, with the exceptions of the CFDT-FNCB and the FNTP. There were no significant differences between sectoral and umbrella associations on either side, though the latter tended to be somewhat more phlegmatic than the former. Both sides had previously and repeatedly voiced their opinions. They viewed the Ministry's proposal as reflective of these previous interventions. Interestingly, no significant differences existed on this issue between unions and employers. The former wanted to safeguard the rights of all employees to standard wages, while the latter regarded foreign competition as a menace to the level of prices on the French market (Table 4.4).

Implementation of the French National Response Strategy: Protecting the Domestic Market

The parliamentary debate on the *Loi Quinquennale* commenced on September 28, 1993 (*Le Monde*, September 29, 1993). On October 1, 1993, the

Table 4.4 The politics of the French national response strategy

Employer Position: Supportive, concerned over unfair competition, downward wage-price spiral
Union Position: Supportive, but fairly passive—unions also seek to avoid social dumping
Government Position: Active; Ministry of Labor drafts respective bill as part of an effort against illegal forms of employment
Other Factors: Government also seeks to discourage immigration
Heavily contested/politicized? No
Internal divisions? None of significance

French parliament (*Assemblée Nationale*) debated Chapter IV on illegal forms of employment in the presence of Minister of Labor Giraud. This package of legislative measures increased fines for employers resorting to illegal forms of employment, notably barring them from submitting bids for public tender for five years or more. It also introduced sentences of up to five years of prison and fines of up to 200,000 francs for intermediaries or procurers of illegal forms of employment. Concerning the question of posted workers, Giraud presented the regulation prepared previously in his ministry (interview FRMEmpSocAff 2001). The text he proposed reads as follows:

If a company not registered in France executes a provision of service on the national territory, then the employees posted temporarily for the execution of such provision shall be subject to the legislation and the regulations as well as the standard wage agreements to which the employees of companies registered in France are subject, taking into consideration and under the limits of international treaties, in regards to social security, *remuneration*, working time and working conditions, within the limits and according to the conditions set forth by decree. (*Journal Officiel* 1993a: 3634, author's emphasis and translation)[10]

This proposal was accepted as amendment 24. The text was then submitted to the Senate on November 8. Here, additional protective social security plans (*protection sociale complémentaire*) were rendered mandatory for posted workers. The regulation was subsumed into the chapter on the employment of foreigners, rather than illegal employment (thus Article 341–5 of the Labor Law). Since the two chambers had adopted different versions of the bill, the *Commission Mixte Paritaire* intervened and revised the new Article 341–5. The final version simply added to the original text: '. . . additional sectoral or intersectoral systems of social protection according to Title III of Book VII of the Social Security Law . . .' (. . . *de régimes complémentaires interprofessionnels ou professionnel relevant du titre III du livre VII du code de la sécurité sociale* . . .) (*Journal Officiel* 1993b: 6090; *Liaisons sociales*, August 25, 1994).

---

[10] The original text in French reads: 'Sous réserve des traités et accords internationaux, lorsqu'une entreprise non établi en France effectue sur le territoire national une prestation de service, les salariés qu'elle détache temporairement pour l'accomplissement de cette prestation sont soumis aux dispositions législatives, réglementaires et conventionnelles applicables aux salariés employés par des entreprises établies en France, en matière de sécurité sociale, de rémunération, de durée du travail et de conditions de travail, dans les limites et selon des modalités déterminées par décret.'

Summary and Detailed Discussion of the French Re-regulation

This final version was accepted on November 15, 1993. The new Article 36 of the *Loi Quinquennale* was then translated into a new decree of July 11, 1994, which modified Article 341-5-1 ff. and D 732–1 of the Labor Law (*Journal Officiel* 1994). A new circulaire was issued on December 30, 1994 to replace the previous one issued on May 2, 1991 (EIRR 1994*c*: 247; Législation Sociale 1995; Ministère des Affaires Sociales et de l'Emploi undated).

The French national response strategy consists of three administrative documents. First came the 1991 *circulaire*, a preliminary internal administrative guideline, was limited to the construction sector. As an internal guideline, it was neither transparent, available to foreign companies, nor technically an actual law. A court would have undoubtedly found it not part of the French Labor Code (*Code du Travail*) and hence could have found it not legally binding on a foreign service provider (Robin 1994). It is best perceived as an expression of the immediate reaction to the Rush Portuguesa case, foreshadowing the actual response strategy and indicating the position of the Ministry of Labor. Second, Article 36 of the 1993 Five Year Law constitutes the heart of the response strategy, which was then thirdly applied into the very detailed *circulaire* of December 30, 1994. Its key components are the following (see also Table 4.5).

1. Broadening the remit of the *lois de police*

The French government deliberately sought to clarify the definition of *lois de police* in the sense of the Rome Convention. Since this Convention was negotiated outside of the EU institutions and since the liberalization of service provision applies to all EEA, not just EU members, the French response strategy is worded so as to apply to *any* foreign company, regardless of its origin. Foreign companies setting up any sort of dependency in France, including just a small office, are immediately considered on equal legal footing with domestic companies. Thus, they are not covered by this regulation, but subject to the whole framework of standard French wages, social security, and social and labor regulations. This applies also if the 'habitual place of employment' of any employee is France. This clause is meant to apply to workers hired specifically or exclusively for purposes of being posted to French territory.

2. Including all service providers

The transnational provision of services is deliberately interpreted in the broadest sense, including temporary and contract labor which are send to France for any work 'of an industrial, commercial, artisan or liberal' character.

3. Rendering (almost) all French wages mandatory

All French laws, regulations, and collectively agreed wages (*conventions collectifs étendus*) are applicable to foreign posted workers *immediately* and regardless of the length of their posting to France. Only collective wage agreements 'seen and approved' by the Ministry of Labor and declared universally applicable (*extension*) can be applied to posted employees. This means in practice that the entire framework of wage brackets (*grille*) may become obligatory in regions and sectors where it has been declared universally applicable. In this case, foreign companies are required to group their posted workers according to their level of qualification into these wage brackets and pay them accordingly. A detailed description of these wage categories and the levels of qualification they correspond to, as well as a general framework of rules and regulations for the construction sector, has been universally applicable since 1958 and updated since, regulating questions of working time, qualification, professional training and labor organization (CFDT-FNCB 1995; *Journal Officiel* 2000). In no way and at no time may a worker be paid below the SMIC, even if the result of the above operation might theoretically produce such outcome, as stipulated in Article 24 of the Ordonnance 82–41 of January 16, 1982 (*Journal Officiel* 2000: 152). For the construction sector, this regulation effectively eliminates the wage differential between posted and domestically employed workers.

4. Rendering the SMIC mandatory

The French national minimum wage SMIC shall heretofore be considered a *loi de police*, thus becoming applicable in any case even if no other collective agreements can be applied. Despite the government's labor inspector repeated insistence and the employer association statements to that end (Medef October 26, 2000; interview Medef 2000; FRMEmpSocAff 2001), this issue had not been previously addressed. Additional employer charges are also payable, as outlined above. Equal wages are to be paid to men and women.

5. Making French labor regulations mandatory

French regulations on working time, rest periods, overtime, and holidays become applicable to posted workers. According to the national accord in the construction sector, which applies to posted workers as well, since it was *extended* by the Ministry of Labor on February 25, 1982, this means in practice that the working day is limited to 10 hours and the working week to 48 hours,[11] with a maximum of nine weekly hours of overtime. The annual paid vacations are thirty days in the construction sector (Article 1–6). French safety (for tools, machinery, and general working place conditions) and health regulations also apply (*Journal Officiel* 2000: 307ff.).

6. Making contributions to French social security mandatory

Foreign companies posting construction workers to France have to contribute to the local sectoral systems of bad weather and vacations funds (*chômage intempéries*) in accordance with articles L. 731-1-731.12 and R.731-2—731-21 of the Labor Code. These funds render payment to workers in case of bad weather and for additional paid holidays. However, companies registered in EEA member states may be exempted from this requirement if they can prove that they have already contributed to equivalent systems in their countries of charter. By contrast, for postings from a EU country of up to one year, no contributions have to be made to the French system of social security. In such cases the régime of the country of origin is applicable under the June 14, 1971 EEC directive 1408/71 with the presentation of an E-101 card. For non-EU member states bilateral agreements between France and their native country may mean that such contributions are not necessary.

7. Clarifying bureaucratic requirements for service providers

Posting companies must submit a declaration to local labor inspectors, indicating details on the posting company itself and the type of work conducted in France. Additional documentation concerning the working time and accommodation arrangements for posted workers must be avail-

---

[11] The most recent 35-hour week legislation of the French Ministry of Labor (loi 200–37 of January 19, 2000) has further revised this regulation. Thus, the social partners agreed upon an amendment to the *convention nationale* hereby the standard work week is now defined as 35 hours. Beyond that, as of January 1, 2001, between the 36th and 43rd hour an overtime charge of 25 percent of the standard salary will apply, above that of 50 percent (*Journal Officiel* 2000, Supplement No. 2).

able on the building sites at all times and may be controlled on a random basis by police, labor inspectors, or customs officers. The authorities are entitled to verify payment of proper wages. Companies are required to provide and have available for on site inspection appropriate information indicating payment of proper wages. French companies employing sub-contractors found in violation of these regulations may be held legally responsible as well.

8. Avoiding linguistic confusion

All documentation regarding the posting of workers is to be provided in French and has to be translated into French in advance if necessary.

[All information derived from the Circulaire DRT 94/18 of December 30, 1995, reprinted in *Législation Sociale* 1995; see also Robin 1994; Moreau 1995.]

In sum, the French national response strategy is a comprehensive meas-ure aimed at preventing social dumping and disparities between the wages and work conditions of posted employees and domestically employed workers. Although not the entire régime of labor regulations applies, the hard core certainly does. By rendering obligatory the SMIC and sectoral collective conventions where they exist, the French national response strategy limits the potential for wage differentials and eradicates it almost altogether in the construction sector, where several regional universally applicable wage agreements exist. In such instances, the entire framework of wage brackets becomes applicable to posted companies, not just the sectoral minimum wage.

The response strategy is a product of the Ministry of Labor, drafted in response to the ECJ Rush Portuguesa case (interview FRMEmpSocAff 2001; FNTP 2001; Medef 2000; Désmazieres de Séchelles 1993; Hennion-Moreau 1994; Moreau 1995). However, while the 1991 *circulaire* can be dismissed as a quick and sectorally limited internal administrative regulation, the com-prehensive 1994 *circulaire*, which grew out of the 1993 Five Year Law's Article 26, was actively supported (FNTP and CFDT-FNCB) or at least accepted (FNB, CNPF, CGT, FO, CFTC) by both unions and employers. The unions saw this regulation on which they were consulted formally and informally by the Ministry of Labor as fulfilling their demands and positions. However, they did not become particularly active about this issue. The employers wanted to avoid *concurrence déloyale* or unfair competition over wage prices, which would result in a downward spiral of prices. They perceived of the LSP as more of a threat than an opportunity. For this reason one sectoral employer association became very active (FNTP) while the others accepted the government regulation as being in their interests.

Amending the French National Response Strategy

Since 1993, three minor amendments have been made to the original French regulation. The first one (Decree 2000–462, published in *Journal Officiel*, May 31, 2000) established that the bilateral industrial tribunals (*conseils de prud'hommes*) would be granted authority to rule over cases in the first instance in which the infringement of posted worker rights was at stake.

In September 2000, a minor amendment of the original Labor Code Article 341–5 (now: Article D 341–5 through D341 5–14) clarified that the imposition of French minimum standards of paid holidays and wages did not apply to sectors outside of construction, where the posting of workers is aimed at the assembly or initial installation of machinery and does not exceed a total period of eight days. This latter change was a reflection of the EU Posted Workers Directive. Ironically, it helped undermine the French standards of regulation, if only in a very limited fashion (Table 4.5).

Finally, a memorandum by the social security agency DSS (DSS/DAEI/July 30, 1998) specifies that posted employees may choose to remain covered by the framework of their home country social security system for the duration of their seconding to France.

Despite a fairly restrictive response strategy, France continues to experience problems with illegal forms of employment in the construction

Table 4.5 An overview of regulation contained within the French response strategy

Does the response strategy cover the entire economy? Yes. This is a very comprehensive and very protectionist response strategy. Not only the construction sector is covered; it applies to the entire economy.

Are there exceptions/loopholes? No, major French labor and social provisions as well as universally applicable wages apply from day onwards.

What regulations become legally binding on foreign service providers? All major French labor and social provisions as well as universally applicable wages and/or the minimum wage SMIC. There are no exceptions. In addition, contributions to the sectoral social security funds also become mandatory, although a recent reform makes exceptions for posted workers whose employers have already made contributions to equivalent systems in their home countries.

sector. Illegal and seasonal employment, involving substandard wages, and commonly also foreign employees, is also prevalent in other low-skill service sectors, such as agriculture, tourism and gastronomy, and transportation. According to government agency DILTI, a total of 8,554 posted employees were registered in France in 2001. However, the actual number comes closer to 18,000–30,000, according to other estimates (EIRO 2003*a*).

The German National Response Strategy

Developments in the German Construction Sector: From CEE to EU Subcontracting

In Germany, the national response strategy was implemented much later and involved a great deal more controversy and conflict than in France. The transnational posting of workers to Germany had commenced in the early 1990s, but increased dramatically in 1994, probably owing somewhat to the psychological effect of the Single Market. According to the construction sector employers, 20,000 workers from EU member states were posted to Germany in 1993. In 1994, this figure reached 106,000, and in 1995 138,000, only to peak at 165,000 in 1996 and 1997 (HDB 1997). In fact, the union estimated even 200,000 posted workers from 1995 onwards (IG BAU, June 28, 1995). The LSP led to the very foundations of the Berlin Republic being constructed by Irish and Portuguese workers, toiling for a fraction of standard German wages. Since the late 1990s, the number of posted workers seems to have decreased, no doubt reflecting the implementation of the German re-regulation. By 2002, the numbers of posted workers for whom contributions were made to the German sectoral construction social security administration ULAK, stood at only 22,121. In addition, these figures reflect a dramatic decrease of posted workers from the sending countries of the 1990s (UK, Ireland, Italy, Portugal) and highlight the continuing importance of posted workers from CEE states, reaching 93,258 in 2002 (EIRO 2003*b*). However, union officials regard these figures with some skepticism.

The posting of workers from CEE states has nothing to do with the LSP. The LSP will not apply to new EU members from CEE during a transition period of seven years and obviously did not apply before EU enlargement in 2004. However, it is important to note that German construction companies were introduced to the benefits of using foreign subcontractor companies through a number of bilateral labor agreements concluded between Germany and her CEE neighbors, commencing in the late 1980s (Reim and Sandbrink 1996; Werner 1996; Menz 2001). Because these treaties helped to establish widespread chains of subcontracting, later exploited by EU companies, their importance should not be underestimated (interviews IG BAU 1999, 2001; HDB 1999, 2001).[12]

Why posting from other EU member states to Germany reached such dramatic proportions in 1993 and not previously can be attributed to a number of factors. Aside from the psychological effect of Maastricht, and the legal clarity that the Rush Portuguesa ruling provided, the large German market became even more attractive that year, given that the French market was sealed off that same year via the French national response strategy. Last but not least, in 1993, the quotas for CEE workers were reduced drastically. One might speak of a *substitution effect* of CEE workers

---

[12] Annual quotas were established for contract workers (*Werkvertragsarbeitnehmer*) from CEE to enter the German labor market for up to 24 months. The workers were formally employed by CEE companies, which acted as subcontractors of German companies. In the treaties the payment of standard German wages to these posted workers was stipulated. In theory, Germany was contributing to the economic revival of CEE by disseminating know-how to CEE workers, reducing pressure on the labor markets, and allowing CEE citizens to earn hard currency which they could then transmit home. In reality, CEE workers were often subject to abusive labor conditions, charged fictitious inflated amounts for accommodation, transport, and use of equipment in order to reduce their de facto salary, and freely transferred between companies as temporary workers, even though this was explicitly prohibited in the German construction sector (Cyrus 1996). Officially, the CEE companies were responsible for the payment of non-wage labor related costs, i.e. social security contributions. CEE companies contributed to their home country vacation funds, not the German one. This proved another perfectly legal mechanism for German construction companies to cut their personnel expenditures. However, larger companies were better apt to take advantage of the quotas then smaller ones and soon downward pressure on bidding offers ensued. In order to ensure fair rules of the game within the construction sector, employers were willing to sign a joint 'Frankfurt Declaration' of July 1993 (Bosch et al. 1999) with the unions, calling on the federal government to replace the annual quotas with limited time work permits for CEE workers, which would then become *direct* employees of German companies. The Kohl government was unwilling to accept this request because it did not intend to alienate its eastern neighbors. Poland, the Czech and Slovak Republics, and Hungary were declared 'safe third countries' in a significant 1993 modification of the German law on political asylum. Henceforth, German immigration and law enforcement officials could immediately deport an applicant for political asylum if it could be proven that this individual had crossed any of these 'safe third countries' en route to Germany. This was a bitter pill to swallow for countries like Poland, which were already turning into countries of transit and even immigration themselves (Koslowski 1999). Thus, rather than accepting the proposals by the social partners, the Kohl government instead drastically reduced the quotas and linked them to developments on the German labor market. These steps could be justified vis-à-vis the CEE governments by the domestic pressure of the social partners in the construction sector. Thus, one might speak of the German government being engaged in and successfully mastering a two-level game.

through EU workers. CEE workers were officially entitled to standard German wages, while posted workers from other EU member states could be paid lower home country wages. Henceforth, EU companies became clearly more attractive, while CEE workers were simply priced out of the market.[13]

Babylon in Berlin, Failure in Brussels: The German Government Attempts to take the European Route

Within the German government at the time, the prevailing sentiment was to negotiate a re-regulation at the EU level and refrain from a national re-regulation (interview DEMLabSocAff 2000). As early as 1989 the economic advisory council to the government (*Sachverständigenrat*) had recommended implementing a law enshrining an internationally binding minimum wage, but this advice went unheeded (*Sachverständigenrat* 1989: 454ff., esp. 464–5). Instead, the German government went to substantial lengths to arrange an EU directive during its presidency in the second half of 1994. Minister of Labor Norbert Blüm became personally involved. However, no such European re-regulation came about until long after national response strategies had been implemented (*Tagesspiegel*, February 1, 1996; Baumann 1995).[14] As mentioned earlier, Germany's proposals were vetoed consistently by Ireland, Portugal, and Britain. Unsurprisingly, nationals of these countries were also well represented among the workers posted to Germany in 1993 and 1994 (*FAZ*, September 10, 1994) and stood to gain most from the lack of EU level re-regulation. The German government arranged for numerous meetings of the Council of Ministers throughout its presidency, until the very end of its presidency. The last meeting was called only four days before Christmas, on December 21, 1994. None of these EU level efforts came to fruition, however.

[13] In its first mention of the practice of outsourcing to Portuguese companies the FAZ describes the pivotal role of the German-Portuguese Chamber of Commerce in Lisbon in arranging such contacts and comments that 'they [Portuguese workers] are barely more expensive than their Polish colleagues but can be legally and freely employed in the European Single Market' (*Die sind kaum teurer als ihre polnischen Kollegen, können aber im europäischen Binnenmarkt frei und legal beschäftigt werden*) (*FAZ*, September 10, 1994). This statement, when read carefully, reveals that Polish workers routinely did not receive the German wages to which they were entitled.

[14] A first unsuccessful effort had been made by the Commission in 1991 when it had issued a Directive on the posting of workers in the framework of the provision of services on August 30, 1991, as mentioned previously.

'Hand in Hand on Our Doorsteps': Sectoral Employers and Unions Lobby the Government

Meanwhile, domestic pressure on the government mounted, as both sectoral union IG BAU and sectoral employer association ZDB and HDB continued their lobbying efforts in favor of a national regulation (Lubanski and Sörries 1997).[15] The government had been approached throughout 1993. In the words of an official at the ministry of labor, ZDB, HDB, and IG BAU had lobbied in 'rare unity' and 'hand in hand on our doorsteps' for a re-regulation of the wages for posted workers. All three associations engaged in massive lobbying, called repeatedly for appointments at the Ministry of Labor, and issued press statements to support their positions (interview DEMLabSocAff 2000). In a joint declaration to the federal government the two employer association HDB and ZDB stated that they would

be able to meet this competition because of the existing discrepancies in wage levels only if the existing distortions of competition endangering jobs and the existence of companies will be ended and fair conditions of competition will be established. Fair competition can only be established, however, if the principle labor conditions of the construction site in question [i.e. host country principle], especially 'same wage for same jobs' is established for all companies involved in construction in Germany. This principle has to apply regardless of the seat of the company and the length of posting. (ZDB 1994, 218)

The Battle Lines Are Drawn: Drafting a Legislative National Response Strategy

The sectoral social partners sought a legislative solution, rather than negotiate a bipartite compromise. The rationale behind this lay in the details of international law: German collective wages are binding only on mem-

---

[15] In an interview with the daily *FAZ*, the president of the ZDB Karl Rohl, representing construction SMEs, called the unfair conditions a "distortion of competition" and mentioned between 100,000 and 200,000 foreign posted workers from Portugal, Spain, Britain, and Greece on German construction sites, offering their services for their home country wages. Under these conditions, increased numbers of bankruptcies and rising unemployment among domestically employed workers were predicted unless a re-regulation was found. HDB President Wilhelm Küchler made similarly worded remarks in an interview, highlighting the situation in Berlin and Leipzig, where German companies were priced out of the market by foreign competitors (*FAZ*, November 25, 1994; December 6, 1994; December 22, 1994; January 11, 1995). In December 1994, the economic ministers of the *Länder* had also called for a national regulation.

bers of German employer association, but do not constitute transnationally binding *lois de police*. In fact, even German-based companies can 'exit' their obligation to pay standard German wages by leaving the employer association. Some legislative solution appeared therefore necessary, given that Germany did not have a legally binding minimum wage. In the absence of any such legally binding wage, subcontractors continued to pay their employees truly minimal Portuguese or Irish wages. Little did the sectoral social partners know that this issue would give rise to a major ideological battle, causing significant conflict and debate and highlighting remarkable ideological vault lines.

The Minister of Labor Blüm was not unsympathetic to the cause. Having failed to secure a directive in Brussels in light of the sustained resistance from low-wage EU states, Blüm decided to draft a national legislative act after all. Just before the Christmas holidays of 1994, he charged an official at the Ministry with preparing a first legislative draft for a national regulation of the wages for posted workers (interview DEMLabSocAff, December 2000). The Minister met with the sectoral social partners in Bonn on January 16, 1995 (*Tagesspiegel*, January 17, 1995). In the course of this meeting, he informed the HDB, ZDB, and IG BAU that his ministry was preparing a legislative draft bill to be presented to the cabinet in the spring. With an estimated 150,000–200,000 posted workers expected on German construction sites in 1994/95 and given the failure to reach a regulation at the European level, the Ministry of Labor felt an immediate need for action. The original draft bill prepared in the Ministry of Labor is not available to the public and still considered confidential. The author was denied access (interview DEMLabSocAff, December 2000). It is safe to assume, however, that the draft was a great deal more ambitious and comprehensive than the final version. During a press conference on March 12, 1995, Minister of Economic Affairs Günter Rexrodt confirmed that the German government was in the process of preparing a national regulation, which would ensure the payment of 'German wages' (*FAZ*, March 13, 1995). However, by that time, significant ideological vault lines within the government and within the labor market interest associations had emerged.

Within the government cabinet a conflict unfolded between CDU Minister of Labor Blüm and the FDP Minister for Economic Affairs Rexrodt. Blüm was both an IG Metall member and former head of the employee organization within the Christian Democratic Party CDA (interview DEMLabSocAff, December 2000; IG Metall 2001, IG BAU 2001; BDA 2001). The Christian social values he represented clashed with the pro-market liberalism of the Free Democrats. The FDP found ideological allies amongst neoliberal academic economists, notably at the Kiel Institute for the Global Economy and at the Walter Eucken Institut in Freiburg, and conservative and business media outlets *Handelsblatt* and *Frankfurter Allgemeine Zeitung* (Gerken/Löwisch/Rieble 1995; Koenigs 1997; *Handelsblatt*, January 11, 1995, May 11, 1995, May 29, 1996).

The issue of the wage regulation for posted workers helped ignite a major ideological confrontation between neoliberal business-friendly supporters of the deregulated status quo and Social Democratic employee-friendly advocates of a national re-regulatory response strategy *à la française*. The sectoral employers partially sided with the unions in calling for an at least temporary limit to the LSP. The controversy unfolded behind the backdrop of a general rise in neoliberal rhetoric in Germany in the mid-1990s, especially among employer and business associations and the liberal FDP. Opponents of a national regulation also skillfully invoked anxiety within the German government about whether such regulation would conform to European law (Eeckhoff 1996) and might indeed not jeopardize Germany's image as a 'model European'. Opponents regarded any such re-regulation a violation of the spirit of the Single Market and a dangerous relapse into protectionism. After all, increased competition and thus lower prices for customers were the proclaimed goals of the Single Market. Any national protectionist measure against it would simply support a 'cartel of prices' (*FAZ*, January 17, 1996).

Bloody Battles along the Rhine: Bellicose Central Employer Association Overrides Sectoral Employers

While the two sectoral employer association had repeatedly expressed their support for re-regulation, other sectoral employer association and the BDA were highly critical of it. The president of the German Association of Large and Export-Oriented Business Michael Fuchs criticized any such measure aimed at 'preventing competition' (*FAZ*, February 21, 1995). The sectoral employer association for the textile sector Gesamttextil had expressed some cautious sympathy for the measure at first, but later completely reversed its position. The association argued that its own companies also had to face competition from low-wage companies from abroad; and in fact much earlier and with even more dramatic consequences than in the case of the construction sector. The association's president Schmidt claimed that high wages in construction were resulting in higher building costs for customers, including textile companies (interview Gesamttextil 2001; personal communication to the author 2001).

Allegedly previously sheltered and spawning inflated wage levels, the sector was now entering a phase of necessary adjustment and restructuring, brought on by foreign low-wage competition. A common argument employed by the employers was an alleged upward wage drift. A high minimum wage for the construction sector (to say nothing of a cross-sectoral minimum wage) would cause an upward spiral of wages across the economy and encourage unions to push for higher wages (interview Gesamtmetall, April 2001). Gesamtmetall pointed out that the construction sector already boasted Germany's highest overall wages. Even the lowest wage bracket in construction exceeded that of the highest wage for skilled workers in other sectors (*FAZ*, August 23, 1995; February 10, 1996; interview Gesamtmetall 2001).

The BDA assumed a somewhat ambiguous position, reflecting the shifting opinions of its sectoral members. In 1995, the BDA remained on the sidelines and did not make any public or press statements. The BDA waited for its sectoral members to take a position, especially mighty Gesamtmetall. This association contributes more than half of the total funding of the BDA. Traditionally, the BDA president is recruited from its ranks. Another reason for the BDA's silence in 1995 was that earlier it had signaled some willingness for compromise informally (interview DEMLabSocAff, December 2000), a position it obviously regretted. Despite evidence to the contrary in the annual report 1994 (BDA 1994*a*: 172),[16] representatives of the association steadfastly denied having ever been supportive of any re-regulation in an interview (interview BDA, April 2001).

By late 1995, the position of the BDA had changed. It categorically rejected a national re-regulation (BDA 1995). The BDA was able to postpone implementation for nine months by refusing to accept universal applicability of the newly created German minimum wage, as will be discussed below.

---

[16] Though the BDA voices 'grave concerns' (*schwerwiegende Bedenken*) against such regulation at the European level and is concerned about possible repercussions for German *Tarifautonomie*, pointing out that the real problem to the construction sector is illegal labor and violations of existing laws, it acknowledges that in light of the problems experienced by its own members in the construction sector the 'question thus imposes itself . . . [whether a strictly limited re-regulation for this sector] could be accepted' (*Es stellt sich deshalb die Frage, ob . . . hingenommen werden könnte*). Close analysis of this document reveals a certain willingness to accept a re-regulation at the European level limited to the construction sector (BDA 1994). Tellingly, the author's considerations of this point are all in the *Konjunktiv*, a grammatical form used to express a possibility in German. On this point, the representative of the French employers remarked that while his association's position had remained constant, the BDA seemed to have shifted over time (interview Medef 2000).

By contrast, the HDB and ZDB had consistently lobbied in favor of a regulation. They were generally fairly satisfied with the first draft of the Law on Posted Workers presented to them in July 1995. In fact, they even supported its extension to all construction-related activities, applicability from day one onwards, and the inclusion of the sectoral vacation funds! They were prepared to have all the existing German wages be declared universally applicable (ZDB, June 28, 1995; HDB, June 28, 1995). This position is remarkably similar to that of the union. In its positive stance towards such regulation the ZDB was somewhat more enthusiastic, but even the HDB, representing larger companies, accepted it as a temporary measure to adapt to the new challenges of the Single Market. While the sectoral employers attempted to maintain a 'common front' and a common position (interviews HDB 1999, 2001; ZDB 2000), some individual construction companies, notably Holzmann, were ostensibly less keen on creating such 'artificial barriers' (*Die Welt*, July 19, 1995) at first, only to revise this position later (interview major German construction company 2001). Nevertheless, a common position was maintained and presented to the public. The larger companies accepted the position of their association, notwithstanding the fact that they had made use of subcontractors paying substandard wages themselves.

'Time is Not on their Side': The German Trade Union Position

The IG BAU had very early on expressed its support for a re-regulation of the LSP. As early as 1991, IG BAU had commented favorably on the EU directive under discussion at the time in a letter addressed to the Minister of Labor. From then onwards, the union's position was clear, as a review of internal policy documents reveals (IG BAU 1991, 1995, June 28, 1995). IG BAU wanted the following:

1. Mandatory application to all areas of the construction sector, in the broadest sense
2. Mandatory inclusion of foreign companies posting workers to Germany into the sectoral funds for bad weather and vacation
3. Rigorous enforcement efforts, involvement of both federal and *Länder* authorities (customs officials, Federal Agency for Labor, police, and even union officials)
4. Harsh fines to ensure compliance
5. No temporal limitation

However, regarding the crucial question of wages, there is a notable *divergence* over time. In 1991, IG BAU demanded the application of the entire framework of German wages to posted workers, if necessary by permitting the Ministry of Labor to declare all German wages in this sector universally applicable. It maintained this position in its immediate response to the government's proposal (IG BAU, June 28, 1995). However, by September (IG BAU 1995) accepted grudgingly that *only the two lowest wage brackets would be declared universally applicable* (Köbele and Leuschner 1995).

IG BAU had consistently demanded the comprehensive re-regulation of the LSP, but eventually caved in somewhat, retreating from its firm demand to ensure standard German wages for all posted workers. As we shall see later, it was forced to retire even further from its original demands in terms of both the coverage of the law and the level of the minimum wage.

The strength of the sectoral employer association Gesamtmetall is matched by its vociferous union counterpart IG Metall. Some of the trades represented, including construction-related activities such as heating, climate control, plumbing, and electrical installation, were also affected by posted workers. Hence, IG Metall supported the demands of IG BAU, although it preferred a re-regulation avoiding universal applicability (IG Metall, June 20, 1995; interview IG Metall 2001). The metal union provided logistical support by participating in parliamentary hearings, and organizing a mail-in campaign to the government among its members in the fall of 1995 (IG Metall, May 31, 1996; interview IG Metall 2001).

Umbrella union association DGB supported the demands of IG BAU as well. It sent its representatives to parliamentary hearings and repeatedly lobbied the Ministry of Labor (interview DGB 2001). DGB coordinated its initiatives with IG BAU, given that this sectoral union was primarily affected and possessed outspoken and well-informed experts on the issue. Initially, DGB demanded coverage of the entire economy, but later accepted coverage of the construction sector only. It supported IG BAU initial demand for the universal applicability of all German wages for posted workers, but followed IG BAU's retreat to demand only the extension of the two lowest wage brackets (interview DGB 2000).

The Politics of the Genesis of the German Response Strategy

As mentioned before, the issue of posted workers pitted the construction sectoral social partners against the central employer association, but also provoked considerable conflict within the center-right coalition

government (see Table 4.6). The ideological differences between the center-left Ministry of Labor and the left wing of the Christian Democrats
represented by Minister Norbert Blüm on the one hand and the liberal pro-
market Free Democrats and Minister of Economic Affairs Günter Rexrodt
were eventually resolved. A compromise was struck during a meeting
between the two ministers on June 27, 1995. The new legislative draft was
significantly toned down compared to the Ministry of Labor's original
draft. Coverage was limited to two years and the construction sector
only. Only the lowest existing wage bracket was extended to posted workers (*Handelsblatt*, June 28, 1995). Based on this compromise draft, the
Committee for Labor and Social Affairs of the lower chamber of parliament
(*Bundestag*) organized a hearing on June 28. Representatives of the HDB,
ZDB, IG BAU, DGB, and IG Metall participated. Based on this session, the
Ministry of Labor presented a revised draft bill on July 17, entitled 'Law on
mandatory labor conditions for transnational service provisions' (*Gesetz
über zwingende Arbeitsbedingungen bei grenzüberschreitenden Dienstleistungen*). This bill aimed at declaring universally applicable the lowest wage
bracket within the construction sector,[17] rendering compulsory a hard
core of German labor law including regulations on vacations and contributions to the sectoral vacation funds. It was limited to two years (interview DEMLabSocAff, December 2000).

   While the position of the coalition government was initially somewhat
divided, the opposition Social Democrats presented their own version of a
draft bill concerning the regulation of wages for posted workers, incorporating up some of the union demands (SPD personal communication
to author, December 2000; interview DEMLabSocAff, December 2000;
Handelsblatt, July 24, 1995). Their very ambitious draft would have rendered
mandatory the *entire framework of labor and social regulations from the first
day onwards in all sectors of the economy for posted workers*.

   Meanwhile, the cabinet officially accepted the revised draft bill on
September 1. It was presented along with the Social Democrats' proposal
to the *Bundestag* on September 28 (*Woche im Bundestag*, October 5, 1995;
interview DEMLabSocAff, December 2000). The Social Democrats
received support in their position through the second chamber of parliament (*Bundesrat*), where they held the majority of votes. Based on a
proposal by the *Land* Berlin, the *Bundesrat* accepted a draft bill on October
13, which was to render mandatory all local German wages for posted

---

[17] This step would have been, it has to be stressed again, contingent on the approval by the
social partners.

Table 4.6 The politics of the German national response strategy

---

Employer Position: Critical, though some division between more conciliatory
    construction sector employers and others—employers sought to obstruct and
    delay national re-regulation
Union Position: Supportive, but would have wished for more comprehensive re-
    regulation—forced to make major concessions on wage levels for posted workers
Government Position: Active, but internal rife between liberals and center-left
    Christian Democrats leads to delays and a relatively more liberal legislative draft
Other Factors: German government seeks European directive first, but is unsuccesful
Heavily contested/politicized? Yes, strongly
Internal divisions? Major internal divisions within the coalition government and
    within the employers camp

---

workers and sharply step up enforcement efforts (interview Berlin Senate Department for Construction 1999; *Tagesspiegel*, September 29, 1995; *FAZ*, November 15, 1995).[18]

A conflict between the two chambers of parliament ensued. Given that the draft bill included enforcement provisions by state-level labor and customs authorities, the *Bundesrat* held veto power. The *Bundesrat*, having had its own draft bill rejected earlier, now rejected the *Bundestag* version on November 15. Subsequently, an arbitration committee (*Vermittlungsausschuss*) was established to find a compromise solution. Once again, the SPD presented its proposal, insisting on coverage of all sectors of the economy. Meanwhile, the IG BAU demanded an extension of the law's validity from two to five years (*FAZ*, December 1, 1995).

Details of the German National Response Strategy

The compromise solution extended coverage of the law to three and a half years, covered the construction sector, including the installation of heating, plumbing, climate control, and electrical installations,[19] as well as the

---

[18] This was perhaps unsurprising, since the state of Berlin had been particularly affected by the posting of workers. Consequently, the Senate Department of Construction had launched an initiative whereby all companies bidding for public tender had to declare that they would pay standard local wages. This declaration was legally binding. It also entailed a declaration that all *subcontractors* would pay standard Berlin wages (*Tariftreueerklärung*) (Berlin Senate 1995; interview with Berlin Senate Department for Construction, 1999).

[19] This was most likely due to the pressure of the IG Metall on this question (interview IG Metall 2001).

tow boat sector,[20] increased fines to up to DM 100,000, and placed responsibility for enforcement with customs and local labor authorities (Worthmann 1998; Deinert 2000). Contributions to the sectoral vacation, bad weather, and unemployment funds were made mandatory, all stipulations applied immediately and without delay (BAMS 1996). On February 6, 1996 the *Bundestag* approved the bill with 598 of 614 votes. The *Bundesrat* followed suit the next day.

The law on mandatory labor conditions for transnational service provision (*Gesetz über zwingende Arbeitsbedingungen bei grenzüberschreitenden Dienstleistungen—Arbeitnehmer-Entsendegesetz—AEntG*) went into effect on March 1, 1996 and was limited until September 1, 1999.[21] It constitutes the German national response strategy.

Its core component is Article 1, Section 1:

The legal conditions of a wage agreement in the construction sector . . . are . . . also compulsory for a work contract between an employer registered abroad and his employee employed in the geographically region to which such wage agreement pertains if and to the extent that

1. the wage agreement contains a minimum wage for all employees covered by it and

2. domestic employers which are registered outside of the geographic zone of coverage set forth in such wage agreement are also bound to this minimum of labor conditions concerning workers employed within the geographic zone covered by the wage agreement. (Bundesgesetzblatt 1996, author's translation)[22]

---

[20] This somewhat curious extension was due to the pressure of the *Land* Hamburg. Mayor Voscherau, a Social Democrat, lobbied for an inclusion of this sector because of the appearance of Dutch towboat companies in the Hamburg harbor which paid their German crews lower Dutch wages and thus were able to undercut their German competitors (interview DEMLab-SocAff December 2000). However, this practice was illegal even under existing legislation since the Dutch companies could be said to maintain dependencies in Germany and would thus have been covered by standard German wage contracts in any case.

[21] However, this temporal limitation was abolished entirely in the revision enacted by the Red-Green coalition in 1998.

[22] In German, this section reads: *Die Rechtsnormen eines für allgemeinverbindlich erklärten Tarifvertrages des Baugewerbes . . . finden . . . auch auf ein Arbeitsverhältnis zwischen einem Arbeitgeber mit Sitz im Ausland und seinem im räumlichen Geltungsbereich dieses Tarifvertrages beschäftigten Arbeitnehmer zwingend Anwendung, wenn und soweit 1. der Tarifvertrag ein für alle unter seinen Geltungsbereich fallenden Arbeitnehmer einheitliches Mindestentgelt enthält und 2. auch inländische Arbeitgeber, die ihren Sitz außerhalb des räumlichen Geltungsbereiches dieses Tarifvertrages haben, ihren im räumlichen Geltungsbereich des Tarifvertrages beschäftigten Arbeitnehmern mindestens diese am Arbeitsort geltende tarifvertragliche Arbeitsbedingung gewähren müssen.*

The length of vacation (30 days a year on average) and the contribution to vacation funds are also covered. Foreign companies must register their posted employees and contribute to the sectoral vacation fund (*Urlaubs-und Lohnausgleichskasse*). *Generally speaking, the act renders mandatory the payment of a minimum wage to workers posted to German construction sites, but only if such minimum wage has been agreed upon and declared universally applicable.* Conditions demanded of foreign employers could not exceed those demanded of domestic ones. Additionally, the act stipulated the following.

1. No transition period

All regulations apply immediately without any delay and to all foreign companies regardless of country of registration.

2. Duty to provide extensive documentation

Companies posting workers must register such intention in advance with the local or regional labor authorities. They must provide documentation concerning the names of the posted employees, the dates of the contract and the exact location of the construction site as well as an affirmation that legally applicable wages will be paid. This declaration must be made in German (Article 3).

3. Increased enforcement efforts and high fines

The Federal Labor Office and its regional dependencies along with custom authorities are charged with enforcement. Foreign employers are required to present documentation concerning wage and labor conditions. Violations of wage or other labor regulations are considered a legal offense and can be fined by up to DM 100,000. Contractors engaging in subcontracting can be fined up to the same amount if the subcontractor is found in violation of any regulations. Companies with a previous record of violations (including by subcontractors) may be excluded from submitting bids to public tender.

4. German working time regulation apply

Standard working time regulations apply, thus the working day is limited to 8 hours a day and six days a week. This 48-hour work week may be extended by up to 2 hours of overtime. Work on Sundays and public holidays is not permitted.

5. No immediate wage-setting

The minimum wage itself is not regulated, as this would constitute a violation of the principle of *Tarifautonomie*. This new and universal minimum wage bracket was eventually set, at a significant 20 percent below the lowest standard German wage bracket, as discussed below (Bundesgesetzblatt 1996; DGB 1996).

The Second Part of the Tragedy: Quarrels, Fights and Bickering over the New Minimum Wage

The core piece of the national response strategy, the exact level of the minimum wage, was left up to regulation by the social partners. The two labor market interest associations not only influenced the deliberation of legislation, but were also directly involved in formulating its implementation. In this process, a clear conflict of interest became obvious within the camp of the employers. While the sectoral construction employer association were much more willing to make concessions, the BDA sought to delay implementation and insisted on a truly minimal minimum wage. For the minimum wage to be declared universally applicable (*allgemeinverbindlich*) a special wage commission within the Ministry of Labor has to agree, composed of three representatives from each camp, though not the associations directly involved.[23]

Without a minimum wage agreement for the construction sector, the German national response strategy had no bite. In early 1996, the lowest wage bracket for skilled domestically employed workers was DM 22.47, DM 20.24 for unskilled domestically employed workers and DM 18.23 for auxiliary unskilled workers (*FAZ*, December 7, 1995). The BDA decided to veto any move making the lowest wage bracket of the construction sector universally applicable. The BDA made it also known that it would not accept a minimum wage of more than DM 15 for the West and DM 13.80 for the East to avoid upward wage drift in other sectors or any gradual wage increases over time (*Tagesspiegel*, September 29, 1995).[24]

---

[23] This is specified in Art. 5 of the Law on Wage Agreements of 1949 (*Tarifvertragsgesetz*).

[24] According to the BDA, in the West German steel industry the lowest wage bracket was DM 14.37, in the metal industry DM 16.01 to DM 16.62, in the paper industry DM 15.86 to DM 16.46, in the textile industry DM 14.51 to DM 15.41 (BDA 1996).

Negotiations between the IG BAU, HDB and ZDB, which had commenced on December 18, 1995, did not produce results. IG BAU initially did not retreat from its position of defending the wage bracket for unskilled workers (DM 20.24 per hour) as the basis for a minimum wage. The sectoral employers refused to accept this level (*FAZ*, November 15, 1995; *FAZ*, January 26, 1996). Eventually, the union accepted DM 19.58, an offer the sectoral employers still rejected. The compromise solution agreed upon by both sides at the sectoral level was to introduce a layered minimum wage of DM 15.30 (14.08) as of April 1, DM 17.00 (15.64) as of September 1, and DM 18.60 (17.11) as of December 1 in the Western (Eastern) *Länder* respectively (*FAZ*, April 15, 1996; *FAZ*, June 16, 1996). This proposal created the new wage bracket VII 2, applicable both for foreign posted workers and newly hired formerly unemployed domestic workers. IG BAU was forced to concede to this.

Tensions Mount: Conflicting Interests within the Employer Camp

But this was not the end of the saga. Even though the sectoral employers and the union had found a compromise solution, the BDA decided to override this solution and torpedo it. During the May 28, 1996 meeting of the wage committee at the Ministry of Labor in Bonn, the employer representatives used their veto to avoid this wage level forming the basis of a minimal wage bracket for posted workers. The BDA announced that its informal guidelines had been ignored (*FAZ*, May 29, 1996). The sectoral employers were appalled. In a referendum, a majority of member companies of both ZDB and HDB voted in favor of quitting the BDA at the earliest possible date, which was December 31, 1996 (*FAZ*, June 13, 1996). This would have been an unparalleled step in the history of German industrial relations.

Both associations continued their negotiations with the IG BAU, attempting to prod and cajole the union into accepting an even lower minimum wage, which the BDA would accept. By late August, the union had conceded to an hourly minimum wage bracket (VII 2) of DM 17 in the West and DM 15.64 in the East (*FAZ*, August 24, 1996). The BDA was willing to accept this wage level, but only if it was limited until May 31, 1997. The IG BAU refused to tolerate any temporal limitation. Limiting the validity of minimum wage to the winter months with little construction activity would have given the compromise very little bite (interview IG BAU, April 2001).

In the meantime, the ever increasing phenomenon of subcontractors employing posted workers crowding out directly employed domestic workers (*Tagesspiegel*, February 1, 1996) undermined the union's bargaining position. After additional stalemates in the wage committee on October 8 and 25, (BDA 1996d, 1996e; interview DGB, December 2000), Minister of Labor Blüm intervened in person and invited representatives of the DGB, BDA, IG BAU, ZDB, and HDB to a meeting in Bonn on November 5 (*FAZ*, October 26, 1996). He suggested a temporarily limited applicability of the agreed wage rates until August 31, 1997 (*FAZ*, November 8, 1996), hence including the summer. Both sides agreed. Universal applicability was accepted by the wage committee on November 12. Blüm thus declared the newly modified framework wage agreement of September 2, 1996, including the new wage bracket VII 2 and the minimum wage, to be universally applicable. The sectoral employer association remained within the BDA. Only now, after nine months of heavy quarreling and fighting, did the German national response strategy start to be effective.

Summary and Detailed Discussion of the German Re-regulation

The German national response strategy was implemented after a lengthy and heated conflict (see Table 4.7). Several cleavages emerged. First, within the employer camp, the BDA and some of its sectoral members (Gesamtmetall, Gesamtextil) supported a truly minimal minimum wage for posted workers, while the HDB and ZDB were more willing to meet the union half-way. The HDB and ZDB generally supported a national re-regulation of the LSP. While they tried to depress wages, they were willing to concede to higher minimum wages than the BDA. The BDA and its allies were fundamentally opposed to a national re-regulation. Even having conceded to one, only a very limited and non-intrusive re-regulation was accepted.

Second, a more predictable line of conflict emerged between the union and the employers. IG BAU and its allies, IG Metall and DGB, desired a comprehensive re-regulation, preferably covering the entire economy and extending standard German wages. In light of fierce resistance, it was forced to significant concessions.

Third, also somewhat predictably, differences between the coalition government and the opposition Social Democrats became clear. The SPD endorsed a national re-regulation closer to union demands.

Fourth, within the government itself diverging interests surfaced. The pro-business fraction of the Christian Democrats, and especially their liberal coalition partner FDP, controlling the Ministry of Economic Affairs, remained highly skeptical of the response strategy, prepared by the Ministry of Labor and supported by the pro-labor left wing of the Christian Democrats.

Finally, and possibly least importantly, some conflicts between the two chambers of parliament became visible over certain details. The *Bundesrat*, dominated by a majority of SPD-ruled *Länder*, insisted on a more comprehensive regulation. However, the importance of this latter arena should not be overestimated. Intervention of the *Bundesrat* and the opposition Social Democrats neither stopped nor delayed implementation, but only modified minute details. The most important outcome of the pressure from the liberal opponents was the law's temporal and sectoral limitation, both of which are absent in the French equivalent.[25]

Without wanting to discount entirely the role of party politics in the formulation of the law, the most pertinent clash of interests had occurred between BDA on the one hand and IG BAU and DGB on the other. The employers used their veto power in the Ministry of Labor committee to impede the universal applicability of a minimum wage until the union had made significant concessions. BDA kept its own sectoral members in check. It pressed the HDB and ZDB, which were potentially somewhat conciliatory towards the union, to negotiate low minimum wages. BDA remained unimpressed by the two sectoral associations' complaints over this tough line and their threat to quit membership. *Its aggressive stance paid off handsomely as IG BAU was forced to agree to a wage differential of significant proportions between the new minimum wage (wage bracket VII 2) and the lowest wage bracket for domestically employed workers.*

Recurring Negotiations and Conflict: The Further Path of Evolution of the German Response Strategy

Given that the wage bracket applicable to posted workers was itself temporarily limited, just as the legislation was in its first incarnation, it had to

---

[25] An important difference to France is also the extent to which the German government had attempted to use the European level first to re-regulate the LSP, before initiating a national response strategy. Only after a stalemate at the European level had become obvious and the efforts of the German presidency in the second half of 1994 had produced no tangible results did the government commence work on a national regulatory response (interview DEMLab-SocAff, December 2000).

be re-negotiated upon expiry. In July 1997, the sectoral social partners and the BDA met for another round of negotiations to set the wage level until the end of August 1999, when the Law on Posted Workers expired. Unable even to defend its current position,[26] IG BAU was forced to concede to a further reduction of this wage bracket to DM 16.00 in the West and DM 15.14 in the East (*FAZ*, July 17, 1997). This solution was declared universally applicable on August 14 and became effective as of September 1, 1997 (*FAZ*, August 15, 1997).[27] Worse yet, this new minimum wage bracket is now applicable to newly hired domestic long-term unemployed workers. At the same time, the sectoral employers were taking advantage of apparent union weakness in securing reduced employer charges, i.e. certain extra payments to employees.

There have since been two reforms of the original 1996 Act. The first was passed by the *Bundestag* on November 28, 1997 as part of the 'First Law on Changes to the Third Book of the Social Law Compendium and other laws' (*Erstes Gesetz zur Änderung des Dritten Buches Sozialgesetzbuch und anderer Gesetze*) (Bundesgesetzblatt 1997). It came into effect on January 1, 1998. It was aimed at improving the practical effects of the original Law on Posted Workers. Measures include:

1. Improved monitoring efforts

Closer coordination and information exchange between customs and labor authorities on the one hand and finance authorities on the other; law enforcement authorities may forward information on past offenses to public authorities soliciting public tenders, fines are increased to up to DM 500,000.

2. Higher standards of documentation required

Required documentation now also has to cover daily working hours so as to make apparent actual hourly wage. All documentation has to be

---

[26] Meanwhile, IG BAU also had to concede to the reduction in the payment of the 13th monthly salary and vacation pay as well as a reduction of the payment during the first three days of illness from 100 percent of the wages to 80 percent (*FAZ*, August 15, 1997).

[27] The minimum wages increased again on September 1, 1999 to DM 18.50 in the West and DM 15.14 in the East, wage levels that the HDB accepted, but the BDA rejected. This time, however, the Minister of Labor could declare these wages universally applicable without the consent of the BDA and based only on the application of the HDB; based on the reform to the Law on Posted Workers described above (*FAZ*, July 12, 1999).

available physically for inspection on actual construction sites subject to posting of workers.

Red-Green Reforms

The second reform was part of the Law on Corrections in Social Insurance and for the Protection of the Rights of Employees (*Gesetz zu Korrekturen in der Sozialversicherung und zur Sicherung der Arbeitnehmerrechte*) passed during the first few months of the Red-Green coalition on December 19, 1998 (BAMS 2000). It went into effect on January 1, 1999 (Bundesgesetzblatt 1998). This second reform adopted the German law to the European Directive on the Posting of Workers, but also provided the German response strategy with more bite. Article 10 of this law, entitled 'Changes to the Law on Posted Workers' (*Änderung des Arbeitnehmer-Entsendegesetzes*) makes the following modifications.

1. Clarification

It is put into much more explicit terms that both the minimum wage, including overtime pay, as well as the vacation regulations and vacation pay are mandatory.

2. Extend life span of old wage agreements

The minimal conditions set forth in the wage agreement are to be applied even in the absence of universal applicability. In practice this means that if an old wage agreement expires its terms remain valid until a new one is agreed upon.

3. Ministry of Labor can impose universal applicability

Most importantly, the Ministry of Labor may declare a wage agreement universally applicable if one party of such contract requests this. The Ministry is not dependent on the approval of the *Bundestag*. It asks both parties for a written comment on this issue, yet is not legally required to take these statements into consideration. This is not considered an infringement on *Tarifautonomie* according to the government because (a) the Ministry does not decree wages, it merely declares wages already agreed upon by the social partners universally applicable, (b) it cannot do so on its own initiative but only following a request by one of the two parties, and (c) this is not a general principle but applies only to the construction sector.

4. Legal responsibility

Companies using subcontractors are legally liable for the payment of proper applicable wages to employees of subcontractors. This includes any 'chains' of subcontractors as well. This principle of contractor liability (*Generalunternehmerhaftung*) was rejected by the HDB (interview HDB 1999).

Same Conflict Lines Re-emerge: BDA versus Sectoral Social Partners

This modified law was to have a practical effect, when during the course of wage negotiations in April 1999 the same conflict lines as before re-emerged. While ZDB and HDB were willing to raise the hourly minimum wage from 1 September 1999 to DM 18.50 in the West and DM 16.28 in the East, the BDA and other sectoral employer association refused to approve of this raise in the Ministry of Labor's wage committee. The very same arguments were advanced by the employers as before: concerns over a wage drift and the relatively high wages in the construction sector. However, using the new authority afforded by the revised response strategy, the Ministry of Labor acted upon an application by IG BAU to declare this new agreement universally applicable in August 1999. The BDA was furious.

Following strike action during June 2002, the employers agreed to further increases in the minimum wage. While the initial German response strategy had been a far cry from the union's demand, with the introduction of a new second tier minimum wage for skilled workers, the union did secure the implementation of one of its demand. From September 2002 (2003), minimum hourly wage brackets were raised by 2.4 percent to EUR 10.12 (10.36) in the West and EUR 8.76 (8.97) in the East. The new bracket for skilled posted workers took effect on September 1, 2003 and was set at EUR 12.47 in the West and EUR 10.01 in the East (EIRO 2002).

A final adjustment to the German national response strategy occurred in the form of a legislative modification, arising from a lost ECJ court case on October 25, 2001 (C-493/99 *Commission vs. Germany*). Germany had long banned temporary labor agencies in the construction sector; only recently had such agencies been permitted to operate, but with the obligation to accept all collective wage agreements in the construction sector, contained in article 1 of the Act on Temporary Employment (BGB II of 1972, p. 1393; *Gesetz zur Regelung der gewerbsmäaigen Arbeitnehmerüberlassung—Arbeitnehmerüberlassungsgesetz*).

The ECJ ruled this limitation to violate the LSP. Subsequently, Art 1b of the law was modified, now permitting foreign construction industries (but still not foreign temporary labor agencies) to engage in the provision of temporary labor procurement services in construction.

The Disintegration of a Union Stronghold: A Three Tier Labor Market in the German Construction Sector

However, despite the legislative efforts, the German national response strategy does not eradicate the wage gap between directly employed workers in Germany, regardless of their nationality, and the posted workers. The former category is entitled to receive wages according to the various wage brackets, while the latter only receive the new minimum wage brackets. However, in light of the slow erosion of the organized German industrial relations system (Hassel and Streeck 2004), especially pronounced in the East, where both unionization and employer association membership are low, this new minimum wage, by virtue of being universally applicable, also applies to directly employed workers and aids their position. Thus, from the perspective of eastern construction workers, this universal applicability brings the advantage of imposing higher wages in Dresden, Leipzig, and Magdeburg than many employers would otherwise be willing to pay. However, given the wage gap between the top and the lower tier, commercial incentives to continue with the employment of subcontractors remain. The once unified and heavily unionized labor market in the German construction sector has thus disintegrated into a three tier structure, composed of a top tier of regularly directly employed workers, posted workers, and illegally employed workers (Menz 2001).

Regardless of any legal obligations and official wage levels, illegal employment remains a substantial problem in the German construction sector. An equally disturbing problem is the shrinking size of the top tier of the labor market. According to IG BAU, unemployment rates among construction workers in the particularly exposed Berlin region stand at 55 percent. While 55,000 workers were employed in the region in 1994, this figure had declined to 10,500 by 2004. A study commissioned by the Berlin social security fund for the construction sector estimates that one third of all construction projects in the region involve the employment of illegal workers and/or substandard wages (*Berliner Morgenpost*, July 7, 2004).

Having implemented a new law against illegal employment in August 2002 (*Gesetz zur Erleichterung der Bekämpfung von illegaler Beschäftigung und Schwarzarbeit*), in 2003 the now re-named Ministry for Labor and Economic Affairs presented a draft proposal for a new law against illegal employment. Presented to parliament on March 2, 2004 (Drucksache 15/2573), this law 'on the intensification of the fight against illegal employment and related tax evasion' (*Gesetz zur Intensivierung der Bekämpfung der Schwarzarbeit und damit zusammenhängender Steuerhinterziehung*) seeks to further increase the authorities that tax and custom enforcement officials can exercise if they suspect illegal employment, tax evasion and evasion of social security payments. The law went into effect on August 1, 2004. While the employer association criticized the 'excessive fines' of up to € 50,000 and the limited redress (BDA, 2003), the construction union generally approved of the new legislation, criticizing only the fairly generous exceptions allotted to unpaid 'help' among 'friends' and neighbors (IG BAU, 2004).

Table 4.7 An overview of regulation contained within the German response strategy

---

Does the response strategy cover the entire economy? No. This is a regulation specifically targeted at the construction sector, plus a few adjacent trades and the towboat sector.

Are there exceptions/loopholes? Yes, the main escape clause proved to be the fact that the law eo ipso does not contain a wage level for posted workers, but left this up to the social partners to negotiate. In the absence of a minimum wage in Germany or a universally applicable sectoral wage in the construction sector, the response strategy therefore had virtually no bite until such sectoral wage level could be agreed upon and was declared universally applicable. Even then, there is a significant wage gap between this minimum sectoral wage and wages for skilled directly employed workers. Subcontracting and outsourcing to foreign service providers henceforth remain lucrative options.

What regulations become legally binding on foreign service providers? The German sectoral wage agreements for the construction sector, but only to the extent that they are universally applicable. In 1999, the government took the extremely rare step of declaring the sectoral wage universally applicable in the face of employer resistance to such measure.

In addition, German labor, working time, and social regulations apply— contributions to the sectoral social security systems likewise become mandatory.

The Austrian National Response Strategy

Developments in the Austrian Construction Sector and the Impact of EU Accession

Austria is a latecomer to the process of European integration. It joined the EU 'waiting room', the EEA, on January 1, 1994 and the European Union on January 1, 1995. The LSP did not apply until 1994, when it came into effect as part of the *acquis communautaire*. In addition, Austria had not signed the Rome Convention of 1980. Therefore, it was still able to regulate autonomously the access to the Austrian labor market and the conditions applicable to posted workers.

The Austrian construction sector was traditionally dominated by SMEs, only after and partly in response to EU membership did some consolidation occur (interview Austrian construction company, April 2001). The need for labor was satisfied domestically. While labor migrants recruited during the 1960s, especially from Yugoslavia and Turkey, were well represented in this sector, they were directly employed by Austrian companies, receiving standard wages. Labor market access by foreigners was regulated by the fairly restrictive Act on the Employment of Foreigners (*Ausländerbeschäftigungsgesetz*). [28]

Discussions about candidacy for EU accession had commenced in the late 1980s. In the summer of 1989 a formal request was submitted. Debates were heated. Opponents feared compromising high standards in environmental and social protection (*Die Presse*, April 2, 1993; June 2, 1993; Falkner 1993). The far right Freedomites invoked images of mass inward migration due to EU membership. The two major political parties, employers and unions abandoned initial hesitation and helped garner support among their rank and file (Heinisch, 1999).

---

[28] The act mandated work permits for any non-Austrian national performing any compensated activity on Austrian territory, as is stated in Article 18. Thus, even though temporary posting of workers to Austria could occur under international private law—i.e. two companies could agree to such practice—the national labor authorities could have intercepted such posting simply by not granting any work permits for posted workers (Eder 1996: 105). According to Article 4 of this Act, work permits to foreigners were issued for one year at a time for a specific job and only after a review of the situation on the Austrian labor market. Such reviews were continued annually for eight years after which the foreign resident was issued a "certificate of exemption" (*Befreiungsschein*) and restrictions were eased somewhat (Article 15). The fairly restrictive Austrian immigration policy was thus heavily flavored by the concept of seasonal or temporary guest workers (*Gastarbeiter*). Migrants were permitted primarily to fill the needs of the domestic labor market without acquiring many rights.

The Union Loses No Time: Moving towards an Austrian Response Strategy

The union was not opposed to EU membership; in fact, it helped swing the vote amongst its clientele (Bieler 2000). Therefore, it cannot be argued that employers had to make concessions to the union to affect a change of heart. However, the umbrella organization ÖGB was concerned about compromising high Austrian standards of social protection and labor laws in the process of adopting the *acquis*. The posting of workers from low-wage EU countries could have been one possible avenue for social dumping.

Sectoral construction and woodworkers' union *Bau-Holz* raised its voice within the ÖGB (Eder 1999: 106ff.; *Die Presse*, April 2, 1993). The aim was to secure status quo wages and social and labor standards for all posted workers. Responding to this input, the ÖGB lost no time and approached the Ministry of Labor and Social Affairs in spring 1993, urging it to develop appropriate legislative action (interviews ÖGB, Bau-Holz 2001). In the 1993 coalition cabinet, the minister Josef Hesoun was a Social Democrat, a former head of the *Bau-Holz* union, and a former construction worker himself (interview Bau-Holz 2001). The ministry developed an initial draft proposal for a law, which would cautiously modify and adapt Austrian labor law to the EU *acquis*, while safeguarding as much of the *status quo* as possible. Comments on this draft were then solicited from all social partners, as is practice in neocorporatist Austria for draft bills concerning labor market and social policy.

The Position of the Employers and the Union in Austria regarding a National Response Strategy

The *union* had already clearly expressed its stance by lobbying the ministry to initiate legislative protection of the status quo. It feared a downward spiral of wages and social protection in the wake of EU membership, not least through somewhat less than obvious channels, as would have been the case with posted workers. There was no internal division within the union on this issue. Although construction union Bau Holz was particularly active, it could not have taken any action independently from the ÖGB. It thus coordinated its lobbying efforts with the umbrella organization, which wholeheartedly supported this issue, since it was considered of potential pertinence to all of its members (interviews ÖGB, Bau-Holz 2001).

The employer association WK was not fervently enthusiastic about such regulation, but also not strictly opposed to it. In fact, its sectoral construction members *Bundesinnung Baugewerbe* and *Fachverband der Bauindustrie* viewed EU membership and the resulting competition from low-wage member states more as a potential threat than as an opportunity to gain access to cheap subcontractors (interview WK 2001). Exiting the relatively high Austrian wages and thus setting in motion a downward spiral in terms of wages and subsequently prices was seen more as a menace to the existing market stability. This attitude might not least be a result of the structure of the Austrian construction sector, dominated by SMEs. These companies did not stand to gain as clearly from outsourcing and applying downward pressure on wages as the few larger companies. In addition, the principle of 'one-member, one-vote' secured substantial influence of SMEs in the WK. Therefore, the WK not only did not oppose such regulation, it was actually itself not unsympathetic to the idea (interview WK 2001).

Swift Union Action, Consenting Employers: Implementation in Austria

Given the political and ideological overlap between the Social Democrats and the union on the one hand and the employers and the conservative Peoples' Party on the other, the two major political parties forming a Grand Coalition adopted the positions of the labor market interest associations. The Social Democrats and the Ministry of Labor controlled by it supported the union initiative wholeheartedly (interview AstMLabEcon Aff 2001). Given that the WK signaled its willingness to accept a national re-regulation, the ÖVP and the Ministry of Economic Affairs did not stand in the way of this initiative (interview AstMEconAff 1999).[29] The three political opposition parties had very little influence. Even so, neither the far right FPÖ, the Greens, nor minute *Liberales Forum* protested against this legislative initiative.

---

[29] Austria's Black-Blue coalition has since united the ministry of labor and social affairs and the ministry of economic affairs into a new Ministry of Labor and Economic Affairs (*Bundesministerium für Wirtschaft und Arbeit*) in 2000. Until then, these ministries had not only been separate, they had also been the traditional domains of the Social Democrats (the 'red camp') and the conservatives (the 'black camp') respectively. Ostensibly, the measure was geared at breaking up this traditional division of power, yet one might also interpret it as an attempt to subsume labor and social affairs under the interests of business, which would reflect the Black-Blue coalition's policy imperatives.

Having been approved by the social partners, the legislative initiative was thus introduced into the lower chamber of parliament *Nationalrat* on May 26, 1993. It was included in a package of legislative measures aimed at bringing labor law into compliance with EU legislation and jurisprudence. Consequently, it is entitled 'Law on Changes to the Labor Code' (*Arbeits-vertragsrechtsanpassungsgesetz*—AVRAG). Relevant Article 7 of this law was approved by the parliamentary committee on Labor and Social Affairs on June 8 and approved unanimously by the *Nationalrat* on June 17. It came into effect on July 1, 1993 and reads as follows:

1. If an employer without dependency in Austria, which is not a member of an association which habitually negotiates wage agreements in Austria, employs a person whose habitual location of employment is Austria, then this employee is entitled to at least those wages set forth by law and wage agreements applicable to comparable employers and employees in this same location.

2. Section 1 is also applicable, notwithstanding the law to be applied to the terms of the labor contract in general, to employees send to Austria from an employer without dependency in Austria for purposes of temporary labor placement or the execution of a continued labor contract for work projects which extend in total over a period of more than four weeks.

3. Section 2 does not apply to posted workers which are employed

    (a) in the course of installation, set-up, and maintenance related to orders of plants or machinery in a company

---

30 In the original German the text reads as follows:

   1. Beschäftigt ein Arbeitgeber ohne Sitz in Österreich, der nicht Mitglied einer kollektivvertrags-fähigen Körperschaft in Österreich ist, einen Arbeitnehmer mit gewöhnlichem Arbeitsort in Österreich, so hat dieser Arbeitnehmer Anspruch zumindest auf jenes gesetzliche oder kollek-tivvertragliche Entgelt, das am Arbeitsort vergleichbaren Arbeitnehmern von vergleichbaren Arbeitgebern gebührt.

   2. Absatz 1 gilt, unbeschadet des auf das Arbeitsverhältnis anzuwendenden Rechts, auch für einen Arbeitnehmer, der von einem Arbeitgeber ohne Sitz in Österreich für Arbeiten, die insgesamt länger als einen Monat dauern, im Rahmen einer Arbeitskräfteüberlassung oder zur Erbringung einer fortgesetzten Arbeitsleistung nach Österreich entsandt wird.

   3. Absatz 2 gilt nicht für einen entsandten Arbeitnehmer, der bei

   1. Montagearbeiten und Reparaturen im Zusammenhang mit Lieferungen von Anlagen und Maschinen an einen Betrieb oder

   2. für die Inbetriebnahme solcher Anlagen und Maschinen nötigen Arbeiten, die von inlän-dischen Arbeitnehmern nicht erbacht werden können, beschäftigt wird, wenn diese Arbeiten insgesamt in Österreich nicht länger als drei Monate dauern.

(b) for setting up such installations and machinery if this work cannot be performed by domestic employees if these activities do not extend for more than three months in Austria.[30]

(Bundesgesetzblatt für die Republik Österreich, 172th piece, No. 459, July 9, 1993, author's translation)

The Austrian national response strategy in detail

1. Comprehensive coverage

The law covers all sectors of the economy, stipulating payment of standard Austrian wages in accordance with the level of qualification. Thus, no obvious wage gap exists between wages for workers employed directly by domestic companies and posted workers. It also covers domestic workers employed within Austria by foreign companies. Although not stated explicitly in the AVRAG, standard overtime pay, vacation pay, and, very importantly, contributions by the employer to accommodation and travel expenses for workers employed outside of their habitual place of employment (*Trennungsgeld*) became mandatory. This also applies to workers posted from abroad and means that such expenses have to be paid to the posted worker *in addition* to his regular wage. Finally, contributions to the sectoral vacation and bad weather funds, if existent, also became obligatory. Contributions to the sectoral funds and rules on overtime payment are stipulated by *law* in Austria and thus could have been considered part of the *ordre public* even before the passage of the national response strategy.

2. All wage brackets are rendered mandatory

The question of universal applicability (*Allgemeinverbindlichkeit*) does not play a central role in Austria, since all Austrian companies are members of the WK and are thus de jure obliged to respect the terms of the wage agreements negotiated by the Chamber on their behalf. Thus, wage agreements are legally binding even without having been officially declared universally applicable by the Federal Arbitration Office (*Bundeseinigungsamt*) to all WK members.

3. 'Window' for short-term postings

The regulation contains an exception for postings of up to four weeks, during which Austrian wages do not apply. This 'window' was implemented to avoid excessive bureaucratic burdens on companies in cases of short-term posting. It allows for some flexibility and was accepted by both social partners (Eder 1999: 107).

Closing the Window: The 1995 Revision of the Austrian Regulation

The national response strategy was implemented without much controversy and based on mutual consent between the social partners and the political parties. However, further developments would prove that the issue of posted workers would create significant political conflict in Austria, too. The four-week 'window', during which Austrian wages did not apply to posted workers, and its exploitation by enterprising Hans-Peter Haselsteiner, CEO of Austria's largest construction company Bau Holding, generated a heated public debate in the summer of 1995 and eventually gave birth to a revision of the original law (*Der Standard*, June 29, 1995; August 29, 1995; August 30, 1995; *Profil*, September 4, 1995).

Haselsteiner announced that he would set up a Portuguese dependency of his company from where workers would be posted to Austria. This would allow Bau Holding to exploit the small gap between the official wage levels (*Soll*-Lohn) and actually paid wages (*Ist*-Lohn), as well as fully exploit this one-month 'loophole' (*Kleine Zeitung*, August 29, 1995; *Tiroler Tageszeitung*, August 24, 1995; *Wirtschaftsblatt*, October 28, 1995; Kirschbaum 1995); interview Austrian construction company 2001). Haselsteiner had obviously not studied the legal regulation of posted workers very closely. There were barely any savings to be realized, given the obligation to pay for the *Trennungsgeld*. By the summer of 1995, Austria had been an EU member for a few months and a few very isolated cases of posting had indeed occurred (Eder 1999). Given the absence of a wage gap, posting of workers was never particularly attractive, assuming the respect of the law, and was limited to a few hundred Portuguese, Britons, and Irish (interview ÖGB 1999, 2001; AstMLabEconAff 2001; WK 2001).

Union Activity Regarding the Revision of the Response Strategy

Bau Holz and ÖGB petitioned the Minister for Labor and Social Affairs in May 1995. They suggested a draft bill strengthening the current legislation, stepping up enforcement, introducing legal liability for Austrian contractors subcontracting to foreign companies found in violation of existing regulations, and, in particular, closing the four week window, which was clearly being exploited by cunning entrepreneurs (interview Bau-Holz 2001). Although the employers were not enthusiastic about such reinforced legislation, it ought to be noted that most construction companies did not support Haselsteiner's position. The concurrent development in Germany, where the posting of workers had reached epidemic proportions by then was very closely monitored by all actors, the unions, the employers, and the government (*Der Standard*, May 2, 1995; September 8, 1995; interview WK 2001). Austrian construction conglomerate Maculan encountered severe economic difficulties following the inability to meet deadlines and deliver consistent quality precisely because it relied on posted workers on some of the East German construction projects in which it was involved.

In early September 1995, the Ministry of Labor and Social Affairs led by Social Democrat Franz Hums presented a draft bill for the revision of the original AVRAG. Its central point was to abolish the one month exemption (*Der Standard*, September 8, 1995).

Late Nights in Vienna: The Politics of the Revision of the Austrian Regulation

ÖGB, AK, and SPÖ supported this project, but even the WK, the ÖVP and the Ministry of Economic Affairs were not fundamentally opposed to it at first. After the draft bill had been formally presented to the social partners

Table 4.8 The politics of the Austrian national response strategy

Employer Position: Accommodationist at first, though slightly more skeptical during revision, especially regarding legal responsibility—strong role of SMEs means that subcontracting is regarded more as menace than as an opportunity

Union Position: Very supportive and active, unions lobbies government ministry for re-regulation

Government Position: Active, during revision some division between more business-friendly Peoples' Party and Social Democrats, but smaller parties help swing the vote

Other Factors: Preceding EU membership, fears of EU-induced 'social dumping' are considerable

Heavily contested/politicized? No, although some conflict over details of the revision

Internal divisions? No

by the Ministry of Labor in October 1995, it did become clear, however, that the employers and the Peoples' Party with it would not support it on all points. Other than abolishing the 'loophole', the bill introduced *legal liability for Austrian companies* involved in illicit forms of employment, tougher spot checks by labor inspectors, and an obligation to present relevant documents detailing compliance with standard wages and work conditions. The WK was particularly concerned about this first point, the legal co-responsibility employers had to bear in case any of their subcontractors were found in violation of any regulation (*Solidarhaftung*) (WK, November 29, 1995; interview WK 2001). It came to be opposed to the abolition of the one month transitory period (VÖI, November 2, 1995; WK, November 29, 1995). The employers considered the legislation already on the books to be sufficient (WK, November 29, 1995; Eder 1997: 110; *Der Standard*, August 28, 1995). No common position could be found between the social partners on the exact content or phrasing of such legislative amendment. A stand-off became obvious during a meeting of the Minister Franz Hums and representatives of the two camps on November 2. By now, the employers proved unwilling to compromise on the issue of the four-week window.

Nevertheless, the bill passed parliament during an all-night session on November 17, 1995, with the votes of the Social Democrats, the Greens, the far-right Freedomites, who had discovered this issue as an 'anti-foreigner' vote and, most surprisingly, a Liberal Forum MP by the name of Haselsteiner! He sought to demonstrate that he distinguished between his private interests and his role as an MP (*Der Standard*, November 22, 1995).[31] The *Bundesrat* approved the new 'Anti-Abuse Law' (*Antimißbrauchsgesetz*) on November 29.

The Revised Austrian Response Strategy in Detail

The new Article 7 of the AVRAG, modified by the 1995 *Antimißbrauchsgesetz*, contained the following amendments to the original bill (see also Table 4.9).

[31] On October 13, the Grand Coalition between the ÖVP and the SPÖ collapsed, yet a special marathon session of parliament was scheduled for the week of November 13–17 in order to pass legislation considered of high relevance before the new elections. On November 13, SPÖ MP Reitsamer introduced a draft bill, based on the Ministry of Labor and Social Affairs proposal from September. His initiative was then referred to the parliamentary committee on labor and social affairs. In the ensuing marathon session from November 15–17 (*Der Standard*, November 4–5, 1995; November 17, 1995; November 18, 1995) support for the so-called Law against Abuses (*Antimißbrauchsgesetz*)was beginning to take on shape both from the Greens and the far right FPÖ.

1. Abolishing the temporary exemption

The original four-week window within which home country wages could be applied was abolished for construction projects. However, the three-month window for installation projects was not modified. A slight change of language announced the character of the new law: payment of wages comparable to Austrian standards was now *mandatory* (*zwingend*).

2. Legal responsibility to pay standard wages—even to subcontractors

In Section 2 the legal responsibility of Austrian companies to ensure payment of standard wages even to employees of any subcontractor employees was specified: 'The immediate employer and its main contractor are legally liable and responsible to the demands by employers regarding these regulations in connection with Section 1.'[32]

3. Increased Documentation Requirements

The central labor inspector office and its regional dependencies are entitled to control documents detailing payment, working time, work conditions, and payments towards social security or sectoral fund systems (Sections 4 and 5). Labor inspectors are encouraged to coordinate their efforts with unions and employers. Fines are also increased to up to Sch240,000 (new Article 7a) and can be imposed both upon the direct employer and the (presumably Austrian) main contractor.

Summary and Detailed Discussion of the Austrian Response Strategy

In sum, the 1995 modification rendered the Austrian response strategy even more comprehensive and effective. It had been implemented in 1993 as a preemptive response to the repercussions of the EU LSP. The original legislation was rendered more restrictive in light of first

---

[32] In German, this section read: '*Der Arbeitgeber und dessen Auftraggeber als Unternehmer haften als Gesamtschuldner für die Ansprüche des Arbeitnehmers gemäß der vorstehenden Bestimmungen in Verbindung mit Abs. 1.*'

The Law on Employment of Foreigners (*Ausländerbeschäftigungsgesetz*) was also modified. Its new Article 28, Sections 6 and 7 reinforced this joint legal responsibility of both main contractor and subcontractor for the employment of illegal workers. As a general new rule, if inspectors found foreigners without work permits on construction sites, the burden of proof of innocence would automatically lie with the employer.

practical experiences and the polemic surrounding the escapades of a major construction company. Although there was slightly more controversy regarding the 1995 modification than with respect to the original, initially not even the WK was vehemently opposed to this modification, though it later modified its position. The passage of this law occurred under the somewhat unusual circumstances of a marathon session and enabled the parliament to override the stand-off between the social partners on this issue. In that sense, its adoption became politicized, with the Freedomites 'discovering' the issue to please their xenophobe clientele and the Greens supporting a law that sought to combat social dumping.

The original AVRAG was a result of remarkably prescient joint action of the ÖGB and Bau-Holz. They enjoyed an excellent direct link to the government in the form of the SPÖ Minister of Labor, a former head of the construction union. The union did not encounter much resistance from the employer camp, which, due to its own organizational design and the structural configuration of the Austrian business community, was skeptical rather than enthusiastic about the impending LSP. Business considered the opening of the labor market more as a threat than an opportunity to exit high Austrian wages. Only two years later did one major company move away from this consensus, causing uproar among the unions and significant public debate. Posting of workers to Austria never reached significant proportions because the legislative response had de-

Table 4.9 An overview of regulation contained within the Austrian response strategy

Does the response strategy cover the entire economy? Yes. This is a very comprehensive and protectionist regulation, covering the entire economy, not only the construction sector.

Are there exceptions/loopholes? Yes, a four-week window during which Austrian wages did not apply, initially implemented to avoid bureaucratic overregulation was exploited by enterprising construction managers. This loophole was closed in the revision of the law. However, for certain other temporary postings temporary exceptions remain. However, in general given the scope and application of this response strategy, outsourcing and subcontracting are hardly financially attractive.

What regulations become legally binding on foreign service providers? All Austrian wage brackets, which are considered to be binding on all employers active on Austrian territory, along with the Austrian labor, working time, and social regulations.

prived companies of most of the advantages and economic incentives this practice offered. Given this attitude on the part of employers, their acceptance, and perhaps even agreement, to the union's initiative becomes understandable (Table 4.9).

Further Modifications of the Austrian Response Strategy

In light of the 1996 EU directive, minor changes were made to the original Austrian regulation in 1999, and slightly more significant ones in 2002. In 1999, a minor modification clarified that the Austrian working time and paid leave entitlements were also applicable to posted workers (*Bundesgesetzblatt* I, No. 20, 1999). In 2002, the definition of 'construction work' was clarified and slightly extended. In addition, foreign companies posting employees to Austria are now required to provide detailed information on these employees to Austrian authorities, including duration, nature, and location of the service provision (*Bundesgesetzblatt* I, No. 459, 2002).

Comparing the Response Strategies

In brief, the national response strategies in Austria and France prove remarkably similar, since both guarantee standard wages for foreign posted employees. In both countries, the issue proved not very divisive. In Austria, employers were willing to concede to a relatively protectionist re-regulation of the EU LSP. Only when this regulation was set to be rendered stricter did they grow somewhat concerned. In France, there was relatively little activity on the side of either camp, but what little activity did occur was favorable. Thus, even French employers, which had brought about the Rush Portuguesa ruling through their actions, were willing to concede to a protectionist national re-regulation.

In Germany, the process of formulating and implementing a national response proved decisively more difficult. Interests diverged widely within the center-right coalition government, where the two camps were each represented by the center-left Minister of Labor and the liberal Minister of Economic Affairs respectively. A major battle was fought between the employers and the unions over the exact wage level for posted workers. The union side was somewhat weakened by the fact that none of the other sectoral unions except for IG Metall came to support IG BAU. Within the employer camp, a cleavage emerged between the somewhat more conciliatory sectoral employers and a belligerent umbrella association that could count on the support of equally relentless sectoral employers such as Gesamtmetall and Gesamttextil.

Therefore, the political battle over the national response strategy proved markedly more bloody, protracted, complicated, and divisive in Germany than either in France or in Austria. In addition, the German (and Dutch) response strategy produced is more limited in scope and more liberal in nature than is true of the Austrian and French ones. Before we compare and interpret the various response strategies and their implications, however, it is useful to consider the re-regulations produced in other high-wage countries. Both of these aims will be pursued in Chapter 5.

5

Response Strategies Elsewhere in Northern Europe and a Comparison of the Response Capacity of National Models

What happened in the other high-wage countries that could have equally attracted posted workers, just like France and later Germany did? Were there similar developments? Given the high wages commonly associated with Scandinavia—and less so the Low Countries—one might expect clever entrepreneurs to capitalize on the wage gap to Southern Europe and dispatch employees to construction sites in Copenhagen, Stockholm, and Oslo.

This chapter explores how the Netherlands, Belgium, Luxembourg, Denmark, Sweden, Norway, and Finland cope with the EU LSP and its implications. As has been argued before, the Netherlands represents an intermediate neocorporatist case, akin to Germany. The six comparative 'shadow' cases can be broadly considered 'strongly' neocorporatist in the case of the Nordic countries, or conforming to the statist model, albeit not perfectly, in the instances of Belgium and Luxembourg.

As will emerge from the discussion, a common pattern of response strategies emerges, with the three categories of politico-economic governance ('strongly' neocorporatist, 'intermediate' neocorporatist and statist) generating distinct re-regulations. Remarkably, the mostly comprehensive 'protectionist' response strategies emerging from the strongly neocorporatist and the statist camp bear remarkable similarities. By contrast, the two 'intermediate' neocorporatist counties implemented much more limited and liberal re-regulations.

Hence, the 'intermediate' neocorporatist Netherlands, comparable to Germany, produced a liberal business-friendly re-regulatory solution that permits short-term 'exceptional' postings of up to four weeks without an obligation to pay more than the Dutch minimum wage. Unlike Germany, however, this regulation was based on a compromise between the social partners in the construction sector, and did not require a legislative basis at first. Only in response to the EU directive a law was being passed, which did not, however, significantly impact the bipartite response strategy.

In strongly neocorporatist Norway, comparable to Austria, a legislative re-regulation was found, which permits future government intervention in the form of declarations of universal applicability if cases of substandard payment to posted workers are reported. Just like in Austria, business resistance to the legislative initiative by the government, in this case, the Ministry for Local and Regional Development, and notably not the Ministry of Labor, was somewhat muted. Employers did oppose this measure on ideological grounds; but their principal concern revolved around a trend of creeping government intervention, rather than higher wages for posted workers. The union was notably less active than in Austria.

In statist Belgium and Luxembourg, comparable to France, the French-style legalistic-juridicial regulation of wages meant that standard wages already possessed *ordre public* character. Thus, there was no explicit national response strategy necessary, unlike France, where the question whether the minimum wage SMIC or other sectoral minima were indeed binding on posted foreigners was not clearly addressed previously. Finland also falls into this group, setting it apart from its Scandinavian neighbors.

Finally, the two Scandinavian countries Denmark and Sweden found re-regulatory responses which do not resemble any of those of the key countries. These 'gentlemen's agreements' consisted of extra-legislative social partner agreements. They grant the union side the dormant right to take action if an infraction should occur. Such solution bears testimony to the power of unions in these two countries. However, it also places the considerable burden of monitoring and enforcement upon them.

After presenting the empirical details of the seven response strategies, this chapter will reflect on the theoretical implications of the divergent response patterns to a common external impetus of liberalization; a theme that is revisited in the concluding chapter as well. Tables 5.1 and 5.2 provide an overview of the re-regulatory response strategies in the seven countries analyzed in this chapter.

Table 5.1 National response strategy in the Low Countries

Netherlands

Regulation: Modified Sectoral Wage Contract for Construction Sector CAO Bouw
  1996; later the 1999 *Wet arbeidsvoorwarden grensoverschrijvende arbeid* was passed
Content: Re-regulation extending standard Dutch wages to posted workers *only in
  the construction sector and only to postings for more than four weeks*
Implementation: Collective wage agreement, based on sectoral union pressure from
  FNV Bouw. Sectoral employers AVBB agreed because four week 'window'
  permitted them enough flexibility, umbrella employers VNO-NCW permitted
  regulation because it was liberal enough and no spillover effects were feared
Dominant actor: Employers
Institutionalist approach most valuable: RCI in general, but historical institutionalism
  draws attention to consensus-oriented decision-making geared towards wage
  moderation in the Netherlands

Belgium

Regulation: Belgian wages are routinely declared universally applicable (*décrets* or
  ârrets royales) and thus are *lois de police*, later the March 5, 2002 'Law on posting of
  workers in the framework of the provision of services' was passed
Content: see above
Implementation: no response strategy necessary
Dominant actor: Government
Institutionalist approach most valuable: Historical institutionalism draws attention to
  statist and legalistic tradition in Belgian industrial relations

Luxembourg

Regulation: All Luxembourg wage and labor regulations possess *lois de police* status,
  following 1959 jurisdiction; in mid-1995 a tripartite declaration restated this line, a
  law of December 20, 2002 implemented the EU directive, but changed little
Content: see above
Implementation: no response strategy necessary, but explicit restatement pursued
  regardless
Dominant actor: Government
Institutionalist approach most valuable: Historical institutionalism emphasizes statist
  and legalistic tradition in Luxembourg industrial relations, but refined RCI draws
  attention to importance of SMEs

The Netherlands: A Liberal National Response Strategy Found by the Social Partners

The Netherlands traditionally is characterized by a very open, internation-
alized economy. Given the small geographical size of the country and its
proximity to major population centers in Belgium and Western Germany,

Table 5.2 National response strategies in the Nordic countries

Denmark

Regulation: Union–Employer Agreement of 1993, restated in January 1999, EU directive
was implemented in a 1999 law, revised in 2001, but changed little

Content: Re-regulation: Employers woe to pay standard Danish wages and will accept
industrial action by union in instances of violation

Implementation: Extra-legislative gentlemen's agreement based on union power, but
pacing the enforcement burden on the unions

Dominant actor: Unions

Institutionalist approach most valuable: RCI in general, but historical institutionalism
draws attention to extralegal form of social partner regulation of labor and social policy
in Denmark

Finland

Regulation: Employment Contracts Act makes all Finnish wages *lois de police*, restated 1996;
1999 implementation of EU directive (modified 1001, 2003) changed little

Content: see above

Implementation: Legislation, no response strategy necessary

Dominant actor: Government

Institutionalist approach most valuable: Historical institutionalism in general highlights
legalistic Finnish industrial relations

Norway

Regulation: Law No. 58 of June 4, 1993 'relating to the imposition of the extension of
collective agreements'; January 2000 implementation of the EU Directive changes little

Content: Government may declare wages universally applicable and can override interest
groups in doing so

Implementation: Legislation, based on Ministry of Local Government and Regional
Development initiative, but endorsed by unions, some limited employer resistance

Dominant actor: Government

Institutionalist approach most valuable: Historical institutionalism in general, highlights
government interventionism after brief spill of neoliberal policy and draws attention to
employers' unwillingness to let foreign competitors undercut wages in the oil sector

Sweden

Regulation: Modification of 1976 Act on Co-Determination in the Workplace
(*medbestämmandelagen*) combined with court case *Lex Britannica* as framework; 1999 *Lag
om utstationering av arbedstagare* clarifies the *lois de police*, but changed little

Content: Union may resort to industrial action if employers pay substandard wages to
posted workers

Implementation: Dormant right for unions, though based on legislative change, so far no
challenged by employers

Dominant actor: Union, though government action aided

Institutionalist approach most valuable: Historical institutionalism in general, highlights
union strength and union-Social Democrat link, though RCI predicts basic stand-off
between unions and employers

short-term trans-border postings to and from these two countries did occur and continue to do so even after national response strategies have been implemented. However, most of these postings did not seek to exploit any wage gap, but instead engaged regional expertise that was difficult to source nationally. For instance, Dutch construction companies have developed considerable expertise in projects involving the reclaiming of land, the construction of dikes, tunnels, channels, and other waterways, as well as working under water.

As has been mentioned earlier, despite considerable immigration to the Netherlands during the postwar decades, the construction sector has recruited relatively few ethnic minorities and labor migrants from Southern Europe, at least partly related to the informal 'old boys' networks that dominate recruitment processes in the Dutch construction sector. At the same time, migration was not a particularly politicized issue until the late 1990s with the electoral rise of the antimigration so-called Livable Rotterdam electoral initiative (*Leifbaar Rotterdam*), spearheaded by maverick leader Pim Fortuyn.

One of the reasons why postings to the Netherlands that aimed at exploiting social gaps were less attractive had to do with the *ex ante* state of regulations. Even before the implementation of any legislation, a certain core of work conditions was mandatory for posted workers, since they constituted part of the legal *ordre public* in the sense of Article 7 of the Rome Convention. This core of labor law was very extensive, including labor conditions, working hour and rest time regulations, *the national minimum wage*, plus overtime payments if applicable, payments for travel expenditures, safety, health and hygiene regulations, restrictions on child and youth employment, and the rules on non-discrimination of men and women (Stichting van de Arbeid 2000: 13). *The minimum wage was therefore always applicable to all workers employed in the Netherlands.* Given the legalistic pattern in Dutch industrial relations, where much regulation possesses legal character, this is fairly unsurprising. It sets the Netherlands apart from its eastern neighbor, where no such national minimum wage existed and where the government was very anxious to avoid intruding on the autonomy of setting-wages.

Active Unions, a Hesitant Government: The First Attempt at a Dutch Response Strategy

In a 1991 letter by the Ministry of Labor and Social Affairs to the social partners, the former made clear that it considered the entire 1919 Labor

Code (*Arbeidswet*) and all Dutch labor conditions to be part of the *ordre public* and thus mandatory for posted workers (Ministerie van Sociale Zaken en Werkgelegenheit (1991); interview NIMinLabSocAff 2000). In practice, the posting of workers never emerged as a significant issue in most sectors of the economy because wage agreements (*collectieve arbeidsovereenkomst—CAO*) were traditionally extended and thus declared universally applicable (*allgemeen verbondlich*) by the Ministry of Labor and Social Affairs. This was not always the case in the construction sector, however (interview FNV 2000). The social partners considered such universally applicable wage agreements to be mandatory for foreign employers posting workers to the Netherlands (interview FNV, VNO-NCW 2000). Although the Ministry was skeptical whether such view would have indeed held up to judicial scrutiny if a case would have been brought up to the ECJ (Ministerie van Sociale Zaken en Werkgelegenheit (1991)), de facto the Dutch CAO were imposed upon foreign employers as long as they were *allgemeen verbondlich*.

In 1991, the two key unions FNV and CNV, especially the former, launched a debate on the introduction of a national response strategy to the LSP. The government had asked the social partners, united in the bipartite think tank *Stichting van de Arbeid*, to respond to social policy issues related to the completion of the Single Market. This included the coverage of foreign employers by Dutch CAOs, as had been practiced up to that point. The study prepared by the unions and the employer organization VNO-NCW in the Stichting, entitled 'Some Aspects of the Social Dimension of Europe 1992', details the common position, specifically the interpretation of the Rome Convention. Accordingly, the 1919 Labor Code (*Arbeidswet*) and the work conditions set forth in the Labor Conditions Act (*Arbeidsomstandigedenwet*) of 1945 were mandatory for all employees employed on Dutch territory. Regarding the issue of wages, the social partners pointed out that the inclusion of posted workers in Dutch CAOs was a question of definition of the term employee (*werknemer*) and employer (*werkgever*) within the CAOs itself. In any case, unions and employers could agree that *allgemeen verbondlich* Dutch wages and labor conditions applied to all work performed in the Netherlands, including temporary work, irrespective of the nationality of the employing company (*dat de arbeidsvoorwaardenbepalingen van de door werkgevers en vakbonden in Nederland gesloten cao en eventuele algemeen verbindendverklaring van bepaling gelden voor alle arbeid, met inbegrip van tijdelijke arbeid, in Nederland*, Stichting 1991: 12). The government remained skeptical on the legality of this position and did not enact a legislative response strategy.[1] Be that as it may, however, as long as the Ministry continued its policy of rendering universally applicable most wage agreements, little or no financial incentive for the employment of foreign subcontractors emerged.

The Consensus Shows Some Cracks: Employers Are Much Less Enthusiastic about Re-regulation than the Unions

In the mid-1990s, and especially in 1994, the Dutch government began to apply pressure on the social partners to reduce the lowest wage brackets in their CAOs. Thus, the gap between the minimum wage and the lowest wage bracket should be closed in order to allow for the labor market entry of low qualified workers. It did so as part of its ongoing efforts to induce wage moderation among the social partners (Visser 1996; interview NIMin-LabSocAff 2000). Alternatively, it could have closed this gap by simply increasing the minimum wage, of course. Yet the government hesitated to do so not only because this was obviously contradictory to a general policy of wage restraint, but also since the level of social assistance is linked to the *minimumloon*, constituting 70 percent of it (interview FNV 2000; interview NIMinLabSocAff 2000).

Irritated by this stance on the part of the government and afraid that the employers might take advantage of a CAO *not* being declared universally applicable, the union wanted to ensure both that posted workers would be mentioned specifically in the individual CAOs and that all wage agreements would then be declared universally applicable (interview FNV 2000). By then, the employers had become less enthusiastic about having Dutch labor law and wages apply to posted workers (interview VNO-NCW 2000; Stichting van de Arbeid 2000: 15).

Reluctant Employers, Active Unions: The Position of the Dutch Actors

The positions of the two camps can be described as follows (see Table 5.3). The *unions* were concerned from very early on about possible negative

---

[1] The ministry was concerned that forcing foreign companies to pay wages which were not mandatory for Dutch companies could have been considered an infraction of EU law against the discrimination of EU companies. However, universally applicable wages and labor conditions were obviously legally binding for Dutch companies, too. Thus, the ministry's concern seems not entirely understandable.

Table 5.3 The politics of the Dutch national response strategy

---

Employer position: Supportive of status quo regulation, but incrasingly less
  enthusiastic about having all wage brackets apply to posted workers; not
  convinced of the need for a national response strategy, unwilling to extend
  response strategy beyond the construction sector
Union position: Supportive of status quo regulation at first, but then concerned
  that this might no be sufficient—union favors a national response strategy that
  would render wage brackets in all sectors of the Dutch economy mandatorily
  applicable to posted workers
Government position: Hesitant, government at first does not perceive of any need
  to draw up a national response strategy. Active, Ministry of Labor drafts respective
  bill as part of an effort against illegal forms of employment
Other factors: No
Heavily contested/politicized? No

---

repercussions of European induced liberalization on the system of Dutch
wages. They were therefore first to demand a legislative re-regulation.
Although unsuccessful, a common position with the employers could be
found in regards to the application of Dutch labor law and wages to posted
workers, as long as those were universally applicable (Stichting van de
Arbeid 1991). This was less optimal than a legislative regulation. Yet, de
facto CAO wages were routinely declared universally applicable by the
Ministry of Labor in most sectors, though not construction. Therefore,
they became binding on foreign employers as well.

The sectoral employers did not resist the payment of standard
CAO wages to posted workers, even though the umbrella organization
had abandoned the more consensual position of 1991 by 2000 (interview
VNO-NCW 2000; AVBB 2000; Stichting van de Arbeid 1991, 2000). The
VNO-NCW did not apply pressure on its sectoral member to 'tow
the line'. The AVBB considered the four week window to constitute a
reasonable mechanism, allowing for enough flexibility, constituting one
standard pay period, and not imposing excessive burdens on the organization's members. Generally, Dutch companies were not pressing for a
wage differential as they saw several problems associated with the use of
foreign posted workers, including conflicts with the unions and with
individual employees at the macrolevel, language problems, and not
least reputation and image as important factors in a small economy (interview AVBB 2000).

The Dutch Response Strategy: Limited to the Construction Sector

In the construction sector, the sectoral construction unions FNV-Bouw and CNV-Bouw had applied significant pressure on the employers from 1991 onwards to agree to specific mentioning of posted workers to ensure that they would be covered by standard CAO wages and not just the minimum wage (interviews FNV-Bouw 2000; AVBB 2000). The sectoral employers finally conceded to this pressure during the negotiations of the CAO for 1995 (interviews FNV-Bouw 2000; AVBB 2000).

Article 1a was added to the collective wage agreement, *stipulating that for workers posted for more than four weeks the Dutch CAO wages were to become applicable in addition to contributions to the pension fund, the sectoral vacation fund, and accident insurance plans.* This regulation was phrased so that it would remain valid until a European regulation concerning this issue was implemented in the Netherlands (CAO Bouwbedrijf 1994–5, 1995–6, 1999–2000).[2] This did occur four years later, when the Law on Mandatory Labor Conditions for Transnational Labor (*Wet Arbeidsvoorwaarden Grensoverschrijdende Arbeid*) was passed on December 2, 1999[3]. Another important change was Article 3 of the CAO which highlighted that employers had to ensure that standard CAO wages

---

[2] In the original Dutch, this article read: *In tegenstelling tot het bepaalde in artikel 1, lid 5, is deze CAO—met inachtneming van de wettelijke regelgeving van het woonland—eerst van toepasing op degene die in het buitenland woonachtig is en Nederland, in dienst van een in het buitenland gevestigde werkgever, werkzaam is, indien deze werkzaamheden langer dan een maand achtereen duren. Zodra Europese regelgeving op dit vlak in Nederland geimplementeerd wordt geldt deze regelgeving.*

[3] In Dutch, the law is known as the *Wet van 2 december 1999 tot uitvoering van de Richtlijn 96/71/EG van het Europees parlement en van de Raad van de Europese Unie van 16 december 1996 betreffende de terbeschikkingstelling van werknemers met het oog op het verrichten van diensten (Wet arbeidsvoorwaarden grensoverschrijdende arbeid*. This implementation of the EU directive changed very other than specify the exact core of mandatory Dutch labor regulations which would become mandatory for posted workers, beyond the wage levels.

However, in defining this core, it remained much below the whole framework of labor conditions ordinarily set forth in the CAO. Specifically, it stipulated that Articles 634 through 642, 645 through 648, 658, and 670 section 2 of the Labor Code (Book 7 of the Civil Laws *Burgerlijk Wetbook*) became applicable to posted workers (Article 1), as did Dutch working time regulations, vacation and vacation pay regulations, minimum wages, including overtime pay, regulations on temporary provision of labor, health, safety, and hygiene regulations, youth and child labor restrictions, and laws on gender equality.

In addition, changes to the Law on the Extension of Collective Agreements (*Wet op het allgemeen verbindend en onverbindend verklaren van bepalingen van collectieve arbeidsovereenkomsten*) became necessary.

were paid by subcontractors to their employees (CAO Bouwbedrijf 1995–6, 1999–2000).

Shortly before implementing the EU directive, the Ministry of Social and Labor Affairs addressed a letter to the Stichting van de Arbeid on November 8, 1999. In doing so, it responded to a request lodged by the second chamber of parliament (*Tweede Kamer*, vergaderjaar 1998–9: 26, 524, nr.10). It sought to inquire whether the social partners would support a legislative measure that would extend the planned new law *beyond* the construction sector. The social partners were divided on the issue, as the resultant Stichting report 'Advice on the implementation of Directive 96/71/EC' reveals (Stichting 2000). The employers were opposed to extending the new Dutch law beyond the construction sector, fearing excessive bureaucracy and citing the liberal EU spirit that such national re-regulation would violate. The unions took the opposite position, arguing that the new EU directive was worker-friendly in spirit and pointing out that the issue of transnational posting would affect other sectors as well, hence there was no logical reason not to extent it to the rest of the economy. However, given the divided position, the ministry did not extend the applicability of the law beyond the construction sector.

As a result, posted workers to the Netherlands are subject to the hard core *lois de police*, part of which is the minimum wage. In addition, in the construction sector *only*, posted workers received the standard Dutch wages for postings extended for more than four weeks. Dutch labor laws that apply to posted workers in the construction sector include, as specified in the 2002–4 CAO for the sector (*CAO voor het bouwbedrijf*):

1. Working time regulations
2. Overtime regulations
3. Guaranteed wages for adults and youths
4. Additional compensatory payments
5. Additional payments for re-arranged working times
6. Bonus for hazardous working conditions
7. Holiday and vacation regulations

A Wage Gap as a Result of the Dutch Re-regulation

Not only did the Dutch re-regulatory response strategy limit itself to the construction sector, it also left a window open for short-term postings of up to four weeks, during which only the Dutch minimum wage is mandatory. Henceforth, for postings of up to four weeks, there remains some incentive for companies to outsource projects to foreign subcontractors, especially outside of the construction sector. For 2000, the sectoral employers' organization AVBB estimated that approximately 20,000 workers were posted to the Netherlands (AVBB 2000), which constitutes approximately 5 percent of the workforce in a sector comprising 417,000 employees in 1999 (AVBB 1999). According to the Central Statistical Office, in 2002, there were 18,870 posted workers from Belgium and 11,115 from Germany, though these postings were most likely the result of specific know-how required from these countries and not inspired by the desire to save on wage expenditures. The office did not collect data on other countries (EIRO 2003c). In general, posting of workers never reached the same epidemic proportions as in Germany, not least because Dutch regulations for the domestic registration of foreign craftsmen and artisans are very strict (AVBB 2000). Therefore, posted workers initially were mainly unskilled. Between the late 1990s and the early 2000s, the Dutch construction sector experienced a labor shortage, though mainly in skilled professions (van der Meer 2000).

In the wage negotiations in 2001, the construction unions were able to secure a minor concession from the employers. Article 1a of the CAO for the sector was modified to clarify that only workers from within the EU would enjoy the 'window' of a four week grace period. However, posted workers from outside the EU, to the very limited extent that they could legally be dispatched to Dutch territory were subject to the whole CAO framework of standard Dutch wages from the first day of the posting

Table 5.4 An overview of regulation contained within the Dutch response strategy

---

Does the response strategy cover the entire economy? No. This is a regulation specifically targeted at the construction sector.

Are there exceptions/loopholes? Yes, there is a gap between the Dutch minimum wage, which applies as the only minimum condition for posting of less than four weeks, and regular Dutch wage brackets. Subcontracting and outsourcing to foreign service providers henceforth remain possible options.

What regulations become legally binding on foreign service providers? The minimum wage, Dutch labor, working time, and social regulations apply. Note that the standard Dutch sectoral wage agreements apply to posted workers only where they have been declared universally applicable.

---

onwards. This modification might have been a preemptive regulation in light of GATS negotiations aimed at temporary transnational LSP.

Summing up the Dutch Response Strategy

In sum, since Dutch wages are routinely declared universally applicable in most sectors and the minimum wage possesses *ordre public* character as well, the posting of workers would have made economic sense from the outset only in sectors where wage agreements were not declared universally applicable, such as the construction sector (see Table 5.4). Thus, the pressure exerted by European liberalization and the LSP was considerably lower in the Netherlands than in other high-wage states. When the Ministry began to exercise pressure on the social partners to lower its entry wages, threatening to refuse universal applicability (*erga omnes*), the sectoral construction union exercised pressure on the employers to agree to a specific mentioning of posted workers in the CAO (interview FNV 2000; FNV-Bouw 2000; interview NIMinLabSocAff 2000). In doing so, however, a concession had to be made. A window of four weeks exists. Short-term posted workers are not covered by Dutch CAO wages in the construction sector, only by the *minimumloon*. The minimum wage is legally enshrined and hence part of the *ordre public*.

The Dutch national response strategy can be described as a liberal compromise, slightly more favorable to the employers than to the unions since they secured a four week exemption window. Yet both sides could claim victory. The sectoral construction union was successful in applying pressure on the employers to agree to an explicit mentioning of posted workers in the 1995 CAO for the construction sector. A major conflict between the union and the employers did not ensue since they had earlier agreed in a position paper on applying a core of universally applicable Dutch labor legislation and wage agreements to posted workers. Although the VNO-NCW was beginning to rethink this stance by 2000, a hard core of labor conditions including the minimum wage was considered *ordre public* in any case, regardless of the employers' attitude. Sectoral employers were less belligerent, since most Dutch companies saw little advantage in outsourcing.

Finally, in 1999 the Netherlands implemented the EU directive of 1996 which practically implied no change at all, other than inscribing explicitly into national law what had previously been considered to constitute international private law in the sense of the Rome Convention. The employers refused to extend the provision of this law beyond the construction sector.

Belgium: A Legalistic National Response Strategy

In Belgium, much of the labor and social regulation is legalistic and had been in place for a very long time. As mentioned earlier, due to geographic and, in part, linguistic proximity with the Netherlands and Germany, postings between these countries had not been uncommon throughout the 1990s, but the aim had not been to save on wage expenditures. Since the Belgian construction sector is dominated by SMEs, one might have expected employers not to be too keen on employing subcontractors, in analogy to the Austrian case. Despite a fairly comprehensive set of legalistic regulations that in theory left little room for lucrative transnational posting to Belgium, substantial posting did occur, most of which aiming to take advantage of gaps in the employer contributions to sectoral vacation funds and similar social security systems. As we shall find below, however, much of this activity unfolded within a legal grey zone, if not being clearly illegal altogether, since the amount of legally binding Belgian *lois de police* was actually substantial.

Most Labor Regulations Posses Loi de Police *Character in Belgium*

In general, Belgian collective agreements on working conditions (*conventions collectives du travail* or CCT) possess the character of laws if declared universally applicable (*obligatoire*) as do indeed most labor regulations. Either employers or unions have to apply for this step. A CCT then becomes a royal decree (*décrets or arrêtés royales*). These then constitute mandatory *lois de police* in the sense of international private law (Dumorthier 1981: 204). Belgian jurisprudence has always clearly supported this line of reasoning. Henceforth, in a number of court rulings, Belgian labor courts made clear that this mandatory character applies to contributions to the Belgian health and unemployment insurance systems (décision Court du Travail de Bruxelles 30 April 1986, later upheld by the ECJ in the decision 28 January 1982 204/90 Bachman; Delarue 1995: 281; Deneve 1995: 182), fiscal legislation (Court du travail du Bruxelles, December 11, 1985), working hours (Court du travail de Bruxelles, June 10, 1976), annual vacations (Tribunal Communautaire de Bruxelles, March 3, 1970), the minimum wage (*rémunération minimale*) (Tribunal du Travail de Bruxelles, February 16, 1976—restated by Court du Travail de Liège, October 22, 1981), and collective wage agreements declared universally applicable (Tribunal du Travail de Bruxelles, April 12, 1988) (Deneve 1995: 182–8).

Hence, the radius of these *lois de police* was extensive and well-defined when the Rome Convention was adopted into Belgian law in 1987 (*Loi de 14 juillet 1987*) (Deneve 1995: 176ff.). It was obvious that Belgian minimum wages and even standard wages were mandatory for posted workers, if declared *obligatoire*. The Mons Court specifically pointed out that *royales décrets or arrêtés* do apply to posted workers in a decision of June 29, 1977, which held up to revision by the *Tribunal du Travail de Bruxelles* (Delarue 1995: 279), and was restated by the latter on 12 April 1988. Since 1975, the minimum wage (*revenu minimum mensuel moyen garanti*) is determined by a legally binding central collective agreement between central employers and unions (EIRR 232, May 1993, 34; EIRR 266, March 1996: 16).[4]

In addition, Belgian regulation is generally very restrictive towards temporary labor agencies. Companies 'putting workers at the disposal' (*mettre à la disposition de main-d-oeuvres*) of others are generally prohibited to operate in Belgium, in accordance with article 31 of *Loi 24 juillet 1987* (EIRO Report 1999). Temporary agencies are not permitted to operate in the construction sector. This ban means in practice that posted workers legally remain employees of the foreign sending company, presumably a company taking on one complete (sub)project. Foreign subcontractors cannot simply hirie out workers to Belgian companies. Hiring workers only for the purpose of posting them to Belgium is generally not permissible. Posted workers must be reimbursed by this foreign company and not by any Belgian main contractor. To the extent that Belgian regulations are considered *lois de police*, they are applicable immediately, i.e. without any transition period (EIRO Report 1999).

Exit Paths for Employers? Loopholes in the Belgian Regulation

The possible exit path for employers would be to refuse the extension of collectively agreed wages. In that case, only the Belgian minimum wage

---

[4] Traditionally, contributions to the Belgian sector-specific funds (*fonds de sécurité d'existence*) for vacations, unemployment (timbres fidélité), and bad weather (*timbres intempéries*) have also been considered obligatory, as exist in the construction sector (*fonds de sécurité d'existence des ouvriers de la construction*) (Ritmeijer 1994: 61ff.). However, the DG III Internal Market and the judicial service of the European Commission addressed a letter to the Belgian government on January 7, 1993 demanding specific details about this obligation for foreign companies, pointing out that such obligation would be contradicting the principles of the LSP (Delarue 1995: 280ff.). The Belgian government therefore dropped the requirement for foreign companies to contribute to these Belgian systems (EIRO Report 1999), but was eventually successful in requiring it for companies that cannot prove to have contributed to equivalent systems in their home countries thanks to a favorable ECJ ruling (C-369/96 Ablade).

would become applicable to the employees of foreign subcontractors. However, the 'level playing field' that universally applicable wages afford might be more attractive than advantages derived from outsourcing, especially in an economy in which small and medium sized enterprises dominate.

The more exciting avenue for circumventing Belgian regulations consisted not of taking advantage of any wage gap—since, if operating within the framework of all applicable laws, there is none—but in a slight gap in the social security contributions. Arising from the fact that posted workers are covered by the social security regime of their country of origin for postings of up to one year (in accordance with directive EC 1401/71), which may be significantly less demanding, savings may thus be realized. A possible 'social security gap' arises. In addition, during the early 1990s, some legal uncertainty remained whether Belgium could indeed insist on requiring foreign companies to contribute to its various systems of sector-specific funds (see fn. 4). Not until the ECJ rulings Arblade (C-369/96) and Leloup (C-376/96)[5] of November 1999, was this principle established without doubt.

Cashing in on this legal uncertainty, a great deal of posting occurred in Belgium in the early 1990s. While in 1991 the total number of posted EU employees reached 71,800, it climbed to 124,000 in 1994, according to estimates by the *Office National de Sécurité Sociale* (EIRO Report 1999). Another mechanism of taking advantage of the social security gap that authorities were concerned with involved companies setting up dependencies in Luxembourg and seconding workers from there, implying lower employer charges.

Finally, illegal practices involving the posting of workers remunerated below the applicable wage levels appeared as serious problems (van Dessel 1995: 287ff.)

The 2002 Implementation of the EU Directive: Restating the Status Quo

Given the extensive character of internationally and nationally binding labor and wage regulations, there was no real need for a specific response

---

[5] These two rulings established that Belgian authorities could demand the presentation of Belgian-style social security contribution documents from posting companies, in these two cases from France. More specifically, the cases revolved around the question whether Belgium could impose sector-specific employer contributions from such foreign subcontractors, as it had wished to do precisely to close the social security gap. The ECJ ruled in favor of the Belgian authorities.

strategy. The main avenue of undercutting Belgian conditions involved taking advantage of some degree of legal uncertainty over the applicability of all sectoral funds and social security contributions. However, after the Ablade and Leloup ruling, it was clear that this exit path for foreign subcontractors would no longer be available.

On March 5, 2002 the new law on posted workers was passed in response to the EU directive. It changed very little from the status quo, but simply restated the already legally binding components of Belgian labor and social conditions. The more interesting part is the second component. This part, rendered an *arrêté royal* on March 29, 2002, sought to simplify and codify exactly what documents foreign posted workers would have to present to Belgian authorities.[6] For short-term postings of up to six months, employers can maintain a reduced number of documents for inspection, which nevertheless needs to contain wage statements, and a declaration with contact details sent to the Belgian social legislation inspectorate. This new law therefore reduces the bureaucratic red tape involved, without impacting the range of mandatory labor and social conditions. In the process of the development of this law, the social partners were consulted in the *Conseil National du Travail/Nationale Arbeidsraad*.[7]

Summing up the Belgian Response Strategy: Legalistic and Comprehensive

In sum, because of the extensive legal regulation, there was no real need for one specific response strategy in Belgium (see Table 5.5). Labor regulation, including wages has legal character and thus the *lex loci* (local law) could be interpreted as *lois de police*. The social partners were thus not actually involved in the formulation of any such re-regulation. The Belgian national response strategy is thus legalistic and was essentially created in a preemptive fashion by jurisprudence. To the extent that the

---

[6] In French the document is called the 'Arrêté royal fixant les modalités d'exécution du régime simplifié d'établissement et de tenue de documents sociaux pour les entreprises qui détachent des travailleurs en Belgique et définissant les activités dans le domaine de la construction visées à l'article 6, § 2, de la loi du 5 mars 2002 transposant la directive 96/71/CE du Parlement européen et du Conseil du 16 décembre 1996 concernant le detachement de travailleurs effectué dans le cadre d'une prestation de services et instaurant un régime simplifié pour la tenue de documents sociaux par les entreprises qui détachent des travailleurs en Belgique'.

[7] It issued largely favorable statements in 1999 (November 17, 1999: Avis 1290) and 2000 (May 30, 2000: Avis 1313).

Table 5.5 An overview of regulation contained within the Belgian response strategy

Does the response strategy cover the entire economy? Yes—to the extent that there is one single response strategy (see discussion in the text).
Are there exceptions/loopholes? Yes, for several years it was unclear whether indeed all social security contributions and especially the sectoral fund employer contributions were mandatory for foreign companies sending employees to Belgium. Two ECJ court cases helped provide clarity. However, even previous to these decisions, most—but not all—social secutiry contributions were indeed manadatory and constituted part of the Belgian *ordre public*.
What regulations become legally binding on foreign service providers? All Belgian labor, working time, and social regulations apply—contributions to the sectoral social security systems likewise become mandatory. The Belgian minimum wage is mandatory, as are all sectoral wage agreements to the extent that they are universally applicable—this generally tends to be the case, as they are routinely extended.

social partners became involved at all, the trade unions supported any additional protection against social dumping, while employers generally approved of the additional legal clarity the 2002 law afforded with some minor concerns over excessive bureaucracy (EIRO 2003*d*).

Luxembourg: A Tripartite Neocorporatist National Response Strategy

In Luxembourg, the employment of foreigners has a long tradition. This is a result of the country's size and a geographical location in the heart of the EU. Luxembourg has attracted a fair share of guest workers, mainly from Portugal, but also from neighboring Belgium, France, and Germany.[8] These are for the most part employed directly by domestic companies. As a founding member of the EU, Luxembourg legislation on the employment of foreign residents and immigration makes obvious exceptions for EU and EEA citizens.[9]

---

[8] There were 27,575 Portuguese registered in Luxembourg in 2004 compared to a total of 650,000 citizens (Statec 2004). Relative to number of inhabitants, Luxembourg has the highest number of foreign residents in the EU, hovering around 20 percent.

[9] See the 'Règlement grand-ducal modifié du 12 mai 1972 déterminant les mesures applicables pour l'emploi des travailleurs étrangers sur le territoire du Grand-Duché de Luxembourg'.

Given the extremely small size of the country, SMEs dominate the construction sector. Relatively little transnational activity occurred with the respect to the Luxembourg construction sector, with the partial exception of postings from there to Belgium, as mentioned earlier. The absence of the phenomenon of posted workers to Luxembourg posing a major challenge is related to a fairly comprehensive legalistic regulation of the labor market, even before the development of any specific national response strategy.

As early as July 2, 1959, a Luxembourg court had decided on that all laws regulating the legal position of workers were to possess the character of *ordre public* (*Kassationsurteil Pasicrisie*, Vol. XVII, p. 443). This broad jurisdiction contained all Luxembourg labor regulations, implying, though not explicitly stating, the payment of wages according to standard collective wage agreements. The Rome Convention was ratified in Luxembourg on March 27, 1986.

Moving towards a Comprehensive Luxembourg Response Strategy: All Sides Agree

Even though the remit of *lois de police* was fairly broad already and there were hence no actual reports of postings to Luxembourg, which would have involved undercutting standard wages, the social partners nevertheless felt compelled to act preemptively. Both unions and employers were afraid of social dumping and feared enterprising companies questioning the precise meaning of the earlier court ruling.

Hence, representatives of both sides met with officials at the ministry of labor in mid-1995 to delineate a more specific national response strategy. Employers viewed the LSP as a mechanism for foreign companies to undercut wages and hence the price structure, jeopardizing social peace with the union. They did not welcome it as an opportunity to cut costs (interview LuxMinLabSocAff 2000). The trade union federation likewise sought to defend current wage levels. Thus, interests between the ministry, the employers and the unions clearly coincided.

The Luxembourg Response: Comprehensive

The Luxembourg national response strategy is contained in Section 4 of the Law of July 31, 1995 on employment and vocational training. The language employed reveals a deep shared concern over LSP as a path towards social dumping. In its preamble, the law invokes the 'fight against social dumping' and the 'avoidance of unfair competition impairing the companies legally registered in Luxembourg'. The law constitutes a very comprehensive response strategy, explicitly referring to the ECJ decision Rush Portuguesa and specifying that its stipulations are to be considered *lois de police* in the sense of Article 7 of the Rome Convention. It stipulations are to apply 'without exception to any work performed on Luxembourg territory, which includes workers posted to Luxembourg territory for purposes of service provision by a company not registered in Luxembourg'.[10]

More specifically, the act details that the following local regulations are now to be considered *lois de police* or *zwingende Bestimmungen des internationalen Rechts*: the employment contract, the minimum wage and its automatic link to the general development of cost of living, working hours and resting periods, paid holidays, statutory public holidays, regulations pertaining to temporary, part-time, and fixed-term contract work, protective regulations pertaining to the employment of youth and pregnant women and the equal treatment between the sexes, and collective wage agreements.

Wage agreements in the construction industry are generally and routinely universally applicable (EIRO Report 1999). In order for such procedure to occur (*déclaration d'obligation générale*) both employers and trade union have to apply for it at the National Arbitration Office and the Trade Chambers have to be consulted.

On December 20, 2002, Luxembourg implemented the EU directive wit ha new law on the 'posting of workers and the control of the application of the labor law'. Once again, the transposition of the directive brought added very little. In this law, three new issues were added to the mandatory canon of regulations, but all of them were already legally binding. The first concerned health and safety at work (Article 1, No. 14), extending the provisions of the already existing legislation of June 17, 1994, the second regarded illegal employment (Article 1, No. 13), and the third extended domestic legislation on mandatory rest periods due to ill weather. One minor impact that the EU directive had was to open a window of eight days for short-term postings aimed at installing machinery machinery, during which the Luxembourg vacation regulations and the collective

---

[10] In the original German, the text reads: '*ausnahmslos für jede auf dem Hoheitsgebiet des Groaherzogtums Luxemburg ausgeführte Arbeit, und zwar auch für von einem nicht in Luxemburg niedergelassenen Unternehmen vorübergehend auf luxemburgisches Gebiet entsandte Arbeitnehmer, die dort eine Dienstleistung zu erbringen haben*'.

Table 5.6 An overview of regulation contained within the Luxembourg response strategy

---

Does the response strategy cover the entire economy? Yes.

Are there exceptions/loopholes? No. In the 2002 revision, there is an exception for the installment of machinery, but this exception is extremely closely curtailed and does not concern the construction sector.

What regulations become legally binding on foreign service providers? All Luxembourg labor, working time, and social regulations apply. All Luxembourg wage agreements, including the national minimum wage, are also legally binding.

---

wage agreements do not apply (Article 3). However, construction sector activities are explicitly exempted from this exception. The law also sought to clarify the relatively extensive list of documents foreign companies need to provide upon inspection.

Summing up Developments in Luxembourg

In sum, the Luxembourg national response strategy was already contained in a very early judicial decision, rendering the posting of workers economically uninteresting (see Table 5.6). However, the status of national wages and labor law was more explicitly restated in a 1995 law, based on the consensus and virtual interest congruence among state, trade union, and employers' organization. Because of the coincidence of interests, no major conflict ensued and the law was passed and implemented rather swiftly. Breaking out of the network of collective wage agreements and labor conditions, to the extent that it is at all legally possible, sets into motion a downward spiral of prices. Employers are not interested in jeopardizing this equilibrium. No major incidents of posted workers have been reported since (EIRO Report 1999), which is not surprising if we consider how universal and all-encompassing in character this law is, allowing for no wage or 'social security' gap of significant proportions.

Denmark: A Union-Dominated National Response Strategy Brokered by the Social Partners

In Denmark, there might have been substantial potential for the posting of workers, given that wage levels in the Danish construction industry are among the highest in Europe, but, in the event, relatively little transnational service provision occurred. In the 1990s, Swedish companies have entered the Danish market, but mainly in the form of mergers and acquisitions. While companies from Sweden, the UK, and Germany were involved in some of the major construction projects of the 1990s, including the major bridges at Storebælt and Øresund as well as the Copenhagen metro, their contribution was based on the know-how they could contribute, rather than significantly lower wage levels.

Scandinavian Gentlemen's Agreements: Moving towards a Danish Response Strategy

Just like in Sweden, the Danish national response strategy hinges on a gentlemen's agreement between the trade unions and employers. While Denmark has passed legislation to implement the EU directive, as so often, this act pails in significance with the much more pivotal bargain struck among the social partners years in advance. The union *Landsforeiningen i Danmark* (LO) and the employers' federation *Dansk Arbejdsgiverforening* (DA) reached an agreement concerning the wages and regulations applicable to posted workers that came into effect on January 1, 1993, perhaps not coincidentally the date of the completion of the Single Market. Previously, practically no posting to Denmark had occurred. Danish employers agreed to admonish foreign subcontractors to pay their employees standard domestic wages. In turn, the union is authorized to monitor compliance and is permitted to take industrial or legal action if companies are found in violation. This right is usually exercised by the local branch of the respective sectoral union. The employer organization will not resist these measures if they are taken in response to improper conduct by individual companies. Posted workers are entitled to standard Danish wages immediately, i.e. without any transitory period. If several construction companies join forces in a consortium, the national level sectoral union Timber Industry and Construction Union (*Forbundet Træ-Industri-Byg—* TIB) becomes active to ensure coverage by a collective wage agreement. TIB cooperates with the larger Federation of Building, Construction and Woodworkers' Union (*Bygge, Anlægs-og Trækartellet*).

The January 1999 'Agreement concerning foreign companies' use of posted employees' signed between TIB, the painters' union *Malerforbundet*, the national union of skilled workers *Specialarbejderforbundet i Danmark*, and the sectoral construction employers organization *Byggeriets Arbejdsgivere* (BYG) essentially restates the terms of the 1993 agreement (EIRO

Report 1999). Foreign companies posting workers to Denmark are thus temporarily admitted into BYG, which means that the collective wage agreements signed by BYG also become binding on them, *regardless* of whether or not their employees are unionized or not. Monitoring compliance with these terms is undertaken by the trade union side.

There seemed to be a consensus between employers and unions on this issue. As in many other small European countries, subcontracting was perceived as more of a menace than an opportunity by employers. In addition, employers were careful not to antagonize the quite powerful trade union movement. The flipside of this agreement is that the considerable burden of monitoring and enforcement rests on the shoulders of the union.

Testing the Limits of the Danish Re-Regulation: The Permasteelisa Case

Without any legislative initiative, the Danish construction market was therefore protected against companies using subcontractors that undercut standard wages. For public jobs, the responsibility to inform foreign (sub)-contractors of relevant obligations while in Denmark rests with the public authorities. This obligation grows out of the International Labor Organization (ILO) Convention 94, which the Danish government is signature to. Just as is the case in the private sector, the union has the right to call for industrial action if a foreign company does not respect domestic wage levels.

However, the limits of the Danish response strategy were soon to be tested. In 1997 specialist Italian company Permasteelisa secured the bid for applying the new glass facades to the Royal Danish Library in Copenhagen. TIB was contacted on June 12 by a representative of the Italian company in order to negotiate wages and work conditions for the 5–16 [sic] employees to be posted to Denmark. While these numbers paled compared to the numbers of workers posted to France, or later Belgium, the Netherlands, and Germany, the Danish union wanted to demonstrate that it did not take this matter lightly. No results were reached and work commenced on August 4. The Italian company paid these workers and hourly wage of DKr 60, about 50 percent below the standard hourly wage rate. TIB hence first announced a picket line (*blockade*). No Danish union members were allowed to work on this site. After the breakdown of negotiations on August 27, the union announced further secondary action (*sympatikonflikt*), blocking off all supplies and services to the construction site. The Italians capitulated and signed an agreement on September 8, allotting its workers the lowest standard Danish wage bracket of DKr 127 per hour and allowing its posted workers formally to become members of TIB. However, the conflict was not over yet. By February 1998, the union secured information according to which the company did not adhere to the terms of this agreement. It thus declared another *blokade* and initiated legal action. Permasteelisa subsequently agreed to pay a lump sum of DKr 700,000 in outstanding salaries to the union (Lind et al. 1998).

Growing Internationalization of the Danish Construction Sector: Swift Union Responses

While the posting of workers traditionally played little role in a Danish construction sector dominated by SMEs, this began to change in the 1990s. Following Swedish and Finnish admission to the EU in 1995, intra-Scandinavian posting began to emerge as a new phenomenon. Swedish companies aggressively entered the Danish market either through acquisition or through direct bids. The major bridge linking Sweden and Denmark across the Øresund was commenced around this time and constructed by a Danish/Swedish/German consortium. The Danish trade union was quick to respond to these developments. TIB signed an agreement with its equivalents in Sweden and Finland regulating posting from these two countries in 1996. TIB thus entered the *Nordisk Bygge og Trae Føderation*. Under the terms of this agreement, posted unionized Nordic workers are automatically considered members of the unions of the receiving countries (Article 1). These respective unions monitor the adherence of companies to the respective (minimum) wages and labor conditions (Article 2). Host country unions also represent the posted employees in case of labor dispute (Article 3). The additional 1998 'Danish-Swedish agreement relating to execution of contract work in the other country' signed between Byggnads in Sweden and the sectoral Danish construction union BAT specifies that exemptions to the above can be made for very short postings (Article 3). Unions are to safeguard that employees are covered by either of the two unemployment insurance schemes (Article 4), they exchange information on pertinent applicable regulations (Article 7) and can negotiate separate collective agreements with companies from the respective other country (Article 9) (EIRO Report 1999). TIB also commenced negotiations with the German sectoral construction union IG BAU, without any results, however.

Implementing the EU Directive in Denmark: Little Change to Status Quo

In response to the EU directive 96/71/EC on posted workers, the Danish government passed a piece of legislation, clarifying the transnationally mandatory *lois de police*. However, as in many other countries, the significance of this act is minor, given that to the extent that there was any challenge to the Danish labor market it came in the form of foreign subcontractors seeking to undercut wages, not any social or labor legislation. Law No. 933 on 'the use of employees' (*Lov om udstationering af lønmodtagere*) was passed on December 15, 1999. This law renders mandatory and thus the Working Environment Act, the Act on Equal Treatment of Men and Women, the Equal Pay Act, Section 7 of the Legal Relationship Act and the Act prohibiting discriminatory treatment (Part 2, Article 5a through e). In addition, the law renders mandatory the allotment of Danish annual holidays and respective holiday pay (Part 2, Article 6). The National Labor Market Authority is charged with informing foreign companies of their obligations (Part 4) (EIRO 1999). In essence, this law does not significantly modify the extra-legislative arrangement found by the *two* social partners as far as the crucial issue of pay is concerned. The act was revised as No. 964 on November 2, 2001, clarifying that Danish working hours were mandatory for posted workers as well. The social partners were consulted before the modification of this act, but raised no objections.

New Lines of Conflict?

Despite the fairly consensual compromise agreement, recent developments have shed some doubt on the future of the gentlemen's agreement. Conflict emerged over a declaration by managing director of sectoral employer association *Dansk Byggeri* in summer 2003 who recommended Danish construction workers to employ Eastern European subcontractors and base their wage calculations on the *lowest* Danish wage bracket (DKr 94 per hour), which is about one half of the *average* hourly wage in the Danish construction sector. BAT protested loudly and announced that it would take industrial action if any such instances would occur. It also cancelled participation in jointly organized conferences (EIRO 2003e).

History seemed to repeat itself during the summer of 2004, when another incident reminiscent of the Permasteelisa case occurred. In June 2004, Polish company Biomax commenced work in renovating the

Table 5.7 An overview of regulation contained within the Danish response strategy

Does the response strategy cover the entire economy? No, it is based on a gentlemen's agreement between the sectoral social partners. However, the legislative act passed in 1999 and amended in 2001 further clarifies a number of social and labor law provisions which apply to posted workers in all sectors.

Are there exceptions/loopholes? No. However, the agreement hinges on the ability of the unions to monitor compliance and take action where and if needed in case of infractions.

What regulations become legally binding on foreign service providers? Danish labor, working time, and social regulations apply. The Danish unions ensure (at least in the construction sector) that Danish wages are being paid.

---

youth hostel Lisbjerghaven near Arhus. Only two weeks later, TIB representatives learned that the company was paying its employees Polish wages. The union threatened action against the company and by July, Biomax agreed to remunerate its workers according to Danish wage levels and reimburse them for the substandard wages its employees had received up to this point (TIB 2004). This incident seemed to confirm fears that EU eastward enlargement would encourage a new wave of social dumping.

Summary of the Danish Response Strategy

In sum, the Danish national response strategy was based on a compromise agreement between the trade union and the employers' organization (see Table 5.7). It can be described as a non-legislative gentlemen's agreement, colored by a strong trade union movement. It places a significant burden upon the shoulders of the unions, namely enforcement and monitoring. Employers only concede to not resisting industrial action in case of non-compliance by a foreign company. However, the high rate of unionization and union militancy may deter employers from violating of the terms of the collective agreements. Indeed, posting of workers has never emerged as a serious issue in Denmark (EIRO Report 1999). Employers agreed to take a somewhat more active role in the revamped 1999 agreement, accepting foreign companies into their ranks and informing them of their obligations. It is significant that *no explicit legislation had existed* until implementation of the EU directive made such law mandatory, but even then this law did not intrude into the realm of the social partners or go beyond what had been agreed upon nearly seven years earlier.

Sweden: Another Scandinavian Gentlemen's Agreement with a Touch of Government Intervention

Sweden joined the EEA on January 1, 1994 and the EU on January 1, 1995. Although foreign construction companies had become active in Sweden in the 1980s, they were obliged to obtain working permits for their posted workers and reached agreements on wages with the sectoral construction union *Svenska Byggnadsarbetareförbundet* (abbreviated as: Byggettan). As an EEA member, Sweden would become subject to the EU LSP and thus had to react accordingly. A national regulation of labor market entry and entry of foreign companies was no longer possible.

A Bilateral Compromise Agreement: Swedish Unions and Employers Strike a Deal

Similar to the Danish re-regulation, the Swedish national response strategy consists of a compromise agreement between union and employers, hinging on the unions' theoretically evocable right to take industrial action if foreign companies posting employees to Sweden pay substandard wages. This agreement grew out of a modification of the original 1976 Act on Co-Determination in the Workplace (*medbestämmandelagen* or MBL) and a 1989 court case involving the question of wages for Swedish employees of the vessel JSS Britannica, chartered in Cyprus. The Swedish unions initiated a strike to force the owners to pay their crew according to Swedish, not Cypriote wage standards. Although this industrial action was ultimately ruled unlawful by a labor court (AD 1989/20) since there was a valid collective wage agreement on board, in 1991, an amendment to the MBL was passed ('Lex Britannica'), then deleted by the subsequent conservative minority government under Carl Bildt, and later reimplemented by the following Social Democratic government (EIRO Report 1999).

The Lex Britannica allows unions to support foreign workers with industrial action *even if these foreign workers are bound by the terms of a valid work contract* including collective wage agreements. This marks a remarkable exception to an otherwise applicable ban on industrial action in instances in which binding collective wage agreements exist. There was some debate whether this law can be upheld in light of the EU regulation pertaining to the liberalization of service provision, including shipping, though no changes were made (Sveriges Riksdag Motion till *riksdagen* 1997/

98: T202, 9 *'Trafikpolitik för tillväxt och god miljö'* and Sveriges Riksdag Motion till *riksdagen* 1999/2000: T616, 4 *'Sjöfartspolitiken'*).

Trade union *Landsorganisationen* (LO) thus possesses the dormant right to take industrial action should foreign employers post employees to Sweden and pay them substandard wages. Although collective wage agreements are not legally binding in Sweden, they are generally followed by employers (*Svenska Arbetsgivareföreningen*—SAF, since renamed: *Svenskt Näringsliv*) exactly because of this fear of industrial action. In general, the union may call a strike if a company is found not to comply with the wage agreement accepted by the SAF, so long as at least one company employee is a union member. Thus, while collective wage agreements are not legally binding or universally applicable, they nevertheless cover an estimated 90 percent of the Swedish workforce (EIRR 243 February 1994b: 24). Given this institutional setup, the threat of industrial action deterred the few foreign companies active in Sweden from violating the terms of Swedish collective agreements.

The employers and unions were therefore able to strike a deal similar to the Danish one, according to which any potential violation by (foreign) employers would legitimate strike action by the union that would force the offending company to reconsider its tactics. As elsewhere, employers were not prepared to challenge the union over this issue, and regarded foreign subcontractors with some degree of suspicion at any rate.

Implementing the EU Directive: Little Change to the Status Quo

Sweden implemented the EU directive on December 16, 1999. Parliament accepted the new Act on Posted Workers (*Lag om utstationering av arbetstagare*) on May 20, 1999. The two social partners were represented in the committee charged with preparing the draft bill. This task was carried out by Eva Helena Kling, a lawyer from the Union for technical and clerical employees (*Svenska Industritjänstemannaförbundet*—SIF) (EIRO Report 1999). The eventual result of these deliberations was a compromise between the two sides with wages notably not covered by the act, in tribute to Swedish de facto *Tarifautonomie*. The employers were not heavily opposed to this new regulation, having contributed to the coverage of foreign companies by Swedish collective agreements to avoid a downward price spiral (EIRO Report 1999). The act upholds the aforementioned section of the MBL and establishes Swedish jurisdiction over claims by posted workers, making action against noncompliant employers easily possible. In addition, the act specifies the *lois de police* to be applied to workers posted to Sweden, including the annual holidays and holiday pay as stipulated in the Annual Leave Act (*semesterlagen*), amounting to a minimum of 25 annual paid holidays, the rules on parental leave (*föräldraledighetslagen*), amounting to protection from dismissal because of asking for or taking parental leave, the Act on equal opportunities for men and women (*jämställdhetslagen*), ethnic discrimination (*lagen om atgärder mot etnisk diskriminering*), disabilities (*lagen mot diskriminering i arbetslivet av personer med funktionshinder*), and sexual orientation (*lagen mot diskriminering i arbetslivet pa grund av sexuell läggning*). Moreover, the stipulations included in the MBL are part of the Law on Posted Workers, including the right for foreign posted workers to join a Swedish union. Finally, the Act on the Work Environment (*arbetsmiljöslagen*) and working hours (*arbetstidslagen*) will become binding for posted workers as well. The National Board of Occupational Safety and Health (*Arbetarskyddsstyrelsen*) will assume the responsibility of informing foreign employers with wages and labor conditions applicable (EIRO Report 1999; EIRO 2003*f*).

Summing up the Swedish Response Strategy

In sum, the Swedish response strategy consisted of a small legislative change aimed at the shipping industry but with implications for all sectors (see Table 5.8). Since then, the trade unions possess the dormant right to take industrial action if substandard wages are being paid and this mere

Table 5.8 An overview of regulation contained within the Swedish response strategy

---

Does the response strategy cover the entire economy? Yes, though it is based on a gentlemen's agreement between the sectoral social partners. Given the Lex Britannica, the general principle applies to all sectors of the economy: unions monitor compliance with the obligation to pay posted workers standard Swedish wages. However, the legislative act passed in 1999 and amended in 2001 further clarifies a number of social and labor law provisions which apply to posted workers in all sectors.

Are there exceptions/loopholes? No. However, the agreement hinges on the ability of the unions to monitor compliance and take action where and if needed in case of infractions.

What regulations become legally binding on foreign service providers? Swedish labor, working time, and social regulations apply. The Swedish unions ensure (at least in the construction sector) that Swedish wages are being paid.

---

possibility has served as a deterrent against the posting of workers. Although the Swedish collective wage agreements, including the lowest wage bracket, which acts as a de facto minimum wage (EIRR 243, February 1994b: 24), did not possess *loi de police* status and do not do so even after implementation of the EU directive, their compliance is assured by the possibility of union action. Since the vast majority of Swedish employers continue to be bound by these agreements, it is in the *employers' interest* as well to avoid a downward spiral of price bids through subcontracting to foreign companies. Lex Britannica was never put to a practical test in the construction industry, which is why we might refer to it as the *dormant right of a very powerful trade union*. Very much like in Denmark, a gentlemen's agreement has been found relying on union power. At the same time, employers are not necessarily interested in setting in motion a downward price-wage spiral. However, unlike Denmark, this possibility hinges on a legislative change made possible by a Social Democratic government.

Norway: Dormant Rights for Government Intervention

Norway entered the EEA on January 1, 1994 and was expected to join the EU together with Austria and its two Nordic neighbors one year later. Although EU entry was rejected by the populace in a referendum and indeed the question of EU accession led to the demise of the conservative Syse government in 1990, membership in the EEA made Norway subject to the LSP and free movement of labor within it as of the date of entry.[11] Traditionally, the Directorate of Immigration (*Utlendingsdirektoratet*) granted work visas only for foreigners if their wage and labor conditions were on par with local ones (EIRO Report 1999). Obviously, this 'unwritten law' could no longer be applied to EEA citizens after 1994, since this could have been considered a violation of EU law and would have probably been struck down by the ECJ.

A Norwegian Government Initiative: Moving Towards a Response Strategy

Given the impending freedom of labor mobility and especially the LSP, the Social Democratic minority government under Gro Harlem Brundtland

---

[11] As noted before, the EEA membership status of Norway is the reason for which the country is considered in this study, even though it is not an EU member state.

perceived the need for a national re-regulation of the LSP, without the social partners having taken any initiative. The Ministry of Local Government and Regional Development prepared a draft bill in February 1993 aimed at the prevention of social dumping (Norwegian Ministry of Local Government and Regional Development (January 2001)). The bill sought to render possible the universal applicability of collective wage agreements, a measure previously not possible in the system of Norwegian industrial relations. Companies not organized in the employer organization *Næringslivets Hovedorganisasjon* (NHO) usually adhere to the terms of the collective wage agreements, but are not formally or legally required to do so (Norwegian Ministry of Local Government and Regional Development (February 2001); EIRR February 1994). Unlike in Austria, NHO membership is not mandatory, either, thus Norway could have been an attractive target for posting of workers from low-wage countries to undercut the high local wages. The Ministry's draft bill made it possible for either national level trade unions or employer organizations, considered 'representative' and thus including at least 10,000 members or 100 companies respectively, to apply for the universal applicability in a given sector, if they believed that instances of social dumping where occurring. This request would then be evaluated by a mediation board composed of three government-nominated experts and one representative of the employers as well as the trade union *Landsorganisasjonen i Norge* (LO).

The Social Partners Agree to the Government Initiative

Although clearly a government initiative, the LO immediately expressed its consent, while employers were at first more reticent. They criticized that *all* companies could be held legally responsible for payment of collective wage agreements, while previously this was voluntary for companies not organized in the employer organization. NHO was therefore more concerned about the ideological principle of possible government intervention, undermining *Tarifautonomie* (Norwegian LO 2001) even though such intervention has been fairly regular in the history of Norwegian industrial relations. This was NHO's main issue of concern.

It ought to be mentioned that the Norwegian economy was and is highly dependent on the export of oil and natural gas: in 1992 (2003), oil and gas (Nkr 110 billion; Nkr 297 billion) amounted to more than half of total exports. The country is the third largest oil exporter worldwide (*FAZ*, March 8, 1993; Norwegian Ministry of Foreign Affairs (2005)). Norwegian companies were concerned that foreign subcontractors not bound to

Norwegian wages and thus undercutting domestic companies might enter this sector, driving Norwegian companies out of business.

Moving Towards Implementation of the Norwegian Response Strategy

Due to the composition of the government, the implementation process proved slightly more protracted than would have been the case otherwise. A peculiarity of Norway is the internal division of the Social Democratic movement. In parliament, the Social Democrats held a minority only and thus needed to secure the support of any of the three amiable opposition parties, the centrist Freedom Party, or, more importantly, either the Socialists or the agrarian Center Party. The conservatives and the right-wing Progress Party remained opposed to this measure. Their opposition reflected the concerns of the employers about state-led intervention into *Tarifautonomie* and the freedom of association for individual companies. In the end, the government managed to secure the support of all 'amiable opposition' parties, but not the conservatives and the Progress Party. The lower house of parliament *Stortinget* agreed to it on May 19, 1993. The Law No. 58 of June 4, 1993 'relating to the imposition of the extension of collective agreements' (*om allmenngjøring av tariffavtaler*—allmenngjøringsloven) went into effect on January 1, 1994. Its provisions did not diverge much from the original draft (Norwegian Ministry of Local Government and Regional Development (12 January 2001)). In its preamble the law states its declared goal to prevent wage dumping in frank terms:

The objective of the Act is to ensure foreign employees of terms of wages and employment equal to those of Norwegian employees, in order to prevent that employees perform work on terms which...are demonstrably inferior to the terms stipulated in existing nationwide collective agreements. (Article 1-1)

Article 1-2, Section 3 extends the coverage to the oil and petroleum sector on all of Norwegian territory continental and offshore regardless of the nationality of the company involved. By contrast, it does not apply to the Norwegian shipping sector. Article 2 outlines the procedures surrounding the creation of a Tariff Board: its chairman and two other members are appointed by the king, while the trade union and the employers each may send one representative. This tariff board is joined by one member of the party making a demand for universal applicability and one from the opposing camp, if such case arises. Applications for an extension of existing sectoral wage agreements may be brought forward to the Tariff Board by either side (Article 3). However, if such extension is deemed in the 'public interest' by the Board it may also become active on its own initiative (Article 3). A positive decision on any such extension must clearly state the date on which it becomes effective and the wage terms that are being made universally applicable (Article 3). Companies found in violation of the terms thus extended are subject to both union action (Article 5), such as boycotts or blockages, and to fines (Article 8).

Implementing the EU Directive: Little Change Needed

In late 1999, the Ministry of Local Government and Regional Development became active again, in order to implement the relevant EU directive 96/71/EC. Its November 5 draft bill submitted to parliament was essentially based on this directive, though it did not include any provision for a statutory minimum wage, which does not exist in Norway. The ministry deemed the existing 1993 law to be an appropriate regulation of the question of wages (Norwegian Ministry of Local Government and Regional Development (January 2001)). Indeed, most Norwegian labor law already possessed the character of *ordre public*. The proposed legislative initiative also modified section XII B of the 1977 Norwegian legislation on worker protection and the working environment (*lov 4. februar 1977 nr 4. om arbeidervern og arbeidsmiljø—arbeidsmiljølova*), rendering these provisions mandatory for posted workers. In addition, the 1999 law bestowed public law character upon provisions which previously had the character of private law only, such as the Norwegian holiday regulations. It restated the principle of no transition period, i.e. Norwegian regulations apply immediately to posted workers. Finally, the bill provided for the establishment of a joint supervision and information office responsible for informing (foreign) employers and unions of their right and duties in Norway, itself reporting to the Directorate of Labor Inspection (*Direktoratet for arbeidstilsynet*) (EIRO Report 1999; EIRO 2003g).

The social partners were consulted and their positions heard, though neither side left an imprint on the draft bill accepted by parliament on December 16, 1999 and becoming effective as of January 1, 2000. The union had called for collective wage agreements becoming applicable to foreign posting companies even without the formal step of universal applicability. In addition, it called for greater access to information about posted workers for trade unions. The employer organization demanded an exemption of the temporary work agencies from the provisions of the act (EIRO Report 1999). The government ignored all of these demands.

Loopholes in the Norwegian Response Strategy?

The theoretical right to declare collective wage agreements universally applicable has not actually been utilized so far. In the 1999 implementation of the EU directive, wages are not directly mentioned, respecting the *Tarifautonomie* of the social partners. The Norwegian response strategy therefore marks a curious combination of government initiative in the face of weak employer resistance, but the legislative act does leave some room for maneuver to the social partners. Despite a relatively comprehensive legislative response strategy, the fact that wage regulation is not immediately binding on posted workers (only where declared universally applicable) ultimately may have contributed to the appearance of posted workers in more significant proportions than elsewhere in Scandinavia. In 2002, tax authorities reported that 1,400 foreign companies were active in Norway, employing 16,600 posted workers. One-third of these workers are employed in the offshore oil and gas industry, while most of the others work in construction. Given that many of these posted workers stem from other Nordic countries, however (EIRO 2003g), this phenomenon might

Table 5.9 An overview of regulation contained within the Norwegian response strategy

---

Does the response strategy cover the entire economy? Yes, although the 1993 law is more about bestowing theoretical rights upon the government to declare sectoral wage agreements universally applicable. In practice, the government has not actually done so yet.

Are there exceptions/loopholes? Yes, to the extent that wages are only binding on foreign subcontractors when and if they are declared universally applicable. There is no minimum wage in Norway. Henceforth, while a core of Norwegian labor and social regulations apply to posted workers in any case, wages do not automatically.

What regulations become legally binding on foreign service providers? Norwegian labor, working time, and social regulations apply. The 2000 implementation of the EU directive sought to slightly broaden the array of applicable social regulations, though the changes were very minor. The main line of attack, as elsewhere in Scandinavia, had more to do with companies being tempted to undercut wages, rather than any applicable social and labor conditions per se.

---

once again be linked more to regional know-how than to the undercutting of wages. Having said that, the union has expressed some concern about posted workers from Central and Eastern Europe receiving substandard wages and labor conditions, while the sectoral employer association *Byggneraeringens Landsforening* has likewise raised the issue of companies bound by sectoral wage agreements being undercut by those that are not and employ foreign subcontractors (EIRO 2003g).

Summing up the Norwegian Response Strategy

In sum, the Norwegian national response strategy can be described as a preemptive government initiative, establishing significant rights for government intervention into wage-setting (see Table 5.9). It provides the legal possibility of extending collective wage agreements to cover foreign posting companies, thus preventing the undercutting of local wages. It is worth mentioning that this clause has never yet been actually put into practice. The number of workers posted to Norway was low in the 1990s (Norwegian Ministry of Local Government and Regional Development (January 2001)), but has increased slightly since. However, many of these posted workers stem from elsewhere in Scandinavia and are employed in the offshore oil industry, making the undercutting of wage levels not a primary consideration. The legal arsenal of responsive capacity by the state is remarkable.

The state-centric character of the Norwegian national response strategy needs to be stressed because it diverges significantly from the two other Scandinavian cases. Within the Tariff Board the government controls a majority of votes. The Tariff Board can also become active on its own initiative. The trade union welcomed the government's plan without having taken itself action on this issue. The employers were more reserved, though not so much because they had planned on taking advantage of wage cutting through outsourcing, but because they resisted state interventionism on ideological grounds. Two reasons might have made Norwegian employers not extremely belligerent to this act. First, universal applicability provides an incentive for companies to join the employer organization so as to be able to manipulate the content of a regulation which will affect them regardless of whether they are members. Second, the act also covered the exploitation of oil and natural gas, notably by foreign companies active on Norwegian territory. A downward price spiral of wages and thus prices for oil exploitation could thus be prevented, which might have proven disadvantageous to Norwegian companies.

Finland: Existing Labor Law Renders National Response Strategy Unnecessary

Finland joined first the EEA on January 1, 1994 and then the EU one year later. Although the EU LSP would have become effective from the first date onwards, industrial relations in Finland are highly legalistic, similar to the situation in Belgium.

Due to the judicial and legal regulation of its system of wages, the entire framework of Finnish wage brackets was universally applicable and could thus be considered ordre public. There was therefore no pressing need for a national response strategy. More specifically, the Employment Contracts Act clearly states that even an employer not party to a collective agreement is bound to the terms of a nationwide sectoral wage agreement (section 17, paragraph 1). Thus, though there is no minimum wage per se, the entire framework of Finnish wages and other employment provisions becomes applicable to *all* employers. The Finnish Supreme Court has interpreted this act to mean that universal applicability of a collective wage agreement is given if the employer federation that signed the treaty organizes at least half of all companies in this sector (EIRO Report 1999; EIRR, February 1994; Finnish Ministry of Labour (23 November 2000)). The Employment Contracts Act was modified on two recent occasions. In 1996, a new paragraph 6 was introduced into section 17, which points out that universal applicability of Finnish collective conventions applies in general. Certain exceptions are permitted to it for short-term service provision by nonresidents including the planning and installment of machinery, its repair and maintenance, and transport through or to Finnish territory (EIRO Report 1999). More recently, the government successfully amended the Act in 2001. Universal applicability now has to be clearly specified and indeed confirmed by a tariff board, ensuring the representative character of the social partners in the sector concerned in accordance with Employment Contract Act 55/2001. Such decision can then be appealed through a tribunal, which has the final decision (EIRO Report 1999; Finnish Ministry of Labour (23 November 2000)).

Implementing the EU Directive: No Real Change to the Status Quo

As an EU member, Finland has signed the Rome Convention in 1999 and implemented the EU Directive in the Act on Posted Workers on December

16, 1999, later amended on June 1, 2001 and January 1, 2003. The implementation renders a number of national labor regulations internationally applicable, roughly following the sketch of the directive. *However, the overall impact of this new law is minimal, since most Finnish labor legislation could be considered to constitute lois de police previously!*

More specifically, the act mentions the following regulations: the Working Hours Act, the Work in Bakeries Act, compliance with working and rest periods set forth in the Working Hours Act, annual holidays, annual holiday pay and holiday compensation as stipulated in the Annual Holidays Act, provisions concerning paternal leave, sick payment, stipulations concerning employee housing contained in the Employment Contracts Act, and the collective wage agreements themselves. Minor exceptions are permitted for short-term installation work of up to eight days, for which the Finnish wage rates and minimum paid annual holidays do not apply. The act also is not applicable to the merchant marine (Finnish Ministry of Labour (23 November 2000)). These two exceptions correspond to the provisions contained in the European directive. In 2003, a bilateral working group was formed to review the need for further amendments to the act, but the employers have been hesitant to endorse any such change (EIRO 2003*h*).

Summing up the Finnish National Response Strategy

A Finnish national response strategy therefore was not essential since existing wage agreements already had the character of being universally applicable and were legally binding (*ordre public*), as specified in the Employment Contracts Act (see Table 5.10). No wage gap existed or exists, nor

Table 5.10 An overview of regulation contained within the Finnish response strategy

---

Does the response strategy cover the entire economy? Yes.

Are there exceptions/loopholes? No. Even before the EU directive, was implemented, which changed little, all Finnish wages, labor and social conditions were binding on employees posted to Finland.

What regulations become legally binding on foreign service providers? Finnish wages, labor, working time, and social regulations apply. The implementation of the EU directive sought to clarify the matter, but changed little compared to the status ante quo.

---

did the EU LSP pose a significant challenge to Finnish wage structure. This, in turn, is a reason for which the number of workers posted to Finland is minimal (EIRO Report 1999; EIRO 2003h). Given the degree of *Verrechtlichung* there was and is no room for strategies of exiting the system of Finnish wages and other labor regulations. Having said that, one might argue that recent government endeavors to reform the status of 'automatic' universal applicability may lead toward some deregulation. However, the room for maneuver for such action rests minimal.

Comparing the National Response Strategies

In general, the power model, assessing the organizational structures of labor market interest associations, generates accurate predictions.

The national response strategies adopted by individual countries are shaped by the most potent labor market interest association. This is the employer association in France, the Netherlands, and Germany, while a legislative response incorporating union preferences is implemented in Austria.

Similar to Austria, government intervention is colored in favor of the presumably more powerful trade union in Norway. Luxembourg, Belgium, and Finland are all cases where comprehensive internationally legally binding labor and social regulations made a national response strategy to the EU LSP not an immediate necessity. However, a re-regulation came about in Luxembourg regardless; this compromise solution incorporates the commonly shared position of labor and business. In the three cases in which bipartite extra-legalistic arrangements were established that at first did not require any government intervention, the response reflects the varying degree of union and employer power. Thus, it varies between being fairly liberal in the Netherlands (powerful employers) and fairly protectionist in Sweden and Denmark (powerful unions). Thus, *organizational power* matters in all cases, even where no government intervention occurs—or only later, in the implementation of the EU directive, which commonly had little or even no real practical discernible impact—and interest associations strike compromise deals of various colors amongst themselves. In Chapter 6, the predictive potential of the two institutionalist approaches will be evaluated in light of the empirical evidence.

Regulatory Patterns: Statist and Strongly Neocorporatist vs. Intermediate Neocorporatist Response Strategies

Although the national response strategies across the high-wage member state of the EU and in EEA member Norway varied considerably, it is nevertheless possible to discern distinct patterns of regulation, a theme which will now be explored in more detail. Generally, these findings dovetail with the emphasis that recent efforts in the comparative political economy literature have placed on individualized strategies and mechanisms of coping and responding to the common external impetus of European liberalization (Crouch and Streeck 1997; Kitschelt et al. 1999; Scharpf and Schmidt 2000; Hall and Soskice 2001; Schmidt 2002). Thus, far from producing a 'one size fits all' common response or necessarily implying simply convergence, as is often feared or even implied in some of the earlier works in this vein (Albert 1991; Streeck 1993, 1997; Boyer and Drache 1996; Berger and Dore 1996), the challenge of EU-induced deregulation highlights institutional differences amongst various organized forms of capitalism.

In the formulation of response strategies, national institutionalized systems of political economy are rendered more, not less important in the context of accelerated and deepened European integration because it is at the national level that top-down and sideways Europeanization is encountered, negotiated, and, to varying degrees counteracted and even diluted. It is here where national response strategies are shaped and generated.

Business Interest vs. Labor Interests in Shaping Response Strategies

Business interests are particularly important in helping account for the nature of the observed response patterns. More specifically, employer association have to take the interest of their composite members into consideration when lobbying governments or negotiating with their trade union counterparts. Just as recent strides in the varieties of capitalism liberalism literature have underlined (Hall and Soskice 2001), the perceived interests of individual firms in maintaining and, where possible, augmenting and improving their specific Ricardian comparative advantage is therefore a crucial variable that will, at the aggregate level, shape the position of the employer association. In light the empirical evidence presented, it would appear as though construction companies in the smaller European countries, often predominantly active at the local or national level, perceive of EU-induced liberalization as a threat to the domestic wage-price structure and hence a potential menace to their market position. This is true in Belgium, Luxembourg, Austria, Norway, Denmark, Finland, and Sweden. By contrast, in the larger and more export-oriented markets of France, Germany, and the Netherlands, construction companies did find it in their interest at least temporarily to employ subcontractors from elsewhere in the EU. Ultimately, however, French companies grew concerned about the implications of widespread use of foreign subcontractors and henceforth agreed to the protectionist re-regulation proposed by the Ministry of Labor that safeguards the French market from a downward wage-price spiral. That is not to say that the powerful internationally active French construction conglomerates can no longer engage in subcontracting *tout court*. It simply means that equal starting conditions are re-established and ruinous competition between the titans in their home market is prevented. In Germany, small and medium enterprises still play an important role, despite market consolidation and increasing international activity since the early 1980s. While the small and medium companies in particular would have been more willing to endorse a protectionist re-regulation, the larger German construction companies were quite interested in employing foreign subcontractors. The result was that the sectoral employer association might have been willing to meet the union half-way in establishing a wage level for posted workers. However, the BDA insisted on challenging the union and imposing a truly minimum wage for posted workers, taking into account the vocal resistance of other sectoral employer association and their perceived interest in maintaining low wages, international competitiveness, and low prices for domestic construction projects. Finally, in the Netherlands, the central employer association did not intervene at first, since the employment of foreign subcontractors seemed to affect primarily the construction sector. The imposition of the Dutch minimum wage—but not the higher sectoral wage brackets—for workers seconded to the Netherlands for up to four weeks permitted a sufficient degree of flexibility for Dutch construction businesses.

Labor typically assumes a protectionist and defensive position. Upon reflection, this is also the wisest and most long-term oriented perspective trade unions could assume. Any wage gap between posted workers and regularly directly employed domestic workers will only undermine the union's position in future negotiation rounds.

'Liberal' Responses lead to Labor Market Segmentation

Having made the case that EU-induced liberalization actually renders more pivotal the particular embedded systems of politico-economic governance, the importance of this external impetus should not be belittled—quite to the contrary, the implications of horizontal Europeanization can be quite dramatic, especially in the interaction with domestic response strategies.

The analysis of the German, and to a lesser extent the Dutch, case is particularly revealing, as it demonstrates how the organizationally superior situation of organized business may translate into a liberal business-friendly re-regulatory outcome that drastically reconfigures the labor market structure.

The regulation of wages for posted workers has pivotal implications for *labor migration*, albeit somewhat indirectly. If the response strategy creates a *wage differential* between the wages for directly employed domestic workers and those for posted workers, then *migration incentives* are being created. Indeed, the practice of outsourcing to EU subcontractors that can rely on low-paid workers posted to higher wage EU countries has the effect of a *wage differential magnet*. Once such wage differential has been implemented, it leads to a disintegration of the formerly unified wage structure, as can be illustrated using the German case. While workers *directly employed* by domestic companies still receive standard wages (top tier), they compete with posted workers on the new sectoral minimum wage (second tier), not to mention illegally employed workers (bottom and third tier). *Mutatis mutandis* this also applies to the Netherlands. By contrast, the absence of a wage differential accounts for the relatively small numbers of posted workers in Austria and France (Menz 2001), as Table 5.11 below illustrates.

The absence of such *wage differential magnet* makes outsourcing to foreign subcontractors less attractive. Generally speaking, the reported number of posted workers from Belgium, Luxembourg, Norway, Sweden, Finland, and Denmark is negligible. This is not to deny that instances of illegal forms of subcontracting have been reported from Denmark and Norway, a temporary social security gap encouraged the posting of workers to Belgium in the mid-1990s, and illegal employment in construction

Table 5.11 Estimates of numbers of posted workers in Germany per year, from 1999 onwards other European countries for comparative purposes

Germany (from 1999 onwards only posted workers for whom contributions to the sectoral vacation funds have been made; 2002 figure includes non-EU workers in brackets)		
1992: 13,000	Austria 1995: a few hundred 2002: 3,550	France 1993: negligible number 2001: 8,554
1993: 20,000	Netherlands 2000: 20,000	
1994: 106,000	2002: 29,985 (includes workers from Belgium and Germany only)	
1995: 132,000		
1996: 165,000		
1997: 165,000		
1998: 150,000		
1999: 35,587		
2000: 29,742		
2001: 25,260		
2002: 22,121 (+93,258)		

remains a major problem, especially in France, but also elsewhere in Europe. But clearly wage regulation has important effects on labor migration public policy responses produce second order effects. Table 5.11 illustrates this point.[12]

One Common Challenge—Four Responses

A comparison of the response strategies reveals *four* patterns. The first one is a preemptive legalistic response, which has existing wage and labor regulations enshrined into law. Where labor and social policy are internationally binding *lois de police* and wages are universally applicable and legally binding, European liberalization has practically no impact. Undercutting wages through an enterprising exploitation of the wage gap between 'high-wage' Northern and 'low-wage' Southern or Northwestern European countries was not legally possible. This response pattern can

---

[12] Sources: for Germany: Hauptverband, 1997 quoted in Bosch and Zühlke-Robinet, 2000: 31; EIRO, 2003*k*; for Austria: interviews OGB, Bundmin Wirt, EIRO, 2003*i*; for France: interviews CNPF/Medef, CFDT-FTP, FNTP, MinduTrav, EIRO 2003*a*; for the Netherlands: interviews AVBB, FNV Bouw, interview Min SozZAk en Werk, EIRO 2003*c*.

be found in *Belgium, Luxembourg, and Finland*. These countries have a highly legalistic tradition of industrial relations. They possess a system of politico-economic governance in which the government plays a prominent role.

We proceed to the analytically more interesting countries in which the EU-induced LSP did have an impact or at least would have had an impact. Here, the empirical evidence suggests three different response patterns that can be plotted as a U-shaped curve. The strongly neocorporatist countries of Scandinavia and Austria are on one end and statist France on the other end of this curve. *Both groups of countries, though distinct, produce similar protectionist response strategies* that help sustain the existing wage conditions, avoid the emergence of a wage gap, and prevent the disintegration of the labor market into grossly divergent tiers. By contrast, the intermediate neocorporatist countries Germany and the Netherlands both *produced response strategies containing the institutionalization of a wage differential* between wages for posted workers and those directly employed domestically. This liberal solution threatens the existing structure of wage regulation. It weakens the union's bargaining position. It may lead to a disintegration of the labor market into different tiers. Table 5.12 illustrates this U-shaped pattern of responses to EU-induced liberalization.

Among the strongly neocorporatist countries we can differentiate between the *Scandinavian gentlemen agreements* in Denmark and Sweden on the one hand and a regulation enshrined into legislation through *government intervention* as in Austria and Norway on the other. The burden of the gentlemen agreements rests on the shoulders of the trade unions. While this regulation pattern attests to the power of trade unions, since employers fear industrial action in case of noncompliance, the unions have to monitor compliance continuously.

The Norwegian and Austrian response enshrines a labor-friendly regulation into law through government intervention, securing the status quo. In Austria, all collective wage agreements are being extended to cover foreign posted workers. In Norway, the government reserves the right to intervene and declare universally applicable existing wage agreements with the expressed explicit aim to prevent the undercutting of standard Norwegian wages.

In systems in which a legalistic (pre)regulation existed, union and employer power matters less. Elsewhere, the influence of these organizations remains crucial. We find the national response strategies to be predominantly protectionist and re-regulatory. *A statist system of politico-economic*

Table 5.12 The U-shaped regulation pattern of response strategies

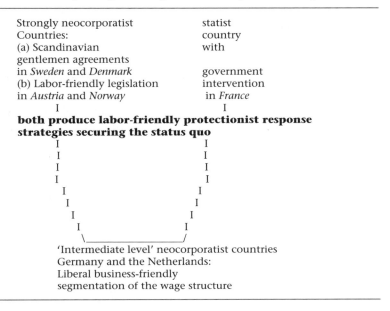

Strongly neocorporatist statist
Countries: country
(a) Scandinavian with
gentlemen agreements
in *Sweden* and *Denmark* government
(b) Labor-friendly legislation intervention
in *Austria* and *Norway* in *France*

**both produce labor-friendly protectionist response
strategies securing the status quo**

'Intermediate level' neocorporatist countries
Germany and the Netherlands:
Liberal business-friendly
segmentation of the wage structure

*governance responds in the same status quo securing fashion as is true of the
strongly neocorporatist group.*

This somewhat counterintuitive response—given organized labor's
weakness and the relative power of employers in France—is a result of
the French employers' willingness to endorse protectionism, as long as it
serves their economic interests. (Neo-Gaullist) government intervention is
shaped by ideational notions such as concerns over dissipating national
sovereignty, Euro-skepticism, and some hesitancy towards economic liberalization. These traits of the French model can be accounted for by an
historical analysis of actors' positions and the role of ideas.

By contrast, the Dutch and the German national responses are both
liberal. They allow for temporary or indefinite avoidance of the standard
local wage brackets. Only the Dutch *minimumloon* is mandatory for postings of up to four weeks. In Germany, a substandard minimum wage
applies to posted workers indefinitely. This result ensues because wage
regulation is left to the social partners without government intervention
into wage-setting. Under these circumstances, the actor with more
relational power shapes the outcome. This actor is business in both countries. In Germany, employers enjoyed the additional advantage of a

liberal-conservative government setting the legislative framework—though not the content—of re-regulation. To the union's dismay other sectoral employers became heavily involved in Germany, fearing wage drift and spillover effects. Gesamtmetall and Gesamttextil encouraged the BDA to pursue a tough stance. Although the Dutch VNO-NCW is as liberally minded as BDA, it tolerated the sectoral solution arranged by AVBB. Other sectoral employers did not become involved. No-one proclaimed to fear spillover effects. VNO-NCW could tolerate this solution, not least since it actually bestows considerable advantages upon employers. Lucrative short-term posting remains possible.

Conclusion: The Response Patterns of Different Varieties of Capitalism and their Implications

In sum, the different varieties of Western European capitalism produce very different responses to the common impetus of economic liberalization induced by the European integration process. This chapter has provided an in-depth empirical study of national response strategies in the Netherlands, Belgium, Luxembourg, Denmark, Sweden, Finland, and Norway.

Response patterns can be sketched in the form of a U-shaped curve. Response strategies generated by strongly neocorporatist Scandinavian countries and Austria resemble the one created by strongly statist France. On the bottom end of this curve are the two medium-level neocorporatist countries Germany and the Netherlands. Both implemented liberal business-friendly regulations.

The discovery of these regulation patterns is not trite. It confirms the relatively powerful position enjoyed by trade unions in Scandinavia and Austria—an assumption which has recently come under some scrutiny (Pestoff 1995; Karlhofer and Tálos 1996; Pontusson and Swenson 1996; Kittel and Talos 1999). However, given reports of violations and in light of the burden placed upon the unions in monitoring compliance to the terms of the gentlemen agreements, it also becomes evident that the national response strategies may act as a strain in years to come.

More extraordinary is the conclusion that re-regulation pursued by such radically different system of politico-economic governance as Austria and France is so remarkably similar. This insight adds further clout to Geoffrey Garrett's (1998) remarkable study that demonstrated not only that globalization was not leading to a convergence on one homogeneous liberal Anglo-American-style model, but that the highly organized neocorporatist/Social Democratic countries were actually able to cope just as well if not better with a globalized market economy than the relatively atomized liberal models. Continental Western European 'models' in which one strong actor is able to implement swiftly a comprehensive re-regulation may be able therefore to counteract and dilute some of the liberal and deregulatory aspects of the European Single Market project. By contrast, in instances in which the responsibility over re-regulation is more diffused, the formulation of a national response strategy will be a more lengthy and protracted process. But re-regulation in the Netherlands and Germany not only was implemented relatively slowly and belatedly. It was also done in a very liberal fashion, allowing employers considerable flexibility. This reflects the organizational advantages enjoyed by employer association over trade unions there as well as their ideological commitment towards labor market deregulation. The declining commitment to the postwar consensus and the very concrete willingness of employers to exit the corset of existing wage determination therefore casts some doubt on the more optimistic and analysis of Thelen (2001: 82–85) that seeks to confirm the continued stability and resilience of the traditional institutions of German industrial relations. This study highlights the incapability of the German union movement to prevent a segmentation of the labor market and the wage structure. This major defeat undermines its future bargaining position. It also creates a substandard wage of workers. *This is a true Achilles' heel of Modell Deutschland* that has previously not been identified even in the more pessimistic accounts on the future of the German model (Streeck 1996). This indication of employers' motivation to profit from European liberalization and exit the existing structure of wage regulation bears witness to the fact that German business is not just becoming more aggressive in its rhetoric (Thelen 2001: 85), but is moving away from its commitment and dedication to the German model.

Indeed one shortcoming of the more recent comparative political economy 'second wave literature' on 'varieties of capitalism' is that it overstates the importance of institutional resilience. While there are scant signs of institutional convergence, changing power dynamics *within existing institutions* may very well mean that the overall outcome of wage-setting, and labor and social policymaking more broadly, in countries like Germany and the Netherlands is notably much more liberal and deregulatory than some of this literature ascertains.

6

Implications and Conclusion

Instead of convergence, we do better talk of European countries going in the same liberalizing direction, but making different policy choices within the more restricted range available; of moving towards greater market orientation while continuing to conform to three national varieties of capitalism...
(Vivien A. Schmidt, *The Futures of European Capitalism*, Oxford: Oxford University Press, 2002, p.310)

When judges convened at the ECJ in Luxembourg in 1990 to make a decision on a seemingly obscure case revolving around Portuguese workers without work visa helping to build a high-speed train track in a Paris suburb, it was far from predictable that this ruling would be in favor of the Portuguese company. Nor was it clear from the outset that the final ruling would set in motion a wave of national response strategies across Europe. In a remarkable parallel, both highly statist and highly neocorporatist countries responded to European liberalization in a protectionist fashion, securing the payment of standard wages to posted workers. No new avenues were opened for corporate strategies of cutting wages by employing foreign subcontractors not bound to domestic wages. Employers were not always interested in these (Luxembourg, to some extent Austria and France), they were held in check by powerful labor unions (Denmark, Sweden), or barred from such strategies by labor-friendly government legislation (Austria, Norway). By contrast, it is highly symbolic that the heart of the Berlin Republic was (re-)built by Polish, Irish, and Portuguese workers, toiling at a fraction of the regular standard German wages. *Spreeland capitalism*, represented by the refurbished *Reichstag* building in central Berlin and its sleek, yet utterly tasteless corporate center around Potsdamer Platz, looks and feels notably different from the more consensus and coherence-oriented ideological principles of Rhineland capitalism, epitomized by sleepy Bonn. The powerful position German business enjoys and its willingness aggressively to challenge unions is well documented in this study. The German re-regulation is the most liberal response of all the ten surveyed. It helps segregate the labor market into distinct tiers. This legal exit option out of the framework of standard wages further augments the bargaining clout of employers.

I submit that the way in which national models respond to a common external impetus of economic liberalization is indicative of the response capacity of such distinct models of politico-economic governance and indeed the varying degrees of power which labor unions and employer association command.

It is also posited that while exaggerated hopes for the future of a Social Europe might be misplaced, nation-states do maintain the capacity to re-regulate aspects of European liberalization within certain imposed constraints. Nation-states may re-regulate national level labor market and wage policy, affected by the consequences of European integration. However, any national re-regulation will be closely monitored by the ECJ. It may not result in a form directly counteracting the principles of the Single Market project.

Moving towards Generalizations: Posted Workers and Europeanization

This study examines the formulation of national responses to economic liberalization induced and initiated by the EU, generated by the interplay of labor market interest associations and national governments. These response strategies, it is argued, are indicative *both* of the way in which 'negative' or 'sideways' Europeanization is counteracted, negotiated, and encountered at the national level *and* the response capacity, the ability to guard resilience, and thus indeed the viability of various European system of politico-economic governance or varieties of capitalism.

Recent inquiries into the effects and implications of (predominantly) top-down Europeanization (Mény et al. 1996; Knill and Lenschow 1998;

Knill 2001, 2002; Börzel and Risse 2000; Cowles et al. 2001; Heritier 2001; Knill and Lehmkuhl 2002; Featherstone and Radaelli 2003) have started to shed some light on the complex dynamics arising from the patterns of inertia, absorption, transformation, and retrenchment in response to Europeanization (Radaelli 2000, 2003). It is now recognized that in a multilevel system of governance, Europeanization is, at least in part, shaped by games played in the national arena. Examining a policy domain—labor and social policy—that remains relatively neglected in favor of environmental policy in the rapidly unfolding literature on Europeanization, it is argued that Europeanization proceeds not only through the implementation of EU directives (top-down), negotiated at the national level, but generally prescribed by Brussels, or the formulation of agenda-setting proposals by member states (bottom-up). It may also take the form of distinct national re-regulatory responses to Scharpf and Taylor's 'negative integration', a dynamic I refer to as 'horizontal Europeanization'. In the implementation of such national re-regulation member states enjoy considerably more autonomy than in the mere implementation of EU directives. Domestic actor coalitions matter, of course; but neither their interests nor the domestic opportunity structure are necessarily shaped by any European impetus, as is alleged in some of the literature (Knill and Lehmkuhl 2002; Radaelli 2003: 40ff.), and they can be assessed and predicted *ex ante*.

The liberalization of service provision opened up fundamentally new corporate strategies involving the transnational posting of employees reimbursed at home country wages. The LSP certainly fits the description of negative integration being entailed in the Single Market project. Yet the LSP is not the product of a specific EU directive. In fact, the abortive 1991 attempt by the Commission to create an EU directive regulating the transnational posting of workers and the toothless 1996 directive demonstrate just how meager an effect top-down Europeanization had. What emerges from the empirical analysis of ten high-wage EU member states is that the implementation of the EU directive had generally very little or almost no tangible effect. The true political battles revolved not around this cause, but around the formulation of proactive re-regulation of a deregulatory 'negative' aspect of the EU Single Market. This dynamic is distinct from the implementation or 'downloading' (Börzel 2002) process, which receives much attention in the existing literature.

In examining the response strategies, it is maintained that the labor market association commanding superior organizational characteristics will be more successful in shaping the overall outcome. Henceforth, it is not simply a matter of whether or not a dominant actor coalition is absent or present (Dimitrova and Steunenberg 2000; Knill and Lehmkuhl 2002), since this is generally the case in organized varieties of capitalism, or what the belief system of such actor coalition may be in the 'pre-liberalization phase' (Heritier et al. 2001), important as though this latter point is. Also, it is not argued that the external liberalizing impetus will change the domestic power balance between actor coalitions, as has been argued by proponents of the 'second image reversed' approach (Gourevitch 1978; Keohane and Milner 1996). Instead, the power balance is assessed *ex ante*, and based on the distribution of power a prediction as to the likely response strategy is then derived.

Moving towards Generalizations: Posted Workers and Comparative Political Economy

It is no gross exaggeration to state that the debate on globalization has dominated the realm of international political economy throughout the 1990s and the early 2000s. Relatedly, a vivid discussion on the future and viability of the 'coordinated market economies' of continental Europe has unfolded (Kitschelt et al. 1999; Coates 2000; Scharpf and Schmidt 2000; Weber 2001; Hall and Soskice 2001; Schmidt 2002; Yamamura and Streeck 2001, 2003). More recent efforts have questioned the convergence thesis developed in earlier works hotly debated in favor of a more nuanced depiction of individual and divergent responses to common external constraints and pressures. Institutionalized divergent varieties of capitalism may prove more resilient than was previously assumed because actors within these systems may find it in their advantage to sustain them, exploiting particular comparative advantages afforded to them, such as the high-quality high-skill production matrix often associated with the Rhineland economies. It might be not least in businesses' interest to uphold organized industrial relations and highly developed systems of education and training (cf. Hall and Soskice 2001; Thelen 2001) rather than clamor for Thatcherite atomization. Other analysts predict 'divergence within convergence' (Deeg and Lütz 2000; cf. Schmidt 2002), or 'hybridization' (Yamamura and Streeck 2003), in other words different coping strategies that do blur previously clear-cut differences between different models of contemporary capitalism.

Some of the insights generated by this literature are valuable, while others need to be amended. In insisting on the potential for re-regulatory responses, this study clearly rejects the simplistic postulate that states possess no room for maneuver vis-à-vis a neoliberal globalization process. In fact, the distinct ways in which European countries re-regulated the EU LSP demonstrates that persistent national traditions of institutionalized governance mechanisms continue to play an important role. This case study of the impact of the EU liberalization of service provision has been examined in order to derive more general observations about the response capacity of different varieties of capitalism to economic liberalization, including strongly neocorporatist (Austria), intermediate neocorporatist (Germany, the Netherlands), and statist (France) models of politico-economic governance. These models and the institutionalized positions and organizational characteristics of interest associations matter strongly. Internal cohesion, coverage, and access to government, will have a profound and distinguishing impact upon the type of response strategy with which states re-regulate the wages for posted workers.

Employer strategies are strongly shaped by the preferences of member firms. The renewed focus on the role of the firm (cf. Hall and Soskice 2001) in seeking to enhance and perpetuate distinct national preferences for certain traditions that ensure comparative advantages (cf. Katzenstein 1984, 1985) is incorporated in this study. Countries with construction sectors composed predominantly of SMEs will most likely favor protectionist re-regulations that do not endanger their own home market position. By contrast, construction markets with internationally active players or companies interested in attracting additional flexible labor or highly skilled labor, including notably France and the Netherlands, saw the widespread use of subcontractors and outsourcing. In France, the national re-regulation has made the use of foreign subcontractors less financially attractive. While it might appear as first perplexing to a foreign observer why French employers might welcome such re-regulation, it might appear less puzzling, if we consider that larger businesses wanted to avoid ruinous competition on their home turf, while smaller companies perceived of the foreign competitors as a potential menace as elsewhere in Europe.

While the focus on the firm is a definite strength of the varieties of capitalism approach, there is a certain danger in overemphasizing institutional resilience. While coordinated market economies might look remarkably unchanged and withstand the twin pressures of globalization and Europeanization surprisingly well at surface level, the policy outcome generated by these very same institutions may be dramatically different from earlier decades. To put it bluntly: Austria, France, Germany, and the Netherlands have not undergone the comprehensive Thatcherite onslaught and have not and probably will not turn into full-fledged clones of post-Thatcher Britain or some form of Anglo-American capitalism. However, this does not mean that policies generated by the coordinated market economies necessarily need to diverge much from an 'embedded neoliberal' (van Apeldoorn 1999) consensus of privatization, market liberalization, monetarist anti-inflationary monetary policy, 'enabling' social and welfare policies, and business-friendly industrial policy.

Due to power imbalances between capital and labor, national response strategies in some countries are notably more liberal and deregulatory than in others. Henceforth, despite relative institutional resilience and stability at surface level, the overall policy outcome in responses to EU-induced economic liberalization in Germany and the Netherlands are business-friendly and allow for labor market flexibilization, thus moving them closer to a regulatory outcome associated with Anglo-Saxon varieties of capitalism than analysts insisting on the continued resilience of coordinated capitalism might expect. The study suggests that both statist systems and strongly neocorporatist systems of economic governance in Europe generate response strategies to EU-induced liberalization that preserve their current labor market structure. By contrast, it is the group of intermediate neocorporatist countries that produces more liberal regulatory outcomes, which endanger the traditional structure of the labor market. In Germany in particular, business is prepared to depart from consensual and concessionary traditions of labor market and social policy regulation, thus adding practical clout to the neoliberal rhetoric espoused in the 1990s. The level of aggression displayed by German employer association BDA in this case is remarkable. Analysts using the varieties of capitalism approach stress that German employers 'cannot get themselves to abandon' this system (Thelen 2001). But by insisting on continued institutional resilience, such assessment might ultimately miss the broader picture. In this case, German employers engaged in a two-tier strategy: employ foreign subcontractors, pay them Portuguese wages, *and* try to block any minimum wage the union might propose. Some employers clearly *did* exit the system of organized industrial relations (and continue to do so), while the BDA used the existing institutional framework to block, delay, and hamper any re-regulation with teeth. As long as it advances their interests, German employers might play along in the existing institutions, but that does not appear to stop them from exiting the system when, where, and if it suits them (see also: Hassel and Streeck 2004).

The distinction provided in the neocorporatist literature between 'stronger' varieties, such as Austria, Sweden, and Norway, and the 'intermediate' cases, including Germany and the Netherlands, might serve as a useful reminder just how heterogeneous the category of 'co-ordinated' or 'organized' market economies really is. Just as the liberal Anglo-American variety of capitalism can be desegregated, given the long legacy of state interventionism and planning in the US and Britain prior to the late 1970s (Goodin 2003), so it might be worth rethinking this category. There would appear to be a world of difference between Sweden and Denmark on the one hand, where trade unions seal gentlemen agreements with employers, monitor compliance, and take swift indus-trial action where necessary, and Germany on the other, where the union is unable to prevent foreign posted construction workers being entitled to a truly minimum wage only. Likewise, the Austrian and Norwegian governments implemented labor-friendly legislation, overrid-ing and ignoring the admittedly feeble resistance of employers. By con-trast, in drafting a legislative initiative the Dutch government listened closely to the concerns of employers and decided not to extend the Dutch regulation to the entire economy.

Reports of the death of neocorporatism and statism appear exaggerated. Coordinated market economies have not unraveled; despite important changes to the structure of polito-economic governance and the role of the state in recent years (Heritier et al. 2001; Schmidt 2002), many of which, at least in the context of continental Europe, were inspired or imposed by European integration. However, common external challenges do not lead to common responses or a trend towards convergence, as this study underlines. Important institutional variations persist in the political economies of Western Europe. What matters is not so much the resilience of these institutions per se, but rather the distribution of power amongst and between them and the way in which traditional institutions are being redefined in the 1990s to serve new political and economic aims, that do set them apart functionally from the arrangements of the 1970s. Similarly, French statism has undergone a metamorphosis. It is no longer character-ized by the traditionally mighty central government steering a business sector characterized by devout national champions. Instead, French busi-ness has outgrown this straitjacket. It manages to influence government decisions in its favor or 'hijack' policy initiatives.

The postwar consensus has evaporated. Business has a credible exit threat. Thus, the balance of power has shifted in its favor. This observation does not imply a general convergence on a more liberal variety of capital-ism. Traditional institutions live on, but they serve new and radically different goals.

Evaluating Rational Choice and Historical Institutionalism

The empirical discussion of the response strategies in Chapters 4 and 5 underlines the persistence of distinct national models of politico-economic governance. It also reflects the shift of power in favor of business. Employers gain the upper hand in all but three cases, Austria, Sweden, and Denmark. However, business interests need not be served by a deregulation of the wages for posted workers. It might share a protectionist interest with unions to avoid a downward spiral of wages and prices. It has been argued that historical and rational choice institutionalism can provide valuable insights in deciding *ex ante* which strategy business is likely to favor.

Rational Choice Institutionalism Evaluated

The predictions generated by the *rational choice institutionalist* approach point into the right direction.

Indeed, with the two strategies predicted for utility maximization for both camps, we capture more sophisticated or at least alternative strategies beyond wage minimization by business and wage maximization by unions. The maximization of the wage gap is not necessarily in business' best interest in economies in which the construction sector is dominated by SMEs, as in Austria, Luxembourg, Belgium, Finland, Norway, and Denmark. Even in countries where larger companies exist like Germany, the Netherlands, and Sweden, the sectoral associations may be prone to avoid conflict and compromise-oriented. Thus, they pursue an alternative strategy of accepting a minimal wage gap to avoid a downward wage-price spiral.

This insight is possibly the root cause behind the conflict between HDB/ ZDB and BDA in Germany and the somewhat conciliatory stance of the Dutch AVBB. Out of this sector-specific interest of maintaining status quo price level on the one hand and the general quest to apply downward pressure on wages on the other, a conflict may arise between the sectoral construction association and the umbrella association, as happened in Germany.

The pursuit of a clear-cut economic rationale seems to have played a role most prominently in Germany. But how can we account for large French companies conceding to the national regulation? Through its use of Portuguese subcontractors, construction giant Bouygues first set in motion the debate and ultimately the passage of the national response strategy, but then later conceded to re-regulation. Given the overwhelming power of the major French construction conglomerates, it is surprising that they chose the alternative strategy of accepting a minimum wage differential, rather than seeking to maximize it and profit from outsourcing. Apparently, business preferred to avoid the ensuing wage-price competition.

The RCI approach is thus generally useful for providing us with road maps leading into the right direction. A difficulty emerges with predicting *ex ante* which one of the alternative two strategies actors will choose to maximize utility. If we contend that in countries in which SMEs dominate employers will choose a more conciliatory strategy (which seems to be the case) this leaves us with the puzzle of the French employers. Likewise, the complexity of the deliberation and games within governments are not fully accounted for. In France, a center-right government passed a protectionist re-regulation, while a German center-right government was internally divided on this issue.

Historical Institutionalism Evaluated

The *historical institutionalist* approach generates more detailed predictions, helps us move beyond the economic rationale, which so dominates the rational choice institutionalist approach, and usefully points to the role of ideology and ideas. Yet it is somewhat hampered by generating fairly vague predictions. In bringing history back in this approach undoubtedly makes a valuable contribution to the analyst's tool chest, yet history can generate a perplexing array of predictions. The organizational power model, developed in this study, serves as a useful addition. Pointing to the structural composition of players in combination with the predictions generated by this theoretical approach helps to arrive at ultimately more refined and pointed hypotheses.

For the employer association we find that the heritage and tradition of individual countries' associations flavored by the role of ideas strongly shape the positions actually taken. Its predictions capture complexities behind decision-making. Thus, the French employer association assumes a fairly protectionist stance in advocating a comprehensive re-regulation. The Austrian association is likewise willing to support a relatively encompassing response, found in consultation with their union counterparts. In the Netherlands, a fairly employer-friendly 'compromise' was found, allowing for wage moderation and enough flexibility for employers. However, this compromise avoids antagonizing the trade unions through the pursuit of a maximum wage differential as in Germany. This fits in very well with the consensual employer-friendly pattern of wage regulation since the Wassenaar agreement. Wage moderation is achieved. Labor acquiescence is secured. By contrast, the German employers pursue a confrontational approach and successfully seek to maximize the wage differential. This strategy is a reflection of the ideological roots of German business, its increasing fascination with neoliberal ideology, and its demands for lower wages and employer charges in the early 1990s.

For the trade unions the predictions about preferences are likewise very accurate. Unions in the two German-speaking countries defended the status quo of coverage for all workers employed on domestic territory—or at least attempted to do so. This continues their tradition of avoiding a gap between wages for 'native workers' and foreign *Gastarbeiter*. This holds true for union preferences across Scandinavia and the Low Countries as well. The French unions supported a re-regulatory response strategy *unisono*. There was no discernible difference in strategy or aim among them despite their ideological cleavages. This factor, highlighted by the historical institutionalist approach, therefore is not relevant. Here, the approach provides unnecessary detail. The ideological cleavage within the Dutch union movement played no role, either.

For the governments this approach usefully underlines the role of the ideological orientations of the coalition partners composing the governments in power at the time. We attain a more sophisticated and wider explanatory potential than with RCI in this instance. Therefore, we are able to move beyond a simple dichotomy of conservative-business friendly and Social Democrat–labor friendly.

Taking into consideration the ideological roots of the Christian Democratic parties in the two *Germanophone* countries in Catholic social thought as well as their electoral indebtedness to small business owners, farmers, and employees, it becomes clearer why these parties were not as outspoken in the support of a liberal response strategy as they might have been otherwise. With some modification, this argument also applies to the French neo-Gaullist RPR, which, unlike Anglo-Saxon parties of the Right, combines staunch patriotism with skepticism towards economic liberalization and an excessive accumulation of power at the European level. Taking these ideological roots into consideration, we can more easily comprehend the relatively swift French response and the Austrian compromise solution between the two main camps. In Germany, the Christian

Democrats were somewhat torn internally. Small liberal coalition partner FDP insisted on a liberal solution without being ultimately able to influence the outcome decisively. In the Netherlands, the center-right government did not become involved in the first bipartite response strategy, while government intervention in Sweden and Norway did confer to the easily predictive pattern of Social Democratic government passing pro-labor legislation.

Merits and Weaknesses of the Two Institutionalist Approaches

The two theoretical approaches utilized have different merits. They stress the role of economic rationale and utility maximization on the one hand and past key decisions, ideological indebtedness, and ideational factors on the other. Based on their predictive capacity, let us turn to a critical assessment of the two neo-institutionalist approaches.

The rational choice institutionalist approach is useful in forcing the analyst to formulate alternative strategies that actors may pursue to maximize utility. Although ultimately based on economic rationale, these strategies need not consist of a simplistic prediction for union and employer behavior. The problem is to choose *ex ante* which strategy actors are most likely to pursue. A number of employer association chose the alternative strategy of accepting a minimal wage gap and most (but not all) of those preside over economies in which SMEs predominate. The price to pay for moving to such level of abstraction is that one may ignore country-specific factors and traditions. The case of the French employers underlines this fallacy. In general, unions pursue a proactive strategy that secures high wages for every worker, including posted ones. Again, it is not clear from the outset, however, what would lead unions to choose a more restrictive strategy of focusing on their core clientele. Could such strategy underlie the relative passivity of the French and Norwegian unions? Perhaps, but this is difficult to predict *ex ante*.

RCI offers parsimoniousness as an advantage. It goes a long way in accounting for the preferences of European labor market interest associations in re-regulating the wages for posted workers. However, they are occasional exceptions. They point to the weakness of this approach, namely its tendency to ignore country-specific variables.

By contrast, the potential fallacies of the historical institutionalist approach lie not in their parsimonious hypotheses, but rather the opposite. An overwhelming plethora of predictive material is being produced. This makes it more challenging to select relevant strings among the ideological and ideational embeddedness of the principal actors. It also creates some potential for personal bias of the analyst, a trap which has been avoided here through the introduction of the combination with the organizational power model. Notwithstanding these potential problems, the historical institutionalist approach clearly generated more predictive source material than the RCI and is better able to allow the analyst a grip on the complex and sometimes convoluted decision-making processes within governments and employers organizations. It is able to capture a wider host of factors and variables. Ultimately, it provides a richer and fuller picture. The useful emphasis on the role of ideas and ideology helps to 'bring back politics'. It can account for decision-making seemingly inconsistent or even contrary to straightforward economic rationale. A direct comparison between the two approaches reveals how useful both can be. However, it is the historically grounded method which ultimately helps to gain the extra analytical mileage beyond what the other can offer.

The EU Liberalization of Service Provision and National Response Strategies: What Implications for 'Social Europe'?

When the architects of the Treaty of Rome laid out the principles of the Single Market, including the liberalization of service provision, one of the ambitions was to promote labor mobility in Europe. It was far from established then and became obvious only through elaboration by the ECJ over the years that such service liberalization included the temporary posting of workers to other member states. Pushing forward the speed and scope of the European integration process conflicts with the national regulatory capacity of the nation-state. Transnational posting of workers could be pursued by enterprising construction companies to take advantage of the wage gap between northern and southern and northwestern Europe in those target countries where wages were not part of the *ordre public*. The issue of posted workers highlights the clash between efforts to create a common market by deregulation and 'negative integration' and attempts to uphold existing high-wage and social standards in some member states. Market integration has been the chief objective of the European integration process. That this would undermine national authority over wage regulation as a second order effect is only consequent. Not all member states, and especially not all labor market interest associations, were prepared to accept this outcome, however. Most member states took advantage of recapturing authority in the aftermath of the Rush Portuguesa decision. Very little room has been devoted in this study to the EU level re-regulation (Directive 96/71/EC). Not only did it come very late—six years after Rush Portuguesa and even after latecomer Germany had passed its own national response strategy—it offered little more than a legal arch spanning over national arrangements already found. It thus had practically no impact.

If such regulatory pattern is indicative of EU labor and social market policy, healthy skepticism towards the prospect of a 'Social Europe' is in order. While market liberalization proceeds in great strides and at jetlike speed, social and labor market policy follows at horse-and-buggy pace. Indeed, European social and labor market policy was concerned primarily with aiding and promoting labor mobility throughout the 1960s and early 1970s. This was followed by modest advances in labor law in the mid-1970s, and a wave of health and safety regulations in the 1980s (Commission européenne 2000: 26–27). Neither the Social Charta of 1989 nor the consultation of social partners growing out of the 1997 Amsterdam Treaty have led to major milestones in truly European social and labor market policy. But this seems hardly surprising given the original underlying aim of market liberalization. Hence, I refrain from using the issue of posted workers as a test case for the future of European social policy.

If we were to do that, the prediction would be gloomy. In fact, the EU attempt to foster transnational mobility of workers by permitting posted workers to remain covered by the home country regime of social security (EC 1408/71) has ironically contributed to the emergence of a 'social security gap', which became of some importance in Belgium. It permits employers to reimburse posted workers at the much lower social security levels of their home countries. Thus, this aspect of 'Social Europe' has backfired completely. It produced another tool to circumvent national regulations in the arms chest of employers.

The LSP and Migration: Implications of the 2004 Round of EU Enlargement

Cunning entrepreneurs take advantage of the newly afforded opportunity to pay substandard wages by outsourcing production to foreign subcontractors. Thus, even in a geographically static service industry, it becomes possible to reduce wage expenditures by importing labor instead of outsourcing production. Construction sites become extralegal zones or 'islands of foreign law' (Hanau 1996). This entails a two-(or even three!) tier legal and wage structure. This disintegration of the labor market in the German construction industry is further advanced through exploitative illegal forms of employment. Obviously, illegal employment in the construction sector also exists elsewhere in Europe. But only in Germany and the Netherlands has such second tier received full legal sanctioning. The new corporate strategy of transnational outsourcing can be used in other service sectors as well, notably in the transportation sector, where the Commission is planning a complete liberalization of local public transportation in 2008. Outsourcing is of course nothing new in manufacturing. Manufacturing companies can compare locales for investment and base their decision on wage levels, absence or presence of labor unions, and degree of social and environmental regulations ('regime shopping'). Yet no comparable development has been previously underway in a sector as geographically static as construction.

With the exception of Sweden, Ireland and the UK, all pre-2004 EU member states have taken measures to limit the transnational service provision and freedom of labor mobility from the 2004 newcomers to the EU. Just like during the Mediterranean rounds of enlargement in the 1980s, temporary bans have been imposed. The Austrian and German governments have been particularly vocal in their demands for limits on the free flow of services and labor. Given the magnitude of the wage gap between current member states and the newcomers, which dwarfs the one within the pre-enlargement EU such concerns are understandable. At the same time, they once again revive some of the fundamental questions that the posted workers issue posed: Should companies from low-wage member states be permitted to take advantage of their main comparative advantage? Or does this constitute social dumping and undermine social and labor standards elsewhere? Can one survive on Portuguese wages in Copenhagen? Can one manage on a Lithuanian salary in Paris?

The nightmare vision of Danish unions and French construction sector employers of having to cope with Czech and Polish subcontractors seems unlikely to materialize, given the limits on service provision imposed on the 2004 newcomers. Clearly, this is one lesson learned from the Rush Portuguesa decision.

The common account of an absence of intra-European integration thus has to be modified. In proposing the concepts of *wage differential magnet* and *migration incentives*, I argue that such economic rationale can be expected to contribute to a migration decision, particularly if language barriers and the recognition of professional degrees do not act as serious impediments. Migrants from lower wage EU member states thus may find themselves being drawn to high-wage member states, especially if both pull (different wage levels) and push (unemployment at home or substitution at home through third country incoming migrants) factors are present. Companies have an incentive to outsource work to foreign subcontractors posting workers to higher wage countries. However, these workers do not receive standard wages in the recipient countries unlike previous migrant workers. They are consigned to second tier of the labor market characterized by inferior wages and labor conditions. It is this sort of labor migration which the LSP and European liberalization has fostered.

Conclusion

Different institutionalized systems of politico-economic governance produce distinct re-regulatory outcomes in reaction to EU-induced liberalization. Such re-regulation at the national level is influenced by the relative distribution of power between business and labor, based on institutional–organizational characteristics. While convergence is therefore not occurring at an institutional level or in terms of policy outcome, national response strategies are protective of existing arrangements only in the statist and strongly neocorporatist countries of Europe, whilst intermediate neocorporatist systems generate regulatory outcomes that are liberal, flexible, and business-friendly in the short-term, but that undermine the structure of the labor market in the long term.

Appendix A
Industrial Relations in Western Europe

Austria

The main Austrian union federation ÖGB is subdivided into sixteen sector-specific and nine regional branches. The employer association WK is even further differentiated with more than 130 sectoral subdivisions and nine regional branches. Both associations remain highly centralized (Traxler 1998). Although subdivisions conduct the annual rounds of wage bargaining, the umbrella organization coordinates and controls wage policies. Within the subdivisions, every company enjoys parity in voting power, i.e. the principle 'one company, one vote' applies. The WK acts as an interest association, a think tank, and an employer association. Given the preponderance of small businesses in the Austrian economy, the think tank of the association of larger industry (VÖI, renamed to IV—*Industriellenvereinigung*) is not particularly influential.

The union effectively controls its affiliates by maintaining thorough control over finances, personnel decisions and legal status. Membership dues are collected by the central ÖGB and then redistributed to affiliates. The ÖGB appoints a large share of its sectoral subdivisions' personnel (Traxler 1999). Finally, these subdivisions do not possess legal standing of their own and engage in bargaining under the authority and the guidelines of the umbrella organization.

Industrial relations in the private sector unfold in a sphere in which social partners enjoy a relatively high degree of autonomy from state intervention. They are bound by the 1919 Labor Contract Act (*Arbeitsvertragsgesetz*—ArbVG). This act establishes works councils in companies with more than five employees. The council is informed on all major management decisions affecting employees, yet actual co-determination (*Mitbestimmung*) is limited to personnel and social issues, and thus considerably more limited than in Germany. Unlike Germany, works councils are de facto controlled by the unions, with up to 90 percent of its representatives being union members (Traxler 1998: 244ff.). This law also mandates that only associations—hence unions and employers—are permitted to engage in collective bargaining. Closed and union shop arrangements are outlawed. Collective bargaining results in commonly agreed wage brackets (*Tarifverträge*) and related agreements on benefits, including overtime and night pay, safety and health regulations, and so on. Since wage agreements are binding for *all* constituents, there is a slight incentive for employees to 'free ride' and not to join the union. Union membership is not mandatory, but contributions to labor's think tank BAK are. WK membership is mandatory for employers, hence, *all companies are bound by collective wages*. This offers the advantage of equal conditions of competition and avoids ruinous wage spirals. However, traditionally there have been company-level wage agreements, which may and often have exceeded sectoral minima. Three bargaining levels exist: macro, encompassing the entire economy, micro, focusing on one sector, and meso, comprising only one company. Lower-level agreements may exceed but never undercut higher-level agreements. In sum, industrial relations in Austria are thus characterized by relatively decentralized bargaining within the framework of bargaining among two key interest associations that are both highly centralized, unitary, quasi-monopolized, and formally nonideological.

France

The French state displays a paternalistic and often patronizing attitude towards societal groups (Keeler 1987; Wilson 1987; Labbé 1996). While closely intertwined with business, the feeble trade unions have rarely been regarded serious partners for negotiation. Instead, the government acts on labor's behalf as a sort of *ersatz union*. Major legislative initiatives leading to labor-friendly innovations in labor law or social policy emerge whenever the government is either composed of left-wing parties (the Popular Front of 1936, Mitterrand's 1981 Auroux Laws) or when it is under nonparliamentary pressure from the Left and/or the populace (1945 after the liberation, 1968 during mass demonstrations against de Gaulle, after the 1995 *refus* by refraining from certain policy steps) (Goetschy 1998).

   While in many ways France combines political, economic, and cultural elements of both Northern and Southern Europe, the structure of French industrial relations is decidedly Southern European. The *relations professionnelles* are highly antagonistic and confrontational; employers are patriarchal and often unwilling to negotiate with unions, which are militant and easily resort to industrial action. Trade unions do not pretend to be ideologically neutral as in Germany, but neither are they as close to the ideological orbit of a political party as in Austria or Scandinavia. Betraying their original anarchist roots, unions attempt to keep some distance to the state as well. Although legalized in 1884, not until 1936 could unions engage in collective bargaining and only since 1968 are they permitted to have representatives at the company level. Unlike the two German-speaking countries and the Netherlands, the French union movement's history (Mouriaux 1993, 1994; Labbé 1996) follows the opposite direction, moving from a unitary movement toward ideological division. The main six French unions CGT, CGT-FO, CFTC, CFDT, CGC, and the FEN have broken away from one common branch. The CGT (*Confédération Générale du Travail*—General Labor Confederation) was once this common root branch, with an affinity to anarcho-syndicalism, radical anticapitalism and confrontational activist-led strikes and demonstrations to overcome capitalism or at least, failing that, improve the condition of the working class. Traditionally the largest union, the CGT still generally rejects collective bargaining and only very recently has begun to sign wage agreements at all, and only at the company level. A fraction of the CGT split off in 1947–8 in protest over the growing dominance of the Communist Party and formed the CGT-FO (*Force Ouvrière*—Workers' Force).

Despite its eclectic and often contradictory ideological composition it has played an important role in wage negotiations. Christian union CFTC (*Confédération Française des travailleurs chrétiens*—French Confederation of Christian Workers) emerged in 1919, a more accommadationist and conservative union, engaging in wage bargaining and eschewing revolutionary rhetoric in favor of Christian values. In 1964 a reformist branch split off, forming the CFDT (*Confédération française démocratique du travail*—French Democratic Confederation of Labor), which grew to become the numerically most important French union.[1] Because of its willingness to engage in collective bargaining, it is arguably the politically most important.

Finally, the numerically smallest union is the salaried employees *cadre* union CFE-CGC (*Confédération française de l'encadrement—Confédération générale des cadres*—French Confederation of Managerial Staff—General Confederation of Managerial Staff) formed in 1944 and focusing exclusively on highly skilled white-collar employees.

The French union movement is ideologically divided, fragmented, internally incoherent, and *predominantly concentrated within the shrinking public sector*. It is also experiencing an even more pronounced and rapid decline in membership than in the rest of Western Europe (Mouriaux 1993; Ebbinghaus and Visser 2000), only partially attributable to structural shifts in the economy. A particular French problem is the union movement's lack of political influence that makes it unattractive to its clientele. Between 1976 and 1994 union membership decreased from 4.93 million total members to 2 million in absolute figures, or from 20 percent of the workforce to less than ten (Bibes and Mouriaux 1990; Jefferys 1996; Hancké 1997). Compared to other Rhineland and Scandinavian countries, the labor movement is more activist, confrontational, and virulent on the one hand, but also in stronger decline and *feeble, particularly outside the rapidly shrinking public sector*. While French unions are generally highly centralized and hierarchical, they often cannot effectively control the rank and file. Internal cohesion is very low. This incapacity to control grassroots activists and suppress wildcat strikes commenced by them or nonunionized workers coupled with the union movement's weakness in sheer numbers renders it an unattractive negotiation partner for business. The CFDT has recently endeavored on a more cooperation-oriented approach with the state and the employers, being particularly willing to cooperate in the *refondation sociale*. Although its membership has consequently increased according to its own figures (EIRO 2004), some skepticism about the viability of this strategy seems appropriate.

---

[1] According to 1994 figures, union membership in total figures is down to 2 million from 4.93 million in 1976. CFDT (500,000) is ahead of the CGT (480,000), the FO (400,000), the FEN (250,000), the CGC (200,000) and the CFTC (170,000). In 1976, the top three positions were as follows: CGT, FO, CFDT (Jefferys 1996). By 2003, the overall ranking had not changed, however, both the CGT and especially the CFDT had claimed to have recruited new members, bringing the CFDT up to 889,000 (EIRO 2004; http://www.eiro.eurofound.eu.int/2004/03/update/tn0403105u.html).

On the employers' side, companies are organized in the unitary CNPF (*Conseil national du patronat française*—National Council of French Employers), recently renamed to Medef (*Mouvement des entreprises françaises*—Movement of French Companies). Originally founded in 1919 and resurrrected in 1945, it is subdivided into eighty-four sectoral affiliates as well as regional subdivisions. CNPF/Medef had traditionally issued recommendations for wage negotiations, but has retired from this practice in the wake of the growing importance of company level bargaining. In fact, collective bargaining never occurs at the national level. This might be a reflection of the power relation between very powerful sectoral associations and a financially dependent umbrella organization. Medef often appears more as an interest association, lobbying group, and think tank than as an employer association, even though it combines all of these roles (Bunel 1997; Hancké 1997). It is much more influential politically and more attractive even to SMEs than the CGPME (*Confédération Générale du Patronat des Petits et Moyennes Entreprises*—General Confederation of Employers in SMEs).

The state plays a strong role in French industrial relations. Not only does it act as an *ersatz union* through occasional bouts of legislative initiatives, as mentioned previously, labor conditions are also highly legalistic, regulated through the encyclopedic Labor Law (*Code du Travail*). While the social partners are consulted on certain legislative measures regarding labor and social policy, these consultations are in no way binding. The state feels under absolutely no obligation to consider them binding. Since the beginning of collective bargaining in France in 1936, the state generally does not intervene directly into collective bargaining. Yet it does determine unilaterally the national minimum wage (SMIC—*salaire minimum industrielle de croissance*), created in 1958, which then becomes legally binding for all employees employed directly by French companies. It may also, based on the initiative of either the Ministry of Labor or one of the social partners, extend (*extension*) a collectively agreed framework of sectoral minimum wages (*grite*), based on level of qualification to cover *all* companies within either a certain sector or a certain region. The Ministry of Labor may also declare the *grite* generally binding for *related* professional sectors, a process known as *enlargissement* (Goetschy 1999: 358ff.).

In sum, French industrial relations are characterized by antagonistic relations between militant, yet relatively weak unions, a traditionally paternalistic *patronat*, and a highly interventionist state, occasionally acting as an 'ersatz union'. The state creates the arenas in which bargaining takes place through legislative measures. It intervenes into wage-setting through the minimum wage and by declaring wage accords universally applicable. It draws unions into consultative bodies at the national level and has strengthened their position at the company level. Yet unions remain fragmented, and have undergone a massive decline in membership. Furthermore, since 1945, but especially since the 1960s, civil servants have become enmeshed with managers in the private sector, opening up broad avenues for potent informal business influence on economic policymaking as has become recently apparent.

Germany

Traditionally, German industrial relations are characterized by highly institution-alized and legally embedded (*verrechtlicht*) interaction between representatives of labor and business, with government playing a supervisory, yet noninterventionist role.

A noteworthy aspect is co-determination (*Mitbestimmung*) of workers in man-agerial decisions. Workers' representatives compose one-third of the delegates on the company's supervisory board in companies with more than 500 employees, while parity of representation is mandated in companies with more than 2,000 employees, in accordance with the 1951 Co-Determination Act (*Mitbestimmungsge-setz*), amended in 1976. The second component of the dual structure of workers' interest representation is the 1952 Works Constitution Act (*Betriebsverfassungsge-setz*). In companies with more than five employees, these workers must be repre-sented at the workplace level through works councils (*Betriebsräte*), which negotiates with management at the macro level concerning issue-areas such as personnel decisions and safety and health regulations. While German works coun-cils have more rights than do their Austrian counterparts, unions are not as well represented among its members[2] as in Austria, commanding only about 80 percent of seats (Jakobi et al. 1998: 211), as opposed to 90 percent in Austria.

Representatives of the 12 sectoral subdivisions of the unions and the 32 sectoral subdivisions of the employers' organizations come together to determine wages in annual rounds of collective bargaining. This is sometimes done alternatively at the regional level, as in the metal industry, but never at the national level (Katzenstein 1987). Traditionally, the company level has also played a negligible role, though this may start to change (Heinisch 2000), as major companies, notably Siemens and VW, negotiate separate agreements that may diverge significantly and in turn have spill-over effects. Commonly, the metal union IG Metall and the corresponding employers organization Gesamtmetall in the southwestern state of Baden-Würt-themberg set the national precedent for consequent rounds of wage bargaining in other sectors.[3] Government agencies intervene only in cases of dispute, in which case an arbitration court (*Schiedsgericht*) becomes involved which attempts to prod both sides to settle on a compromise solution. As a general principle, however, the autonomy of employers and unions to settle on wage levels (*Tarifautonomie*) is being upheld and respected by the state a laid down in the 1949 Collective Agree-ment Act (*TVG—Tarifvertragsgesetz*) and Article 9 III of the Basic Law. These rounds of collective bargaining, in the course of which wage brackets (*Tarifverträge*) and

---

[2] 21.9 percent of works councils members are nonunionists.

[3] Baden-Würthemberg is home to the headquarters and substantial production facilities of Bosch, Porsche, and Daimler-Benz (since 1998 Daimler-Chrysler). Since this region and this sector is thus particularly export-oriented, business considers crucial wage regulation in this sector. However, in 1999 the employers in the southwest metal sector publicly announced that their settlement would no longer 'send a signal' (Stumpfe, quoted in Heinisch 2000).

other work-related benefits are being established, carry significant weight because their results cover approximately 80 percent of all German employees. Union membership in Germany is a mere 32.2 percent of the work force or 9.35 million (Jacobi et al. 1998: 201). Resulting from the emphasis on sectoral and regional bargaining, sectoral unions are much more powerful than the umbrella association DGB (Markovits 1986; Thelen 1991). However, the BDA does issue wage recommendations to its members and attempts to coordinate their policy more actively. Yet in both associations, the sectoral metal groups are the strongest, with Gesamtmetall disposing of substantial funds used to supply member companies in cases of strike (Jacobi et al. 1998: 205).

Unions and employer association influence extends beyond their actual clientele because they negotiate the sector-specific comprehensive wage agreements (*Tarifverträge*). Although only a small fraction were declared legally binding—most of them in the construction industry—most employers find it in their interests to adhere to the negotiated terms, especially since the 'decisions of collective bargainers actually follow the labor market' (Jacobi et al. 1998: 217) and usually constitute compromise solutions.[4]

The Netherlands, Belgium, and Luxembourg

The three Benelux countries are characterized by a peculiar mixture of French *étatisme* and German neocorporatism. Generally, the three come closer to the German model, given the relatively powerful union movements. However, state intervention into the economy in general and collective bargaining in particular (or at least the threat thereof) are common features both of the Netherlands and Luxemburg. Belgian industrial relations are highly legalistic. The Belgian government has restrained the room for maneuver left to the social partners and has placed them 'under house arrest' (Vilrokx 1998) in the 1990s. This brings Belgium

---

[4] Wage agreements can be declared generally binding or 'universally applicable' (*allgemeinverbindlich*) by the Ministry of Labor. However, the procedure is notably different from the French *extension*: According to Article 5 of the TVG the Ministry of Labor and Social Affairs may declare an agreement universally applicable if and only if the simple majority of a commission at the Ministry composed of three representatives of the employers (the BDA and two other sectoral associations, but never from the sector concerned) and three of the union (the DGB and two other sectoral associations, again not from the sector itself) known as the *Tarifausschuss* has agreed. Of 51,500 agreements in Germany, only 498 were declared universally applicable as of October 2000. In the construction sector, a general framework on labor conditions (not implying wage levels!) had been declared generally applicable as of February 3, 1981, one on sectoral education as 29 January 1987, and one for sectoral social funds on December 20, 1999 (BAS 2000: 3, 16). The question of universal applicability became a crucial one in attempts to devise a national response strategy because any minimum wage for posted workers had to jump through this institutional loop, otherwise it could have been struck down as discriminatory by the ECJ, since it would have applied to foreign companies only, but not to their German counterparts. This point will be discussed in more detail in Chapter 3.

somewhat closer to the French rather than the German model. All three countries have small, open economies that host a number of powerful multinational corporations alongside a numerically predominantly *Mittelstand*. Given the economic, political, and cultural implications of being situated in the borderland region between France and Germany, all three countries are traditionally ardent supporters of trade liberalization. Since the 1980s, the Netherlands in particular have also shifted towards a very pronouncedly liberal position in terms of the role of the state in the economy, more restrictive and 'enabling' social and welfare policies (Visser and Hemerijck 1998).

In all three Benelux countries, the union movements are divided into a Socialist and a Catholic branch, along with additional subdivisions that vary by country. In the Netherlands, the CNV (Christian National Workers' Federation—*Christelijk Nationaal Vakverbond*) and the FNV (Federation of Dutch Trade Unions—*Federatie Nederlandse Vakbeweging*) coexist.[5] The Catholic General Christian Trade Union ACV/CSC (*Algemeen Christlijk Vakverbond/Confédération des Syndicats Chrétiens*) and the Socialist General Belgian Trade Union Federation ABVV/FGTB (*Algemeen Belgisch Vakverbond/Fédération Générale du Travail de Belgique*) compete in Belgium.[6] Tiny Luxembourg has both the originally socialist Independent Trade Union Confederation of Luxembourg OGB-L (*Onofhängege Gewerkschaftsbond Lëtzebuerg*) and the Luxemburg Confederation of Christian Trade Unions LCGB (*Lëtzebuerger Chrëstleche Gewerkschaftsbond*).[7] While unions organize around 50 percent of the work force in Luxembourg and 60 percent in Belgium, this figure only stands at 25 percent in the Netherlands.

Employers, by contrast, enjoy a relatively high degree of organizational coverage, yet were traditionally hampered by an internal division and even organizational atomization in the Netherlands and a continuing linguistic cleavage in Belgium. This trend has recently been reversed in the Netherlands, following the famous 1982 Wassenaar Agreement. The two major employer association NCW and VNO merged, creating the Federation of Dutch Employers VNO-NCW (*Vereniging van*

---

[5] These two are the numerically most important (membership figures stood at 1,226,000 and 355,000 respectively in 2003; EIRO 2004). The FNV has abandoned its socialist roots, which, in combination with a general decrease of the religious and ideological cleavages in Holland, has rendered it the most important union. However, there is also the white collar union VHP with 160,560 and the General Union Federation AVC with 104,885 members. In the construction sector, there is also the so-called Black Corps of Workers *Zwarte Vakverbond,* a specific sectoral union.

[6] Unlike Holland, the Christian union in Belgium is numerically more important, boasting 1,201,000 members versus 1,637,000 members respectively in 2003. Note that there is also a smaller liberal union, the General Confederation of Liberal Trade Unions (*Algemene Centrale der Libeale Vakverbonden van Belgie/Confédération Générale des Syndicats Libéraux de Belgique*), which united 223,000 members in 2003. Unlike the two larger unions, this latter one has been more successful in resisting the trend towards a disintegration along linguistic cleavages (EIRO 2004).

[7] In addition, there is a separate union for private sector white collar employees, the FEP/FITC and a Neutral Trade Union of Luxembourg NGL (*Neutral Gewerkschaft Lëtzebuerg*) that organizes individual crafts unions (EIRO 2004).

Nederlandse Ondernemers—Nederlands Christelijke Werkgeversverbond). Collective agreements can be extended by the Ministry of Labor to cover all employees in the economy which are not bound by any company-level agreement under the terms of the 1937 Law on Extension and Nullification of Collective Agreements (interview NIMinLabSocAff 2000). The 1927 Law on Collective Agreements renders such agreements legally binding on member firms of signatory employer association. Thus, as in Germany, companies have to pay their employees the wages specified in this agreement regardless of whether or not these are union members or not, thereby posing a similar free riding incentive as in Germany.

In Belgium, there is likewise little internal rivalry. The main Federation of Belgian Enterprises VBO/FEB (*Verbond van Belgische Ondernemingen/ Fédération des Entreprises de Belgique*) is subdivided into 36 sectoral associations.

In Luxembourg, the main Federation of Luxemburg Industrialists FEDIL (*Fédération des Industriels Luxembourgeois*) organizes most employers (Tunsch 1998).

For collective bargaining, the sectoral level is the most important arena in all three countries. In Luxemburg and Belgium industrial relations are legalistic. Thus, the Luxembourg Ministry of Labor can declare universally applicable a sectoral collective bargaining agreement as set forth in the 1965 law on collective agreement while in Belgium agreements by the National Labor Council (*Nationale Arbeidraad/ Conseil National du Travail*), which commonly cover topics such as working time, wages, holiday regulations, are commonly declared legally binding and thus royal decrees by the Ministry of Labor.

The Nordic Countries: Sweden, Norway, Denmark, Finland

The Nordic countries Sweden, Norway, Denmark, and Finland have been commonly considered highly neocorporatist. This characterization is based on the traditionally high degree of coverage by unions and employers, peak level negotiations, and high levels of autonomy from the state in wage bargaining. Unlike the Benelux countries, which have certain common features but differ significantly on a number of dimensions, it was accurate to speak of one Nordic model in different varieties until the 1980s, characterized by Social Democratic hegemony, an activist 'decommodifying social policy', a substantial public sector and frequent government intervention into the economy, and powerful trade unions. However, recent developments complicate or even eradicate this traditional sketch of the Scandinavian model—a decentralization of wage negotiations and the exit of employers from neocorporatist associations in Sweden (Pontusson 1997; Dolvik and Martin 1997; Kjellberg 1998; Due et al. 1995), less pronounced in Denmark, coupled with an embrace of more liberal economic policy under the conservative governments of Sweden and Denmark in the 1980s and early 1990s, and EMU-induced cuts in social spending and privatization programs all seem to point towards a move away from the classic Scandinavian model towards something resembling more the German model. While Norway and Finland seemed to follow the Swedish flirt with neoliberalism in the 1980s, Norway has since moved back towards classic Social Democracy coupled with statist elements, no doubt helped along by substantial oil revenues.

While the Nordic countries have successfully transformed themselves from being producers of agricultural commodities to filling sophisticated industrial (niche) markets, Finland proved somewhat of a laggard. This shift was helped along by the 'Nordic model', which grew out of 'peace accords' between unitary employers and unions in the 1930s to promote economic and political stability and escape tendencies towards socialist or fascist totalitarianism present in other European countries at the time (Katzenstein 1985).

It operated on the basis of the following factors: a relative power parity between employers and unions, Social Democratic hegemony, unitary and highly centralized unions and employer association with a high degree of coverage, particular union strength not least derived from the administration of retirement funds, pivotal agreements at the national level acting as umbrellas for more specific sectoral and company-level agreements, a 'high trust' environment among the social partners, and a commitment to wage equality across sectors correlated with a universalistic welfare state aimed at 'decommodifying labor' (Esping-Andersen 1990). It is important to note that *Tarifautonomie* existed de facto but certainly not de jure in Sweden and Denmark. In fact, because of SAF's more confrontational attitude in bargaining, state mediation and arbitration has actually increased over time in Sweden. State intervention in wage bargaining and macroeconomic policy formulation more broadly was and is not uncommon in Norway and Finland, either.

The organizational structure of unions and employers varies little prima facie: unitary secular union movements, (*Landsorganisationen*—LO in Sweden, *Landsorganisasjonen i Norge*—LO in Norway, *Landsorganisationen i Danmark*—LO in Denmark, and *Suomen Ammattiliitojen Keskusjärjestö*—SAK in Finland) and their respective sectoral subdivisions face the employers association (SAF—*Svenska Arbeidsgivarföreningen* in Sweden, NHO—*Nærignslivets Hovedorganisasjon* in Norway, DA—*Dansk Arbejdsgiverforening* in Denmark, and TT—*Teollisuus ja Työnantajat* in Finland).

Despite the many similarities, differences amongst the various systems exist and will be briefly discussed. This analysis is all the more pertinent as recent developments have undermined the relative unitary character of the Nordic countries' systems of industrial relations and macroeconomic governance.

Sweden—and more recently Finland as well—is host to a number of important multinational corporations, while always a small open economy, has grown increasingly liberal in its domestic macroeconomic policies. It was not least due to the growing pressure of these large internationally active companies that wage bargaining became more decentralized and liberalized with many observers proclaiming the death of the 'Swedish model' (Pontusson 1997). However, other factors played a role as well: LO faced growing competition from white-collar unions TCO and SACO (Kjellberg 1998: 78), and wage increases were effectively decoupled from productivity growth causing inflation and rendered international competitiveness more difficult. The employers became increasingly more neoliberal in the 1980s, withdrawing first from central-level bargaining and subsequently from all neocorporatist institutions. In receding from a self-regulatory modus vivendi based on what I call *gentlemen's agreements*—resting and being nurtured by on the high trust environment and relative power equality among social partners—the SAF involuntarily opened the path for more government intervention in the 1990s leading to a series of wage freezes, wage decrees and, ironically, culminating in a short-lived revival of tripartism in the form of the 1990–3 government commission on wage mediation (Rehnberg Commission). The SAF continues to push for a decentralization of wage bargaining as a means to break union power. Meanwhile, the Swedish trade union movement is suffering severe attrition, internal separation and division between blue-collar and white-collar employees, none of which is counterbalanced by a slightly increasing tendency of the state to prod the social partners into wage agreements by threatening intervention or offering mediation (Dolvik and Martin 1997: 304ff.).

In Denmark, a trend towards decentralization in wage bargaining and a more and Knudsen neoliberal policy direction seemed discernible as early as the early 1980s (Lind and Knudsen 1998) in a political economy and a system of industrial relations very similar to Sweden. However, it seems as though these developments have had little lasting impact. Membership in unions (90 percent of workforce) and in employer association (50 percent) remains high (Danish Ministry of Labour 1991). In fact, state interventionism seems to recede and the essentially voluntarist model of industrial relations with de facto *Tarifautonomie* is thus still predominant in Denmark (Lind and Knudsen 1998). The Danish model thus remains more constant than is true of Sweden.

In Norway, after a brief flirt with neoliberalism and a consequent shift away from concertation at the national level in the mid-1980s, more recent developments point into the opposite direction. Indeed, state interventionism has reappeared in the governance of the Norwegian political economy. Undoubtedly the economic difficulties experienced in the 1980s helped provide a conducive climate to the government's initiative to revive tripartism in the form of a national level Solidarity Alternative, giving birth to a Employment Commission in 1992 (Dølvik and Martin 1997) to discuss steps to curtail inflationary wage growth. Norwegian tripartite neocorporatism coupled with substantial state interventionism into the economy has thus actually experienced a revival in the 1990s. It must be realized that this development hinged on three factors, some of which somewhat idiosyncratic: First, a perceived failure of 'market-led' wage determination and a more general association between neoliberal experiments and economic problems, providing fertile intellectual ground for state interventionism. Second, Norway has a long history of state interventionism in the political economy and industrial relations more specifically. The state is thus relatively powerful vis-à-vis trade unions and employers. Third, revived concertation occurred under the impression of the need for austerity measures and wage moderation. Norway as a de facto EU and de jure EEA member was preparing for full EU membership in 1995, which necessitated adjustment to the Maastricht criteria. Membership was only prevented by the negative popular referendum.

In Finland, national level tripartite concertation on macroeconomic issues has a long history. Social pacts have been used as a successful tool in dealing with the challenges involved in shifting from a predominantly agricultural economy to the predominance of the tertiary sector, losing the most important trading partner with the disintegration of the Soviet Union in 1991, and meeting the criteria for membership in the EU and the EMU in 1995 and 1999 respectively. Such tripartite agreements have permitted for a downward shift of wage bargaining to lower levels of negotiation (Kauppinen 1998), yet discussions on major policy issues continue to be held at the national level. One might thus regard Finland as yet another case of the survival of organized capitalism and neocorporatist institutions, which had to cope with the external economic pressures of EU membership and the Maastricht criteria, and a very different external environment.

Appendix B
A Discussion of the Two Institutionalist Approaches and a Detailed Introduction to the Hypotheses Derived from Them

A Brief Introduction to Historical Institutionalism

The historical institutionalist approach highlights the historical roots and legacy of institutions. While organizations arise under the influence of social and political forces at time of inception, they may also act as intermediaries (Steinmo et al. 1992) between societal demands and policy outcome. Political phenomena, developments, degrees of internal power configuration, even social and ethnic stratification, and indeed the very structure of institutions themselves (Thelen and Steinmo 1992: 2–4), can be accounted for by different historical paths taken following key trajectories or 'critical junctures' (Collier and Collier 1991) in the political history. Institutions continue to shape policy based on structurally institutionalized choices made in their design (Skocpol 1992), thus perpetuating 'path dependency' (Krasner 1983; Pierson 2000) or "preexisting legacies of public policies" (Weir and Skocpol 1985: 109).

Indeed, the re-emerging field of comparative political economy similarly emphasizes the structuring role of historically shaped politico-economic institutions, though commonly without explicitly referring to this approach. This approach implies the following questions for this study: To what extent do such past legacies inform the preferences of trade unions, employers and governments regarding wages for posted workers? Will the past preference of some employers prevail to avoid conflict or to pursue a protectionist stance vis-à-vis foreign companies entering the market? Will the past preference of unions to guarantee equal wages for all employees shape the union position on posted workers? Will a historical legacy of Euroskepticism or Euroenthusiasm, liberalism or protectionism, continue to shape the decision-making of political parties composing the governments? Regarding strategies or actions, will past patterns of cooperative decision-making between social partners continue to shape actors in Scandinavia and Austria?

An important strand of this approach stresses the role of ideas in (re)configuring institutions, particularly if they happen to arrive under amiable circumstances, such as moments of crisis or 'critical junctures' (Collier and Collier 1991).[1] The potential role of such ideas will therefore be examined regarding all actors. We need to extract such ideas from patterns of past behavior and ideological preference.

---

[1] Academic experts may play a particularly pivotal role first in the formulation and later in the dissemination of ideas, an insight first formulated by Keynes (1936), and later re-discovered in the wake of the constructivist turn in international relations theory (Checkel 1993; Risse-

Unfortunately, it is very difficult to predict the occurrence of a critical juncture ex ante. Regarding the cases examined in this study, unification, the fall of the Iron Curtain, and accession to the EU may have served as such major moments of transformation in Germany and Austria (and, by extension, Sweden and Finland). For this reason, these countries deserve particular scrutiny for signs of the role of ideas. The difficulty encountered in defining moments of crisis or critical junctures point to a more general potential problem associated with the historical institutionalist approach, namely a certain tautological tendency, pointed out by Peters (1999).[2]

A Brief Introduction to Rational Choice Institutionalism

The rational choice approach is heavily indebted to neoclassical economics and, as a consequence, assumes a certain relation between preferences, beliefs, resources,

Kappen 1994; Katzenstein 1996; Adler 1997). Scholars in this tradition had discovered institutions earlier as 'regimes' (Krasner 1983) and discussed them as constraining and regulating arenas of interest intermediation, self-perpetuating even after the decline of the hegemon (Keohane 1984). For instance, the role of ideas as 'cognitive roadmaps' (Goldstein and Keohane 1993) has led to a gradual intellectual hegemony of the monetarism of the 1980s over the Keynesianism of the 1970s to (Hall 1989) and to a subsequent often radical recast of many public institutions under the banner of reinventing the role of government. Another often used example of the role of ideas in international relations theory is the peaceful reorientation of Gorbachev's Soviet Union in its foreign and domestic policy (Checkel 1997; Evangelista 1999).

[2] In continuing to identify some weaknesses of this approach, let us consider some practical examples. In Katzenstein's (1985) work on small states, the 'peace treaties' between capital and labor signed in the early 1930s are critical junctures. Given the economic and political crisis situation of Europe at the time, concerted macroeconomic policymaking seemed like an adequate way to avoid the economic difficulties and political radicalization which ushered in the rise of fascism in Italy and Germany. But then how do we account for the rise and persistence of corporatism in Austria, which was subject first to domestic then to forcefully imported fascism and thus missed this critical juncture by about twenty years? There are more outliers: How can we account for the gradual unraveling of centralized neocorporatism in Sweden in the 1980s, but its concurrent revival in the Netherlands despite similar international constraints of increased economic internationalization?

While Hall demonstrates the historical embeddedness of the divergent macroeconomic directions France and Britain took in the early 1980s, the subsequent gradual withdrawal of the French state from *plannification* and *dirigisme* seems to negate any notion of path dependency. The influence of ideas on political institutions and developments, nourished by the new theoretical turn in the international relations literature towards constructivism after the end of the Cold War, is often conceived of in a highly abstract fashion (Goldstein and Keohane 1993) and illustrated with an excessive focus on only one empirical case, the shift in policy orientation of the Soviet Union in the 1980s (Checkel 1993, Risse-Kappen 1994). When and under what circumstances will which ideas become implemented? Though the concept of 'veto points' (Immergut 1992) may appear helpful at first in responding to this challenge, the problem with it is that it is difficult to predict under what circumstances which veto point will become effective.

and actions (Elster 1987: 68). Individuals pursue their preferences, motivated by rational weighing of options given costs and limitations. Rational choice institutionalism (RCI) either takes institutions as exogenously given, which influence the rules of the game (North 1990). These then exert pressure on players to adapt their behavior and thus affect the incentive and preference structure (North 1981, 1984; Olson 1965, 1982; Bates 1981, 1983; Tsebelis 1990). Alternatively, institutions may be conceptualized as endogenous, as the result of attempts to promote utility maximization and to discourage rent seeking (North 1981, 1984; Shepsle 1989; Shepsle and Weingast 1995; Tsebelis 1995). They have often grown out of attempts to overcome collective action problems (Axelrod 1984; Ostrom 1990). Hence, Shepsle (1986) distinguishes between institutions that can *provide* an equilibrium of policy outcome (institutional equilibrium) and those institutions that are *stable themselves* (equilibrium institutions).

In sum, individuals are both constrained and influenced by the institutions or rules of the game they partake in. They will have to adapt their strategies accordingly to maximize utility successfully. These motives can be usefully adapted to explore the preferences of actors in this study. Relevant questions inspired by RCI include: What is the desired rational choice of employers and unions in terms of wages for posted workers? Which equilibrium do they seek to achieve? Given that preference formation will be informed by utility maximization, which strategies will be pursued to achieve higher or lower wage levels respectively?

As with HI, a potential problem with RCI is the tautological *post hoc* justification (acknowledged by Tsebelis 1990: 42) of certain choices as 'rational'.

Hypotheses Flowing from the Rational Choice Institutionalist Approach

RCI highlights the desire to maximize utility. However, institutions act as 'rules of the game' that need to be taken into consideration in the process. The game theoretically oriented thrust and Tsebelis' notion of 'nested games' (1990) remind us that the structure of such games may be very opaque and complex. Based on this perspective, what type of concrete actions and policy preferences can we expect from the key actors? The hypotheses about preferences generated by RCI should hold true across all countries. We shall return later to the possibility of more complex and complicated multilevel games being played.

Employers' associations in all high-wage countries both at the sectoral and the general level seek utility maximization and thus profit maximization. They represent their members' interests. These companies seek to maximize their profits. In a service sector industry like construction, wages make up a substantial portion of operating expenditures. Thus, *prima facie* employers can be expected to *push for the lowest wage possible for posted workers*. Still assuming the same preference—profit maximization—an alternative strategy thus becomes conceivable: *concede to a small*

wage differential between wages for domestically employed and posted workers to avoid a
ruinous downward wage-price spiral.

What Strategy can We Expect Employers to Pursue to Attain their Preference?

Either they pursue cost minimization, which translates into the pursuit of a maximal gulf between the wages for posted workers and those for directly employed workers. In that case, employers will push for minimal regulation. In case of a national response strategy being devised, business will either obstruct passage, minimize the efficiency and coverage of such response strategy *or* enshrine its preferences into this strategy by formalizing a wage differential if the default status quo is favorable to its position. We would expect the interests of sectoral associations and national umbrella associations to coincide because lower wage costs for one sector might have a spillover effect in the form of a downward wage drift.

Alternatively, employers can concede to a minimal wage gulf between posted workers and directly employed workers so as to avoid setting in motion a ruinous downward wage-price spiral. In such case, they would strive for an equilibrium of a higher wage for posted workers and be more conciliatory towards a national response strategy that enshrines such regulation.

Trade unions represent the interests of their due-paying members, or even by virtue of representative monopoly the interests of *all* employees regardless of their membership status. They attempt to 'improve' working conditions including wages. Utility maximization consists of raising their members' wage levels and fending off challenges to these salaries. *Trade unions can be expected to support the maintenance or upward amendment of high labor standards and wages of their clientele.*

What strategy will trade unions employ? First and foremost, they will seek to guarantee or even increase their clientele's wages. However, by their very nature posted workers might not be considered part of their clientele. The fact that unions are representing free riders has been characterized as part of their distinct 'logic of collective action' (Offe and Wiesenthal 1980). One potential strategy might thus be to neglect posted workers entirely. This is admittedly a short-sighted and even precarious strategy. A more long-term-oriented strategy would consist of support-ing a national response strategy that prevents the disintegration and stratification of the wage structure into several tiers. Trade unions might fear functional *replace-ment* of domestic employees by posted workers. This would cause downward pres-sure on wages, a stronger bargaining position for business, and a loss of influence for unions. *Trade unions will therefore likely support a highly effective, all-encompassing national response strategy to be implemented quickly preserving a maximum level of wages and extending the* lois de police *as far as possible.* Presumably, this strategy will be the same for all trade unions in all high-wage member states. *Alternatively, they neglect posted workers and concentrate on wages for directly domestically employed workers.* The union could then forego a closure of the wage differential in order to receive higher wages for its domestic constituents in return.

Government also maximizes utility, though it is difficult to predict *ex ante* how utility is defined. In addition, government is not a unitary actor. Although the Ministry of Labor is generally responsible for drafting legislative initiatives in labor market policy, governments can potentially be engaged in a myriad nested games: appealing to particular parts of the electorate; internal rifts, games, and trade-offs in a coalition government; games and trade-offs with particular labor market interest associations. For simplicity sake and to avoid *post hoc* justifications, a very straightforward economic interest based definition of utility maximization will be used. Thus, utility maximization is interpreted to mean that governments dominated by the political left support implementation of a national response strategy avoiding a wage differential, while a government dominated by the political right (or liberal parties) will endorse a wage differential as a means towards liberalization of the wage structure.

Other factors, such as internal games among coalition governments are possible, yet impossible to predict *ex ante*. Concessions by government towards either labor or capital are incorporated in that a more business-friendly attitude is assumed among a conservative/liberal government, while a more labor-friendly attitude is assumed under a leftist/social democratic government. As *Tarifautonomie* exists in some countries *de jure* (Germany) and in others *de facto* (Austria, Denmark) government has to accept this institution as a constraining rule in choosing its strategy. It cannot intervene directly into wage-setting or will be very hesitant to do so. Thus, it either has to remain on the sidelines and merely influence the social partners to accept the response strategy it favors or else implement a response strategy which does not impinge directly on the *Autonomie* of unions and employers. If the government acts unilaterally, it might be prudent, though it is not required, to consult with the social partners.

Hypotheses for Actors in France

In France, trade unions have been traditionally characterized by militancy, a confrontational stance, strong commitment to the respective ideological roots, and organizational atomization (Mouriaux 1994). The issue of wages for posted workers naturally affects the clientele of all major trade unions. Despite their ideological differences, it is unlikely that any union will taciturnly accept a segmentation of the wage structure and thus a long-term undermining of its members' interests without any sort of compensation or trade-off. Yet the strategies employed to defend their members' interests will differ depending on the underlying ideological orientation: the CGT has traditionally refused to sign sectoral or national wage agreements with management and only most recently has begun to do so at the enterprise level. We expect it to take the most radical and militant position and most likely to favor industrial action if necessary. The CGT-FO has become more pragmatic over time, but still is wedded to a radical Socialist perspective, making compromise and trade-off deals with business equally unlikely. By contrast, the CFDT and especially the CFTC are characterized by a much more pragmatic attitude and have been more willing to bargain with employers. If it is perceived to serve the long-term interests of their clientele, the latter two unions may be inclined to engage in a trade-off or to strike a deal with employers. Critical junctures or 'ideas' do not seem to be relevant in this context, unless we are willing to refer to the divergent ideological positions as 'ideas'. However, these are very much historically embedded and possess a long-standing tradition. A sudden change is therefore highly unlikely.

Given the internal division of the French trade union movement, the overarching goal may be similar, but the more militant unions on the one hand and the more accommodationist unions on the other may employ different strategies. While all trade unions will seek to guarantee their clientele's wages, the less radical CFDT and CFTC are more likely to strike a deal with business. It is therefore possible to imagine a situation in which the union position is undermined by employers playing off the different unions against each other (*divide et impera*).

The French employers (CNPF/Medef) continue to be wary of engaging in negotiations with trade unions, especially the more radical ones. Given the polar structure of the French construction sector—and indeed the economy as a whole—we expect the difference between larger, internationally active corporations and SMEs to be particularly crucial. Regionally based, politically weak SMEs have traditionally stood in the shadow of the larger dominant 'national champions'. Over time, subcontracting along chains of dependent SMEs has become more prevalent both in manufacturing and the service sector. The domestic SMEs are not necessarily interested in lower wages for posted workers, because such competitive advantage would enable their foreign competitors to replace them in the subcontractor chain. Yet even the larger French construction companies may not favor further liberalization of the wage structure, given that the status quo already affords them with substantial leverage on SMEs, *including the ability to apply downward pressure on wages on the lower ends of the subcontracting chain.* Larger companies value this potential to apply pressure, but do not necessarily push for a national response strategy enshrining a segmentation of the wage structure, given that they can realize savings under the current distribution of power structures. Therefore, it is not essential to enshrine such cost advantage into a response strategy. The French employers have also been traditionally characterized as 'protectionist' (Ebbinghaus and Visser 1994) and thus not necessarily been embracing liberalization. In terms of the 'ideational' attitude towards the process of European integration and concurrent market liberalization employers traditionally have maintained some skepticism, though this attitude has begun to change since the mid-1990s, just as the balance of power between government and business has shifted notably in favor of the latter (Schmidt 1996a; Levy 1999; Hancké 1999). The influence of 'ideas' of more 'pro market' orientation on French business has thus grown only recently. Internal competition is not the highest priority of French business, since corporate structures of larger companies are characterized by cross-holdings and interwoven multisector conglomerates with substantial involvement by large institutional owners such as banks and insurances (Hancké 1999). The relatively stable oligopolist distribution of power may thus very well impede the all-out competition neoclassical economic theory would predict. This in turn has pivotal implications for business' overall attitude. If major companies are unwilling to rock the boat and neoliberal pro market 'ideas' play little role, the cost advantage afforded by posted workers becomes less attractive, since such downward pressure on wages also implies *increased competitive pressure* both from foreign competitors and internally between companies employing foreign subcontractors and those which do not. A downward price spiral is set in motion, which need not be in the interest of business, since lower wages and increased competition also translate into lower overall price levels and thus lower profit margins!

In considering the historical position and attitude of French business, a hypothesis about their overall incentive structure is difficult to formulate. While French business obviously is not adverse to lowering wages and rendering the wage structure more 'flexible', it has traditionally not been influenced by neoliberal notions of deregulation and increased competition. In fact, given the threats of replacement by SMEs and the oligopolist structure of larger companies, increased competition and a downward spiral of wages and thus price levels might be considered as potentially precarious and jeopardizing the status quo, and not desirable. French business will therefore be less committed to advocating deregulation. However, given the historical hesitancy to negotiate with unions, business is also unlikely to use this issue as a bargaining chip in attempting to strike a deal. One might go so far as to say that due to the historically conditioned imbalance between business and labor in France, the former sees less of a pressing need to extract further concessions from labor.

The French government has historically managed to insulate itself from societal pressure relatively successful (Zysman 1977).

The close nexus between business and capital has been underlined in Chapter 2, along with the role of the state as an *ersatz* union, culminating in occasional great leaps forward in social and labor market policy. De facto government it is often influenced by the informal ties, interest overlaps, and the similar socialization and educational background of the business and government elite. Such common intellectual and mental mindset translates into a similar attitude towards problem-solving (Hancké 1999). While substantial congruency between government and business' interests exists, the question must be raised whether the issue of posted workers could have served to trigger a 'great leap forward'. Historical evidence indicates that such state intervention occurs only under certain circumstances: a major economic and/or political crisis, substantial ideological delegitimization of the previous government, and a left-wing government in power. To consider the 1993 *Loi Quinquennale* another instance of massive state intervention into social and labor market policy, as Goetschy (1998) does, only under reverse— right-wing liberal—ideological templates, inflates its importance and exaggerates the role of high unemployment as triggering a 'crisis'. If we do follow her argument, we would expect the state as an ersatz union to act 'under reverse templates', hence deregulating, liberalizing, and flexibilizing the labor market and reducing interest representation by labor.

A detailed historical analysis of actors' preferences has to examine the exact impact of ideological orientation on policy preferences. Therefore, relevant 'ideas' influencing policymakers are briefly assessed, particularly regarding the two central *topoi* of economic liberalization and immigration. Most recently, the old division between left and right seems to have been superseded in France by new cleavage lines, at least in regard to these issues and the related question of further European integration: the Communist PCF and the Greens (*Les Vertes*) are skeptical of both, just as the neo-Gaullist RPR and even more so the right-wing *Front Nationale* (FN). By contrast, the Socialist PS and the liberal UPR both seem to be more favorably inclined.

Traditionally, the neo-Gaullists perceived of European integration as a means of securing French influence over Europe, more specifically to keep in check Germany, while offering its own model of bureaucracy as one to emulate by the emerging administration in Brussels. But this embrace of a *Europe des patries* does not entail much enthusiasm for an intrusive European *super polis* or for Europe to serve as a vehicle for market liberalization. Similarly, the small UPR, though more favorably inclined towards liberalization, is by no means a staunch advocate of full-fledged neoliberalism. The two parties of the moderate right have been analyzed in close detail, since they formed the coalition government in 1993, at which time the national response strategy was implemented.[3]

In sum, the French government in the early 1990s would seem most inclined to act in relative autonomy from any influence by the labor market interest associations. However, there is a strong tilt towards the interests of business with which an informal nexus of interest *Akkordierung* exists. Few of the necessary conditions are present for the state taking 'a great leap forward' and acting in lieu of the union movement. The ideational/ideological orientation of the French neo-Gaullist right in power during the period under examination does not embrace market liberalization. Instead, skepticism towards economic liberalization prevails among the moderate right.

Hypotheses for Actors in Austria

In Austria, a unitary trade union movement exists since 1945 united underneath the umbrella of the ÖGB. There are no internal cleavages. The union, while pragmatic and willing to engage in negotiation and bargaining with business, has firmly and outspokenly represented the interests of its members in the past. Since the 1970s, it has conceded to wage moderation and a hard currency policy. However, it did so convinced that this would promote economic growth, limit inflation, ensure the

---

[3] The far right (FN) and far left (PCF and Greens) have been even more skeptical, if not overtly hostile, to European integration, market liberalization, and also immigration. The *Parti Socialiste* was characterized by a Keynesian, if not Socialist position, until its leadership performed a remarkable U-turn in economic policy orientation.

country's international competitiveness and thus serve the interests of its members in the long term (Scharpf 1991; Traxler 1996). Unlike its counterparts in Scandinavian countries, notably Sweden, the union has not opposed unequal wage distribution across sectors or between genders. Nevertheless, the migrant workers which were recruited to come to Austria from the 1960s onwards were always included in the standard wage brackets. Therefore, no tradition of a substandard wage sector exists. Based on historical precedent, the union can thus be expected to insist on the *minimization of a wage differential between wages of posted and domestic workers*. Though not renown for its militancy—partially due to legal restrictions on industrial action—the union movement is unified, hierarchical, tightly organized, and highly centralized. It thus 'carries a big stick' during negotiations. It appears unlikely that the Austrian union movement would take up any position other than *a strong advocacy of a comprehensive response strategy involving a maximum coverage of the* lois de police. Because of its degree of centralization and the subordination of the sectoral associations, the ÖGB will either take up and represent or repress entirely concerns of sectoral associations. There is little history of internal union strife in Austria, instead the umbrella organization takes up concerns from its sectoral members and represents them.[4]

Austrian employers, united in the *Wirtschaftskammer* (WK), have profited from wage moderation and unequal pay among sectors, but have not previously advocated a low-wage sector or used chains of subcontracting to apply downward pressure on wages, a result of the predominance in size *and* power of SMEs in the WK. Given compulsory membership in the WK and the 'one member–one vote' principle, the balance of power in the WK directly reflects the Austrian corporate structure. There has not been a pronounced difference between the interests of larger companies and SMEs historically, since larger companies tended to be part of the comprehensive public sector.

The degree of consensus that dominates decision-making on macroeconomic policymaking in Austria is remarkable and could perhaps be considered a perpetual and persistent *idea* shaping Austrian politics. Neoliberal tenets have made inroads into the ideational discourse only most recently. Even so, 'free market' ideas tend to be limited to the larger industry association VÖI, which is less central in importance, since it does not act as an employer association nor speak for the majority of business. This consensual compromise-oriented tradition of wage policymaking is a pivotal factor because it suggests an aversion to risk and certainly to outright

---

[4] We will note in passing that the historically unique situation of Austria as a new member negotiating its accession leads one analyst to speculate that it was during this 'window of opportunity' of the early 1990s (Eichhorst 1998), when social dumping was a prevalent (Falkner 1993, 1996) but not dominant popular concern, that the union enjoyed a situational bonus generated by circumstances. This argument is not compelling. By 1993, the Austrian labor movement had not only accepted EU membership, but was actively promoting this cause, urging its members to vote in favor during the referendum (Heinisch 1999). Under these conditions, the union could no longer use its agreement to membership, already once offered and even actively promoted, as a bargaining chip.

confrontation. Negotiated solutions are preferred by both sides. This makes a trade-off or some form of deal a likely outcome.

From a historical perspective, employers have learned to profit from wage differentiation and moderation, yet they have been held in check by a mighty union movement and, to a lesser extent, by a self-internalized tradition of compromise-seeking. We therefore *do not expect Austrian employers to risk full head-on clashes with unions over an issue they might not consider of chief importance, seeing that most companies have difficulties profiting from outsourcing due to their small size anyway. Instead, a compromise solution or a trade-off appears as a likely outcome.*

In the Second Republic, the Austrian government has always allotted great weight to the voice of the social partners, and historically has been closely inter-linked with them (*Personalunion*). Given the close connections and overlap between the Social Democrats and the unions on the one hand and the Peoples' Party and the employer association on the other, government—historically came close to being 'captured' by the social partners. Parliament was reduced to rubber-stamp bills already submitted to and approved by the two camps in advance. The balance has shifted slightly since the early 1980s (Tálos 1993; Traxler 1996; Kittel and Talos 1999; Karlhofer and Talos 1999) and even more so under the Black-Blue coalition since 1999. Nevertheless, the influence of unions and employers remains substantial in core sectors like economic, social, and labor market policy (Kittel and Talos 1999). While it is true that a government will be closer to the respective camp whose colors it flies, the long tradition of grand coalitions, covering the year 1993 in which the Austrian national response strategy was implemented, has meant that the government is unlikely to give undue preference to any one side. Once again, *compromise and consensus typically prevail.*

The role of ideas needs to be examined with close scrutiny, as EU accession in 1995 might constitute a 'critical juncture', as indicated earlier. Both major parties overcame their initial Euroskepticism by 1989, when application for membership was made. However, given the fears among the agricultural clientele of the People's Party who feared cheap agricultural exports flooding the Austrian market and their own small farms suffering from the common agricultural policy, EU membership was not an easy sell (Bieler 2000). The party is traditionally wedded to Catholic social values. Though staunchly conservative, the party did not endorse economic liberalization strongly until it switched coalition partners in 2000. By contrast, the Social Democrats had cautiously begun to embrace a more liberal economic orientation, since the privatizations of the 1980s under Chancellor Kreisky (Müller 1986). However, while Austrokeynesianism may have lost appeal to the leadership, the party's blue-collar rank and file were concerned about negative repercussion of EU membership (Falkner 1993; Bieler 2000).[5]

---

[5] Let us briefly consider the other political parties not in power in 1993: The Freedom Party (FPÖ) traditionally combined both a liberal and a nationalist ideological orientation. In 1984, Haider became party leader and has since abandoned (political) liberalism, though the economic policies supported by the party since it ascended to power in 2000 can be characterized

While EU accession did not afford the unions with additional bargaining power, some of the adaptations and consequences of membership were foreseen and the government attempted (and largely managed) to negotiate relatively favorable accession terms. The social partners would have certainly been granted the opportunity to leave their imprint upon the issue of posted workers, however, as has remained standard practice in the core 'turf' of social and labor market policy (Kittel and Talos 1999).

In sum, based on historical precedent the government can be expected to permit the social partners formidable influence in decision-making. Given that the government in 1993 was composed of a grand coalition, a consensual 'middle of the road' compromise seem the most likely outcome.

Hypotheses for Actors in Germany

In Germany, the trade union is unified under the auspices of the DGB, which presides over its sixteen sectoral associations less strictly its Austrian counterpart. Although the wage policy pursued by the unions has been less solidarist than in Scandinavian countries, the union has always sought to uphold maximum coverage of employees by standard wage brackets and prevented a stratification of the labor market. It supported the coverage of the 1960s wave of migrant workers by standard wage brackets. Based on historical precedence, there is no reason to assume any other preference than a *minimization of the potential wage differential*.

However, wage bargaining is conducted by sectoral associations, and sometimes innovative new labor market policy is designed at this level. *If other sectoral unions did not actively lend their support to the DGB and the sectoral construction union on this issue as they did not feel directly affected, overall union strength on this issue might have been compromised.* The DGB relies on the financial and logistical clout of its sectoral associations and is relatively weak on its own devices. This is not least a result of the federal structure and the deep distrust towards any centralized authority, pivotal leitmotifs in postwar West Germany.

The employer association BDA has traditionally found it advantageous to engage in collective bargaining and negotiations with the unions, though without ever reaching the Austrian commitment to consensus. Historically, the German employers endorsed a liberal *Ordnungspolitik*, while accepting improved workers' representation as a concession to the trade unions and the Social Democrats during the 1960s and 1970s. Ideologically, there are signs of departing from this traditional acceptance of established institutions, ideology, and mechanisms of the social

as populist neoliberal. The *Liberales Forum* split off from the Freedom Party in 1986 in protest over the movement towards a right-wing nationalist position and has sought to defend core liberal values, though it has never managed to secure much electoral support. The Austrian Green Party *Die Grünen*, a product of the antinuclear and pro-environmental citizens' movements of the 1980s, has similarly struggled to secure representation in parliament. Traditionally, the party remained the only party critical of EU membership and adverse to economic liberalization, though most recently this is beginning to change.

market economy in the 1990s, when both BDA and a vociferous president of larger business association BDI launched a public debate about Germany as a location for future investment (*Wirtschaftsstandort Deutschland*). The ensuing polemic revealed employers' discontent over presumably inflated wages, taxes, and social security charges. Both associations clearly flirted with neoliberal rhetoric and ideas, and became more aggressive in word and deed. The BDA was somewhat less outspoken in rhetorically charges against German model, given that the organization itself is very much a component and product thereof. In fact, the employer association faced declining membership figures as companies sought to avoid being bound by its wage agreements (*Verbandsflucht*), particularly in the East (Hassel 1999) and would have been ill-advised to question the relevance its own existence.

Though the German model of industrial relations and macoreconomic policy steering had offered business the advantages of social peace, low levels of industrial action, and accommodation of the strong unions and the Social Democrats, liberal ideology always persevered amongst business quarters and made a notable (re)-appearance in the neoliberal 'pro market' rhetoric of the 1990s.

Given this historical legacy, *German employers' preference thus lies in maximizing the wage differential*. This permits a legal escape option from what was portrayed as an excessive level both of wages and of non-wage labor-related costs. Forcing the unions into accepting wage moderation and possibly further future concessions based on a deteriorating bargaining position can also only be congruent with employers' interests.

Due to the tradition of *Tarifautonomie*, a sacred cow in Germany, government is most reluctant to take policy measures which are seen as treading on territory reserved for the social partners. While the independent *Bundesbank* makes known its preferences for the outcome of bargaining, these recommendations are not binding and therefore cannot be considered government intervention. The government has used other instruments for macroeconomic fine-tuning, notably tax policy. It has never relied on a substantial public sector. The German government cannot simply impose wages, which obviously affects the type of response strategy it can devise. It is fair to assume that government will be more open to the concerns of the labor market interest associations it is ideologically close to, yet state-society relations are in the center of an imaginary continuum between "overlap" in Austria on the one end and 'state insulation' in France on the other. From 1982 to 1998 Germany was governed by a coalition of the Christian Democrat CDU and the Free Liberal FDP. We will therefore briefly explore the ideological positions of both.

The CDU grew out of the Weimar Republic Catholic *Zentrumspartei*, and hence shares its intellectual heritage in Christian social thought with its Austrian counterpart.[6] As a catch-all *Volkspartei*, it encompasses a wide variety of social strata, including farmers, small business owners (*Mittelstand*) and even employees,

---

[6] Highlighting this ideological link to Christian social thought is the name of the Bavarian version of the CDU, the CSU or *Christliche Soziale Union*. Since this party is in perennial coalition with the CDU, the following observations apply to the CSU as well.

organized in the CDA. Since the CDU-FDP coalition's ascension to power in 1982, it has pursued a modestly liberalizing economic course, which continued the business-friendly center-right economic policy of the 1950s and 1960s and Ludwig Erhard's *Ordnungspolitik*. Being deeply convinced of the benefits of European integration and having declared the issue one of 'war and peace' Chancellor Kohl and the party with him adopted a very pro-European course in the 1980s, accepting and even embracing resulting measures aimed at market liberalization. Germany, always committed to the EU as part of its ties to the west, reinforced this commitment in the 1980s, which gave rise to its image as a 'model European'. The argument has often been advanced that the country was eager to embrace an European identity as a substitute for its own heavily tainted national identity.

The Free Liberal FDP endorses liberal ideas, both in civil rights and economic policy. It is not a *Volkspartei* but a clientele party, relying on the support of the upper middle class, including well-off major business owners, doctors, lawyers, and architects. As a staunchly liberal party, the FDP generally remains skeptical of state intervention into the economy. The party therefore eagerly welcomed impulses for liberalization emanating from the EU.[7]

We have analyzed the potential role of ideas in great detail, not least because reunification might have served as a 'critical juncture'. In any event, the German government was committed to rebuilding the East, primarily through tax incentives for investors in apartment buildings and commercial space, but certainly also by moving the capital to Berlin. Given that this was a political priority, re-regulating the wages for construction workers might have been less central than getting the job done with.

Given the ideational and ideological roots of the three parties forming the German government coalition in 1996 (CDU, CSU, FDP), we can therefore expect a business-friendly national response strategy. In light of the FDP's commitment to an unfettered market economy and its hesitancy towards state interventionism, we expect a legislative regulation, if passed at all, to leave the actual wage setting to the social partners and generally not be particularly intrusive. An important 'idea' informing

[7] Let us briefly consider the other political parties: The postwar Social Democrats had abandoned their Socialist roots in the revised Godesberg party program of 1954. However, they maintained their commitment to moderate redistribution, worker codetermination and regulative state interventionism. These elements influenced the economic policy pursued while they were in office, especially during the first half of the 1970s. Market liberalization was traditionally regarded with much skepticism and support for European integration remained somewhat lackluster. Both attitudes were completely reversed after the Red-Green coalition government of 1998 took over power leading to the predominance of the conservative business-friendly wing within the SPD and the government (*Neue Mitte*). Similarly, the Greens had remained extremely skeptical of market liberalization given their roots in the heritage of the student protest movement of 1968 and the antinuclear and environmental movements of the 1970s and 1980s. This attitude has changed dramatically since their inclusion in national government in 1998. The only party which remains skeptical of further European integration and market liberalization is the socialist PDS, the successor party to East Germany's state socialist party SED. However, this party attracts relatively weak electoral support at the national level.

the CDU/CSU/FDP coalition during the 1980s and early 1990s was its support for European integration and EC/EU measures. We therefore expect the German national response strategy to reflect this embrace of Europe. However, given the CDU's ideological roots and its electoral and societal clientele, the party is likely to support a less radically pro-market oriented solution than its smaller coalition partner.

Hypotheses for Actors in the Nordic Countries

As has been pointed out before, the governance of the economy and industrial relations in the Nordic countries has traditionally been characterized by neocorporatist consensus-oriented decision-making, based on the parameters of a powerful highly centralized, rigidly hierarchical, and comprehensive union movement, an employers' organization preferring negotiated concessions to industrial action in light of their export dependency, and a state dominated by a Social Democratic party dedicated to relative wage equality and redistributive policies. If this traditional picture of Northern Europe had not begun to change in the mid-1980s and early 1990s, notably in Sweden, but to a lesser extent also in Denmark and Norway, the historical precedent of an egalitarian and generous wage policy would have generated a clear and unambiguous prediction on the nature and coloring of the national response strategy to liberalization. Though the legacy of Social Democratic hegemony and union strength still lingers on, employers' organizations are no longer willing to accept without challenge peak-level negotiations and intersectoral wage equality. They have clamored for decentralization of wage bargaining, more flexibility and less constraints in wage determination. This led to a decentralization of bargaining in Sweden and Denmark, while similar developments in Norway and Finland have since been reversed.[8] However, this more aggressive stance of Danish and Swedish employers does not automatically mean that they want to withdraw completely from a system of well-organized industrial relations, because this creates considerable transaction costs, which are avoided in the traditional high-trust environment.

In the Nordic countries, wage policy is considered a domain left to the social partners, yet governments may choose to become involved directly (as in Denmark) or through arbitration of wage level disputes (as in Norway). In the traditionally highly neocorporatist systems of Northern Europe, the issue of wages for posted workers would have nevertheless most likely be left up to the social partners to negotiate in the first instance. The outcome of this bargaining may or may not have been passed into legislation. Given union strength and the legacy of wage equality, the most likely outcome of such negotiations would have been equal wages for all workers, domestically employed or not. The Social Democratic

---

[8] Thus, in Norway and especially in Finland, there has been a shift back towards centralized wage bargaining. Interestingly, the same constraints of international competition and exposure to the world market, which were previously used as to justify peak-level bargaining, are now used as arguments in favor of decentralization and even atomization of wage bargaining.

hegemony over government would then have assured the egalitarian nature of any ensuing legislation. A brief review of the individual Nordic countries examines whether the somewhat generalizing 'thumbnail' prediction can indeed be sustained for all the individual countries.

In Finland macrolevel bargaining retained its importance throughout the economic recession of the early 1990s, spurred on by the collapse of the most important export market, the USSR. Employers have favored more room for maneuver for wage bargaining at the microlevel, but *have not espoused neoliberal ideas* or expressed major discontent with the status quo. The unions can be expected to *reject univocally any segmentation of the wage structure*, especially given Finland's tradition of wage equality (Lilja 1998).

The government continued to be dominated by the Social Democrats throughout the 1990s. Finland entered the EU in 1995, thus creating the demand for adaptation of existing legislation. Finland can therefore be expected to *confer to the general hypothesis* about the nature of the national response strategies in Nordic countries outlined above.

Norway has bucked the trend of wage decentralization following a brief and fairly disastrous experiment in that direction during the first half of the 1980s. Since the 1990s, centralized bargaining has reappeared (Traxler 1995: 16; Dølvik and Stokke 1998) in a tripartite fashion, thus implying a substantive role of government in wage-setting, further underlined by its role in dispute arbitration. Norway adopted a series of austerity measures and a general policy of wage moderation in response to the economic difficulties of the early 1990s, not least in reference to the Maastricht criteria, further underlining its status as a *quasi member* of the EU. Yet despite this perceived need for wage moderation, the principle of wage solidarity has not been abandoned, and neither has union power decreased to an appreciable degree. Given the delegitimation of neoliberal tenets owing to the experiments of the 1980s, *employers are not likely to promote the segmentation of the wage structure*. The Norwegian trade union movement have traditionally defended the Scandinavian tradition of equalitarianism in wages, it can thus be expected to *resist attempts to introduce a wage differential*. In the early 1990s, Norway was governed by a Social Democratic minority government relying on the parliamentary support of the bourgeoise center to center right parties. The country entered the EEA in 1993, thus adopting substantial segments of the EU *acquis communautaire*. Given aforementioned dependency on conservative support, *government intervention will consist of a middle of the road compromise solution, likely to be mildly protectionist, given the traditional policy orientation of Norwegian conservatives.*

Decentralization of wage bargaining has gone furthest in Sweden, following the sustained campaign of the employer association SAF against the principle of intersectoral wage solidarity and the tradition of substantial wage drift that had characterized macrolevel wage bargaining in Sweden between 1952 and the mid-1980s (Kjellberg 1998). SAF has clothed this campaign in explicitly neoliberal terms, arguing that growing international competition called for a reversal of its demands of the 1940s and 1950s for higher centralization (Pestoff 1995). Wage-level bargaining at the sectoral and company level has facilitated a disintegration of the formerly highly centralized union organization LO, which is further marred by intra-union competition and internal divisions between white-collar and blue-collar employees. In light of more recent trends, *employers can be expected to push for segmentation of the wage structure* and thus endorse a wage differential. Yet any such demands must meet with the *fierce resistance of a still powerful, well-endorsed, and numerically important union movement.* If the *government* does become involved in the formulation of a national response strategy, *it cannot be automatically expected to endorse the principle of wage equality* since this principle has become discredited and even the Swedish Social Democrats have moved to the right considerably. Having said that, prevailing Euroskepticism in Sweden may prove a prominent 'idea' and would push the outcome in a more protectionist re-regulatory direction, making its overall assessment most challenging.

Denmark has historically complied with the Nordic 'model', yet has taken cautious steps towards decentralization of bargaining in the 1980s. The country has been governed by a conservative government since 1982 and has witnessed some challenge to the representational monopoly previously enjoyed by its union movement LO. Cautious steps towards decentralization have been taken, but Denmark did not experience the same amount of employers' resistance to central collective bargaining as in Sweden. Government intervention into wage setting is not uncommon and takes the form of arbitration settlement, such arbitration can be initiated even before the breakdown of negotiations. Social and labor market policy is commonly initiated and based on a compromise solution between labor and business, it is then later written into law (Due et al. 1995: 122 ff.).

Based on the historical antecedents, we can therefore expect to find regulation of the wages for posted workers and the basis of the national response strategy to be rooted in a solution brokered between the social partners and then possibly written into law by government. The latter will be probable if a universal coverage of the entire labor market seems desirable. *Business will push for lower wages, although it might be hesitant to engage the unions head-on if encountering sustained resistance.* The trade unions can be expected *fiercely to defend the current wage structure.* is not necessarily firmly determined to push for a segmentation of the wage structure. The government, though composed of a conservative Christian Democratic party, has not espoused neoliberal ideology, yet it has begun a movement towards moderate market liberalization (Schwartz 1994). *Government intervention* into the issue may therefore color it in a *slightly liberal fashion.*

Hypotheses for Actors in the Low Countries

The hypotheses for the national response strategies of the three Low Countries based on historical institutionalism differ notably from those of Scandinavia. First, there is no common 'model'; second, the overall structure of industrial relations in all three countries has oscillated considerably between different poles over time. This gives rise to a third point, the sometimes confusing degree of variation of state interventionism. Fourth, none of the Low Countries can be said to have been dominated by Social Democratic Parties, *au contraire*, Christian Democratic parties and ideology play pronounced and significant roles. Fifth, the nature of the political economy in these countries is not easily captured by labels such as neocorporatist or liberal/Anglo-Saxon. Finally, religious and linguistic cleavages have produced eclectic additional lines of divisions in contrast to the relatively homogeneous Nordic countries where the key line of division is social class.

Government intervention into wage bargaining was quite common in the Netherlands in the 1970s and 1980s. With the more recent revival of Dutch neocorporatism (Visser and Hemerijck 1998)—though with templates notably different from those of the 1970s—the social partners have regained some of their de facto autonomy over the domain of wage bargaining and they have consolidated organizationally following the heralded 1982 agreement of Wassenaar. Since the early 1980s macrolevel institutions like the *Stichting van de Arbeid* and the *Social-Economische Raad* have regained prominence as arenas for deliberation of macroeconomic policy ideas. This organized market economy's attempt to regain international competitiveness after an economically disastrous decade (Visser and Hemerijck 1998) and implement 'competitive corporatism' under the conservative Lubbers government of the 1980s is allowing labor market interest associations to regain influence over wage-setting, but under the premise of the primacy of business over labor. *Dutch employers are likely to push for a wage differential* given a liberal orientation and a past preference for wage moderation. Meanwhile, *the union movement*, though still divided, can be expected to *unanimously favor the avoidance of a segmentation of the wage structure*. The issue could be addressed by a compromise solution between the two social partners. *Government may intervene*, however, for instance by extending the agreement to all companies in the economy, taking advantage of a 1937 law permitting such erga omnes practices (Visser 1998). In case of *unilateral government intervention*, we would expect the outcome to be liberally oriented and *thus endorsing a wage gap*, given the conservative government's past efforts at maintaining wage moderation.

In Belgium, the state traditionally granted considerable autonomy to the social partners in wage bargaining and involved them in the administration of part of the welfare state system, notably unemployment insurance, but always maintained some degree of control and more recently has begun to take back some of this autonomy little by little. Frustrated by failed efforts to fashion a national tripartite pact on employment in 1993 (Hassel 1999), the Belgian government imposed a wage freeze for two years, mandated maximum values for future wage increases, and linked wage increases to developments in neighboring France, Germany, and the Netherlands. The state thus sets the parameters of wage bargaining. The government attempted to coax the social partners into an agreement and, after this approach failed, locked them into a corset. Given these circumstances, the national response strategy in Belgium becomes difficult to predict following the historical institutionalist school: *Will the past legacy of relative autonomy prevail over the more recent changes?* Given the scope and degree of these latter, their impact appears more formidable, which gives rise to the hypothesis that *the state's preference will be the defining and dominating core to a national response strategy*, which may however be somewhat conditioned by the impact of the social partners' preferences. The *union's position* would appear to be in *disfavor of a wage segmentation* based on a tradition of wage equality in Belgium. The *employers will favor a substantial wage gap*. The Belgian *government's* position on this issue can be expected to be generally liberal and *thus in favor of a segmentation* of what was perceived as an excessively high-wage structure. However, we will note in passing that just like in the Netherlands, a tradition or 'idea' of Christian social values exists in Belgium, which might tip the scale in favor of a more equal wage structure.

Finally, in Luxembourg government plays a pronounced role in wage regulation and so do national tripartite macroeconomic institutions. Though collective bargaining occurs on a bilateral basis between employers and unions, the collective results must then be approved by the Ministry of Labor. Tripartite institutions such as the *Conseil Economique et Social* and the parietetic *Comité de Coordination Tripartite* and the *Comité de Conjonture* serve as common fori in which issues of macroeconomic governance are being discussed among actors. Given the small size of the country, the high level of organizational hierarchy is perhaps less than surprising. *This points to a national response strategy devised by the interplay of all three actors*. In a small state dominated by small companies, employers might perceive of foreign subcontractors more as a threat than as an opportunity and thus could be reluctant to maximize a wage differential and more interested in maintaining social peace with the unions.

Bibliography

Interviews conducted (list only includes formal interviews)

June 1999: Representative of Austrian Umbrella Union ÖGB in Vienna

June 1999: Representative of Austrian Ministry of Economic Affairs in Vienna

July 1999: Representative of Central Association of German Construction HDB in Berlin

July 1999: Representative of Berlin Senate Department of Construction and Housing in Berlin

July 1999: Representative of Berlin Region Sectoral Construction Union IG BAU in Berlin

July 1999: Representative of German Sectoral Construction Sector Union IG BAU in Frankfurt

July 2000: Representative of French Ministry of Labor and Social Affairs in Paris

October 2000: Representative of French Umbrella Union CFDT in Paris

November 2000: Representative of Sectoral Construction Sector Union FNCB-CFDT in Paris

November 2000: Representative with French Umbrella Union CGT in Paris

November 2000: Representative of Dutch Umbrella Union FNV in Amsterdam

November 2000: Representative of Dutch Employers Umbrella Association VNO-NCW in The Hague

November 2000: Representative of Dutch Ministry of Labor and Social Affairs in The Hague

November 2000: Representative of Dutch Sectoral Construction Employers Association AVBB in The Hague

November 2000: Representative of Dutch Sectoral Construction Union FVN-Bouw in Woerden

December 2000: Representative of Association of Small Construction Companies in Artisans ZDB in Berlin

December 2000: Representative of Luxembourg Ministry of Labor and Social Affairs

December 2000: Representative of German Umbrella Union DGB in Berlin

December 2000: Representative of German Ministry of Labor and Social Affairs in Bonn

December 2000: Representative of French Employer Umbrella Association Medef in Paris

December 2000: Representative of French Council on Social and Economic Affairs in Paris

January 2001: Representatives of French Sectoral Construction Association FNTP in Paris

January 2001: Representative of French Sectoral Construction Association FFB in Paris

March 2001: Representative of French Ministry for Employment and Social Affairs in Paris

April 2001 Representative of Austrian construction company, Vienna

April 2001: Representative of German Employers Umbrella Association BDA in Berlin

April 2001: Representative of Central Association of German Construction HDB in Berlin

April 2001 Representative of Austrian construction company, Vienna

April 2001 Representative of Austrian construction company, Vienna

April 2001: Representative of Austrian Umbrella Union ÖGB in Vienna

April 2001: Representative of Austrian Umbrella Employers WK in Vienna

April 2001: Representative of Austrian Sectoral Union Bau-Holz in Vienna

April 2001: Representative of Austrian Ministry of Labor and Economic Affairs in Vienna

April 2001: Representative of major German construction company

April 2001: Representative of German Sectoral Employers Association for the Metal Sector Gesamtmetall in Berlin

April 2001: Representative of German Sectoral Union for the Metal Sector IG Metall in Frankfurt

April 2001: Representative of German Sectoral Construction Union IG BAU in Frankfurt

April 2001: Representative of German Sectoral Employer Association for the Textile Sector Gesamttextil in Eschborn

July 2001: Representative of German Umbrella Union DGB in Berlin

Primary sources

Action juridique (March 1994), no. 105

L'Année Politique (1991). [Annual summary of developments in French politics].

AVBB (2000) De Bouw in cijfers [Key figures for the construction sector], Den Haag: AVBB.

AVBB (2001) personal communication to the author

BAMS (German) Bundesministerium für Arbeit und Sozialordnung (1996). *Pressemitteilung: Vermittlungsausschuss erreicht Einigung zum Arbeitnehmer-Entsendegesetz* [Press Release: Commitee reaches agreement on Law on Posted Workers], February 2, 1996.

AVBB (2000) *Het bouw en Kerncijfers* [Central data on the Construction Sector], The Hague: AVBB.

AVBB (2004) *Kerncijfers* [Central data on the Construction Sector], The Hague: AVBB.

BAM – Koninjlijke BAM Groep (2004) *Jaarrapport 2003* [Annual report 2003]

BAMS (2000). *Pressemitteilung: Bundesarbeitsminister Walter Riester: Voraussetzung für fairen Wettbewerb auf Baustellen ist geschaffen* [Press Release: Federal Minister of

Labor Walter Riester: Conditions have been created for fair competition on construction sites], March 2, 2000.

BAMS (2000). *Verzeichnis der für allgemeinverbindlich erklärten Tarifverträge* [Directory of Collective Agreements declared universally applicable] Bonn: BMAS (also available at http://www.bma.de).

BDA (1991). *Euro-Info 10–91*, p. 7.

BDA (1994). *Jahresbericht* [Annual Report 1994], BDA: Köln.

BDA (Bundesvereinigung Deutscher Arbeitgeber) (1995a). *Arbeitgeber zum Entsendegesetz* [Press Release: Employers on the Law on Posted Workers], 27 September 1995.

BDA (1995b). *Stellungnahme zu dem Gesetz der Bundesregierung* [Position paper regarding the law under consideration by the federal government].

BDA (1996). *Göhner: Verschiebung ist bedauerlich und unverständlich* [Press Release: Postponement is deplorable and hard to understand], October 9, 1996.

Berlin Senate Department for Construction (*Senatsverwaltung für Bau- und Wohnungswesen*) (1995). internal Rundschreiben BauWohn VI 7/1995.

BIT (Bureau International du Travail) (2000). *Repertoire des instruments internationaux de sécurité sociale* [Collection of international instruments in social security]. Bureau International du Travail: Geneva.

Bouygues, S. A. (2000). *Le groupe Bouygues* Paris: Bouygues [Corporate Information Brochure for Shareholders].

Bouygues, S.A. (2004) *Rapport annuel 2003*, Paris: Bouygues [Annual Report for 2003]

Bundesgesetzblatt (1996). Teil I Nr. 11 vom 26. Februar 1996, *Gesetz über zwingende Arbeitsbedingungen bei grenzüberschreitenden Dienstleistungen—Arbeitnehmer-Entsendegesetz—AEntG.*

Bundesgesetzblatt (1997). I Nr. 84 February 19, 1997, *Erstes Gesetz zur Änderung des Dritten Buches Sozialgesetzbuch und anderer Gesetze.*

Bundesgesetzblatt (1998). TEIl I Nr. 85 vom 28. Dezember 1998, *Gesetz zu Korrekturen in der Sozialversicherung und zur Sicherung der Arbeitnehmerrechte.*

CAO Bouwbedrijf (1994–5), CAO Bouwbedrijf (1995–6), CAO Bouwbedrijf (1999–2000)

CFDT-FNCB (1995). *Reponses au Questionnaire Friedrich Ebert Stiftung sur la negotiation collective dans le BTP* [Responses to the Questionnaire of the Friedrich Ebert Stiftung about collective negotiations in the construction sector], Paris.

CFDT-FNCB (2000). *L'Action constructive.*

CFDT-FNCB (23 May 1995). Letter by Secretary-General Joseph Murgia to Minister of Labor Barrot.

CFDT Magazine (May 1994). *La loi quinquennale sur l'emploi.*

CFTC (10 October 2000). personal electronic communication to author

Centre de Sécurité Sociale des Travailleurs Migrants (1996) 'Le détachement'.

Commission of the European Communities (1991) COM (91) 230 final XXX – 30 August 1991

Commission of the European Communities (1993) COM (593) 225 final XXX

Commission of the European Communities (1996) COM (96/71) EC final XXX

Conseil Economique et Sociale (1993). 'Avis et Rapport du Conseil Economique et Social: Avant-Projet de Loi Quinquennale relatif au travail, a l'emploi et a la formation professionnelle' [Opinion and Report of the Economic and Social Council: The Preliminary Draft of the Five Year Law on work, employment, and professional education], Paris: Journal Officiel de la République Française 1993, Séances de 7 et 8 septembre, 18, September 10, 1993.

Commission européenne (2000) *Les relations du travail en Europe*, Luxembourg: European Communities

Danish Ministry of Labour (1991) *Labour Relations in Denmark: The Self-Regulatory System*. Copenhagen: Danish Ministry of Labour.

Destatis – Statistisches Bundesamt Deutschland (2004) *Statistik-Portal 2004*, Wiesbaden: destatis.

DGB (Deutscher Gewerkschaftsbund) (1 December 1994). letter to the Ministry of Labor.

DGB (December 23, 1994). *Diskussionspapier über Möglichkeiten einer nationalen Regelung nach dem Scheitern der EU-Entsenderichtlinie* [Discussion Paper on Possibilities of a National Regulation after the Failure of an EU Directive].

DGB (May 9, 1995). *DGB-Positionen zur Regelung des grenzüberschreitenden Einsatzes von Arbeitskräften* [DGB Positions concerning the Regulation of Posting Workers Transnationally].

DGB (July 13, 1995). *Stellungnahme zum Entwurf eines Gesetzes über zwingende Arbeitsbedingungen bei grenzüberschreitenden Dienstleistungen AentG* [Position on the Law on Labor Conditions for Posted Workers].

DGB (August 2, 1995). *Notiz über das Abstimmungsgesprach zwischen IGBSE, IGM und DGB* [Note on the Coordination Talks between IG BAU, IG METALL and DGB].

DGB (1996). *Das Arbeitnehmer-Entsendegesetz* [The Law on Posted Workers], unpublished internal documentation.

DILTI (1999). *La verbalisation du travail illégal: les chiffres de l'année 1997*, Paris: Délégation interministérielle à la lutte contre le travail illégal a la Ministère de l'emploi et de la solidarité.

European Commission (1991). *Proposal for a Council Directive concerning the posting of workers in the framework of the provision of services*, COM (91) 230.

Eurostat (2003) "Arbeitskostenerhebung 2000–EU-Mitgliedsstaaten und Beitrittskandidaten. Statistik Kurz gefasst, Bevölkerung und soziale Bedingungen". Luxembourg: Eurostat 3–18/2003.

FAZ (8 March 1993) "Dolce vital am Polarkreis – Norwegen bleibt ein Subventionsstaat" [Dolce vita near the polar circle – Norway remains dependent on subsidies]

FAZ (21 February 2000) *Schwedens Bauwirtschaft weiter im Aufschwung* [Swedish construction sector continues to boom]

FFB-Fédération Française du Batiment (1999). *Les indicateurs sociaux du bâtiment*, [Social Figures in the Construction Sector]. Paris: FFB.

FFB-Fédération Française due Batiment (2004) *Le bâtiment en chiffres 2003*, [Figures on the Construction Sector] Paris: FFB

Finnish Ministry of Labor (23 November 2000) personal communication to the author

FNB—Fédération Nationale du Batiment (1996). *Pour venir à bout du travail noir—les 10 propositions de la FNB* [Getting to the Roots of Illegal Labor—the 10 propositions of the FNB]. FNB: Paris.

FNCB-CFDT (2000). *L'Action constructive*. Paris: FNCB-CFDT.

Force Ouvrière (1993). 'La Loi Quinquennale sur l'emploi—tout sur la loi qui bouleverse le code du travail' [The Five Year Law on Employment—All about the law which perturbates the French Labor Law], No. 2195. Paris: Force Ouvrière.

HDB (Hauptverband der Deutschen Bauindustrie) (June 28, 1995). *Stellungnahme zu dem Entwurf einer EU-Entsenderichtlinie und zu dem Vorhaben einer nationalen Entsende-Regelung*, [Position regarding the EU Draft Directive and a National Initative regardingthe Posting of Workers]. Wiesbaden: HDB.

HDB (1997). [Main Federation of the German Construction Industry], *Baukonjunkturelle Lage im Herbst 1997* [Economic Situation in the Fall of 1997], Wiesbaden: HDB.

HDB (1999). *Bauwirtschaft im Zahlenbild 1999*, [Figures for the Construction Sector]. Berlin: HDB.

HDB (2001). *Perspektiven 2001*, [Perspectives for 2001]. Berlin: HDB.

HDB – Hauptverband der Deutschen Bauindustrie (2004) *Wichtige Baudaten 2004*, [Important statistics about the construction sector] Berlin: HDB

IG BAU—Industriegewerkschaft Bauen, Agrar, Umwelt (1991). *Brief an den Bundesminister für Arbeit und Sozialordnung* [Letter to the Ministry of Labor and Social Affairs].

IG Bau (28 June 1995). *Stellungnahme der Industriegewerkschaft Bau-Steine-Erden zur Anhörung im Bundestagsausschuaß für Arbeit und Sozialordnung am 28. Juni 1995 in Bonn* [Position of the IG BAU during the Parliamentary Hearing by the Bundestag Committee on Labor and Social Affairs on June 28, 1995 in Bonn].

IG BAU (1995). *Stellungnahme . . . zum Entwurf eines Arbeitnehmer-Entsendegesetzes* [Reaction paper to the draft version of a Law on Posted Workers], *Rundschreiben 21/1995*, Frankfurt.

IG BAU (1997). *Zur gesamt- und bauwirtschaftlichen Entwicklung sowie zur Einkommenssituation* [About the general macroeconomic situation and that of the construction sector as well as the wage situation], internal unpublished document.

IG BAU (2004) *Gesetz zur Bekämpfung illegaler Beschäftigung tritt in Kraft: IG BAU nimmt Generalunternehmer und Auftragggeber ins Visier* [Law on efforts against illegal forms of employment becomes effective: IG BAU targets main contractors]

IG Metall (June 20, 1995). *Entsenderichtlinie/Anhörung am 28.6.1995* [Law on Posted Workers/Hearing of June 28, 1995].

IG Metall (31 May 1996). *IG Metall: Chronologie zum Entsendegesetz* [IG METALL: A Chronology of Events surrounding the Genesis on the Law of Posted Workers]. Journal Officiel de la République Française (1993a). Débats Parlementaires, Assemblée Nationale, 10ème Législature, 12ème séance, Compte Rendu Intégral, 3ème séance du vendredi 1er octobre 1993.

Journal Officiel de la République Française (1993*b*). Débats Parlementaires, Assemblée Nationale, 10ème Législature, 72ème séance, Compte Rendu Intégral, séance du jeudi 18 novembre 1993.

Journal Officiel de la République Française (1994). 'Décret No. 94–573 du 11 juillet 1994 pris pour l'application de l'article 36 de la loi quinquennale relative à l'emploi, au travail et à la formation professionnelle', July 12, 1994, p. 10041ff.

Journal Officiel de la République Française (2000). 'Conventions Collectives Nationales—Bâtiment (ETAM-IAC)', May 2000.

Lardy-Pélissier, B., Pélissier, J. Roset, A. and Tholy L. (2000). *Le code du travail annoté* [The annotatetd Labor Law], Paris: Groupe Revue Fiduciaire.

Législation Sociale (1995). 'Circulaire Ministérielle DRT 94/18 du 30 décembre 1994 relative à la situation des salariés d'entreprises étrangères détachés temporairement en France pour l'exécution d'une prestation de service' [Ministerial Document regarding the situation of foreign posted workers temporarily seconded to France for the provision of a service] *Législation Sociale* 7197, January 30, 1995.

Liaisons sociales (May 21, 1991). No 6254, 'Sous-traitance par une entreprise de la CEE' [Subcontracting by a EU company].

Liaisons sociales (August 25, 1994). No. 7097 'Salariés d'entreprises étrangères temporairement détachés en France: Loi quinquennale' [Employees of a foreign company temporarily seconded to France: The Five Year Law]. *Liaisons sociales* (March 11, 1997). No 12377.

Liaisons sociales (6 February 1997). No 12354 'Détachement de travailleurs dans le cadre d'une prestation de services' [Posting of Workers for the Purpose of Service Provision].

Medef (October 26, 2000). personal electronic communication to author.

Ministère des Affaires Sociales et de l'Emploi (undated). L'application combinée du droit interne, du droit communautaire, et du droit internationale aux entreprises étrangères en France occupant du personnel salarié [The Combined Application of Domestic, Communal and International Law to foreign companies in France employing workers] Paris.

Ministère du Travail, de l'Emploi et de la formation Professionnelle (1994). *Circulaire DRT 94/18 du 30 décembre 1994 relative à la situation d'entreprises étrangères détachés temporairement en France pour l'exécution d'une prestation de service* [Ministerial Directive regarding the situation of foreign companies temporarily posted to France for the provision of a service].

Ministère du Travail, de l'Emploi et de la formation Professionnelle (1991). *Circulaire DRT 91/12 du 2 Mai 1991 précisant les règles à appliquer aux entreprises de la Communauté Economique Européenne temporairement effectuer une prestation de services en France dans le domaine de bâtiment et du génie civil* [Ministerial Directive clarifying the applicable rules for EU companies temporarily providing a service in France in the sector of construction and civil engineering].

Ministère de la Justice (1999). *Le travail illégal et sa répression*, [Illegal Employment and its Repression] Infostat Justice, No.54, December 1999.

Ministère du Travail, de l'Emploi et de la Formation Professionnelle (May 2, 1991). *Règles a appliquer aux entreprises de la Communauté Economique Européenne venant temporairement effectuer une prestation de services en France dans le domaine du bâtiment et du génie civil* [Rules to apply to companies from the EU that come to France temporarily to provide a service in the secotr of construction and civil engineering].

Ministerie van Sociale Zaken en Werkgelegenheid (September 25, 1991). Letter to the Stichting van de Arbeid (reprinted in Stichting van de Arbeid 'Advies inzake de utivoering van Richtlijn 96/71/EG' [Advice regarding the implementation of EU directive 96/71/EC]. Den Haag: Stichting van de Arbeid.

Norwegian Ministry of Local Government and Regional Development (January 2001) personal communication to the author

Norwegian LO (2001) personal communication to the author

Norwegian Ministry of Local Government and Regional Development (12 January 2001) personal communication to the author

Norwegian Ministry of Local Government and Regional Development (January 2001) personal communication to the author

Norwegian Ministry of Foreign Affairs (2005) Business: Oil and Gas, available online at http://www.norway.org.uk/business (internet accessed 19 January 2005)

Norwegian Ministry of Foreign Affairs (2005). 'The Norwegian Economy', available at: http://www.norway.org.uk/business/oil/oilgas.htm

Sachverständigenrat zur Begutachtung der gesamtwirtschaftlichen Entwicklung (1989). *Jahresbericht 1989–1990* [Annual Report 1989–1990].

Senatsverwaltung für Bauen, Wohnen und Verkehr (1999). [Berlin Senate Department for Construction, Housing and Transportation], 'Vierteljahresbericht über die Entwicklung in der Berliner Bauwirtschaft' [Quarterly Report on the Development in the Construction Sector in Berlin].

Statec (2004) Informations statistiques, Luxembourg: Statec

Statistik Austria (2004) *Statistisches Jahrbuch Österreichs 2004*, Vienna: Statistik Austria

Stichting van de Arbeid (3 February 1991) Advies 'Enkele aspecten van de sociale dimensie van Europa 1992' [Advice regarding some aspects with respect to the social dimension of Europe 1992] Den Haag: Stichting van de Arbeid.

Stichting van de Arbeid (4 October 2000) Advies inzake de uitvoering van Richtlijn 96/71/EG, [Advice regarding the implementation of EU directive 96/71/EC], Publication 11/2000, Den Haag: Stichting van de Arbeid.

Sveriges Riksdag Motion till riksdagen 1997/98 T202, 9, 'Trafikpolitik för tillväxt och god miljö' [Environmentally Friendly Transportation Policy].

Sveriges Riksdag Motion till riksdagen (1999/2000). T616, 4 'Sjöfartspolitiken' [Policies in Shipping].

TIB (2004). 'Polsk firma i retten for social dumping' [Polish company involved in protecting against social dumping], August 12, 2004, http://www.tib.dk/Artikler/ Polsk%20firma%20i%20Arbejdsretten%20for%20social%20dumping.aspx.

VÖI Vereinigung Österreichischer Industriellen (November 2, 1995). *Stellungnahme zum Entwurf eines Bundesgesetzes, mit dem das Arbeitsvertragsrechts-Anpassungsgesetz geändert wird* [Position paper regarding a federal law with which the Law on Change to the Labor Code will be changed].

WK (Wirtschaftskammer Österreich) (November 29, 1995). *Antimißbrauchgesetz* [Position Paper on the Law against Abuses].

ZDB (Zentralverband des Deutschen Baugewerbes) (1994). *Baujahr 1994* [Annual Report 1994]. ZDB: Bonn.

ZDB (Zentralverband des Deutschen Baugewerbes) (June 28, 1995). *Stellungnahme zu...Grundsätze für eine EU-Entsenderichtlinie sowie eine nationale Regelung bis zu deren Realisierung*, [Position Paper regarding the . . . outline of an EU Directive and a National Regulation concerning the Posting of Workers]. ZDB: Bonn.

ZDB (Zentralverband des Deutschen Baugewerbes), *Baumarkt '99* [Construction Sector 1999]. ZDB: Berlin.

ZDB – Zentralverband des Deutschen Baugewerbes (2004), *Baumarkt 2003*, [Construction Sector 2003] ZDB: Berlin.

Secondary sources

Adler, E. (1997). 'Seizing the Middle Ground: Constructivism in World Politics', *European Journal of International* Relations, 3 (3) 319–63.

Albert, M. (1991). *Capitalisme contre capitalisme*. Paris: Le Seuil.

Albert, M. (1993). *Capitalism vs. Capitalism*. New York: Four Walls Eight Windows.

Allen, C. (1989). 'The Underdevelopment of Keynesianism in the Federal Republic of Germany', in P. Hall (ed.) *The Political Power of Economic Ideas*. Princeton, NJ: Princeton University Press, 263–90.

Amable, B. (2003). *The Diversity of Modern Capitalism*. Oxford/New York: Oxford University Press.

Andersen, J. G. (1992). 'Denmark: The Progress Party—Populist Neo-Liberalism and Welfare State Chauvinism', in Hainsworth, P. (ed.) *The Extreme Right in Europe and the USA*. London: Pinter.

Andersen, S. and K. Eliassen (1993). *Making Policy in Europe: The Europeification of National Policy-Making*. London: Sage.

APA Journal (December 18, 1995). 'Triste Stimmung im Baugewerbe' [Sober mood in the construction sector].

van Apeldoorn, Bastiaan (1999). 'Transnationalisation and the Restructuring of Europe's Socio-Economic Order: Social Forces in the Construction of "Embedded Neoliberalism" ', *International Journal of Political Economy*, 28 (1): 12–53.

Aust, A. (1999) *Irlands Entwicklung im europäischen Binnenmarkt*, Wiesbaden: Deutscher Universitäsverlag.

Axelrod, Robert (1984) *The Evolution of Cooperation*, New York, Basic Books.

Bates, Robert (1981) *Markets and State in Tropical Africa*, Berkeley: University of California Press.

Bates, Robert (1983) *Essays on the Political Economy of Rural Africa*, Cambridge: Cambridge University Press.

Baumann, H. (1995). 'Von nationalstaatlichen zu europäischen Arbeits-und Sozialbeziehungen?', *Basler Schriften zur Europäischen Union*. Universität Basel.

Becker, U. (2001). 'A Dutch Miracle? Employment Growth by Corporatist Consensus and Wage Restraint? A Critical Account of an Idyllic View', *New Political Economy* March, 6 (1): 19–43.

Berger, S. and Dore, R. (eds.) (1996). *National Diversity and Global Capitalism*. Ithaca, NY: Cornell University Press.

—— and Piore, M. J. (1980). *Dualism and Discontinuity in Industrial Societies*. Cambridge/New York: Cambridge University Press.

Berliner Morgenpost (July 7, 2004). 'Jagd auf Schwarzarbeiter in Berlin' [Hunt for Illegal Workers in Berlin].

Berliner Zeitung (November 30, 1995). 'Union und FDP gegen Lohndumping' [Christian Democrats and Free Democrats Against 'Dumping' Wages].

—— (April 12, 1996). 'Bau einigt sich auf Tarifkompromiss' [Construction Sector Finds Compromise on Wage Levels].

—— (March 11, 1997). 'Stundenlöhne unter fünf Mark' [Hourly Wages of Less than Five Marks].

Berthier, J.-P. (1992). 'Une analyse sur 20 ans de l'activite du batiment-trvaux publics', *Economie et Statistiques*, 253 (April) 3–13.

von Beyme, K. (1977). *Gewerkschaften und Arbeitsbeziehungen in kapitalistischen Ländern* [Unions and Industrial Relations in Capitalist Countries]. Munich: Piper-Verlag.

Bibes, G. and Mouriaux, R. (1990) (eds.). *Les Syndicats Européens à l'epreuve*. Paris: Fondation Nationale des Sciences Politiques.

Bieler, A. (2000). *Path to EU Membership in Austria and Sweden*. London: Routledge.

Blyth, M. (2003). 'Same as it Never Was: Typology and Temporality in the Varieties of Capitalism', *Comparative European Politics* 1 (2): 215–25.

Börzel, T. and Risse, T. (2000). 'When Europe Hits Home: Europeanization and Domestic Change', *EUI Working Paper*, RSC 2000/56. Florence: EUI.

Börzel, T. (2002). *Nations and Regions in the European Union: Institutional Adaptation in Germany and Spain*. Cambridge: Cambridge University Press.

Boltho, A. (1996). 'Has France Converged on Germany? Policies and Institutions since 1958', in S. Berger and R. Dore, ibid., 89–104.

Bonnechere, M. (1995). 'La libre circulation des travailleurs dans l'Union Européenne', *Le Droit Ouvrier*, 561: 319–40.

Bosch, G., Worthmann, G., and Zühlke-Robinet, K. (1999). 'Verschärfte Konkurrenz zwischen deutschen und ausländischen gewerblichen Bauarbeitern', in H.Mayrzedt (ed.) *Arbeitsmarkt und erfolgsorientiertes Personalmangement im Bau*. Düsseldorf: Werner-Verlag.

—— and Zühlke-Robinet, K. (1999). 'Der Bauarbeitsmarkt in Deutschland: Zum Zusammenhang von Produktionsstrukturen, Arbeitsmarkt und Regulierungssystem' [The Labor Market in the German Construction Industry: On the Relation between Production Structures, Labor Market and the Regulatory System], *Industrielle Beziehungen*, 6 (3): 239–67.

—— and Zühlke-Robinet, K. (2000). 'The labour market in the German construction industry', paper presented at conference on 'Structural Change in the Building Industry Labour Market', October 19–20, Gelsenkirchen, Germany.

Boyer, R. (1984). 'Wage Labor, Capital Accumulation, and the Crisis, 1968–82', in Mark Kesselman (ed.) *The French Workers' Movement: Economic Crisis and Political Change*. London/Boston: Allen & Unwin, 17–39.

Boyer, R. (1996). 'The Convergence Hypothesis Revisited: Globalization but Still the Century of Nations?', in S. Berger and R. Dore, ibid., 29–59.

—— (1997). 'French Statism at the crossroads', in Crouch, Colin and Streeck (eds.) *Political Economy of Modern Capitalism*. London/Thousand Oaks, CA: Sage, pp. 71–101.

—— and Drache, D. (eds.) (1996). *States Against Markets—The Limits of Globalization*. London/New York: Routledge.

Brouwer, M. (2002). 'Dutch Building Fraud Rampant', Radio Netherlands, August 22, 2002—available at: http://www.rnw.nl/hotspots/html/nedii020822.html.

Brubaker, R. (1992). *Citizenship and Nationhood in France and Germany*, Cambridge, MA: Harvard University Press.

Bunel, J. (1997). 'Représentation patronale et réprésentativité des organisations patronales', *Travail et Emploi*, 70, 1/97: 3–20.

Calmfors, L. and Driffill, J. (1988). 'Centralization of Wage Bargaining', *Economic Policy*, 6: 13–61.

Cerny, P.G. (1993) "American decline and the emergence of embedded financial Orthodoxy", in Philip G. Cerny (ed) *Finance and World Politics: Markets, Regimes and States in the Post-hegemonic Era*. Hants, UK: Edward Elgar: 155–185.

Cerny, P.G. (1997) "Paradoxes of the Competition State: The Dynamics of Political Globalization", *Government and Opposition*, 32 (2) (Spring): 251–274.

Chapman, H., Kesselman, M. and Schain, M. (eds.) (1998). *A Century of Organized Labor in France: A Union Movement for the Twenty-first Century?* New York : St. Martin's Press.

Checkel, J. T. (1993). 'Ideas, Institutions, and the Gorbachev Foreign Policy Revolution', *World Politics* 45 (2): 271–300.

—— (1997). *Ideas and International Political Change: Soviet/Russian Behavior and the End of the Cold War*. New Haven, CT: Yale University Press.

Coates, D. (2000). *Models of Capitalism: Growth and Stagnation in the Modern Era*. Cambridge: Polity Press.

Collier, R. and Collier, D. (1991). *Shaping the Political Arena: Critical Junctures, the Labor Movement, and Regime Dynamics in Latin America*. Princeton: Princeton University Press.

Cornelius, W. A., Martin, P. L. and Hollifield, J. F. (eds.) (1994). *Controlling Immigration: A Global Perspective*. Stanford, CA: Stanford University Press.

Cowles, M. and Risse, T. (2001). 'Europeanization and Domestic Change: Conclusions', in M. Cowles, J. Caporaso, and T. Risse (eds.) *Transforming Europe: Europeanization and Domestic Change*. Ithaca, NY: Cornell University Press.

—— Caporaso, J., and Risse, T. (eds.) (2001). *Transforming Europe: Europeanization and Domestic Change*. Ithaca, NY: Cornell University Press.

Crepaz, M. (1994). 'From Semisovereingty to Sovereignty: The Decline of Corporatism and Rise of Parliament in Austria', *Comparative Politics*, 1: 45–65.

Crouch, C. and Streeck, W. (eds.) (1996). *Les capitalismes en Europe*. Paris: La Découverte.

—— —— (eds.) (1997). *Political Economy of Modern Capitalism: Mapping Convergence and Diversity*, London/Thousand Oaks, CA: Sage.

—— and Traxler, F. (eds.) (1995). *Organized Industrial Relations in Europe: What Future?* Aldershot, Hants, UK; Brookfield, VT: Avebury.

Cyrus, N. (1996). 'Moderne Migrationspolitik im alten Gewand', paper presented at the Friedrich Ebert Stiftung Conference on 'Moderne Migrationspolitik', available at www.polskarada.de (Internet accessed on February 1, 2001).

Daley, A. (1998). 'Reconceptualizing the Relationship between Unions and Politics in France', in H. Chapman, M. Kesselman, and M. Schain (eds.) *A Century of Organized Labor in France: A Union Movement for the Twenty-first Century?* New York: St. Martin's Press.

—— (1999). 'The Hollowing Out of French Unions: Politics and Industrial Relations After 1981', in A. Martin and G. Ross (eds.) *The Brave New World of European Labor: European Trade Unions at the Millennium*. New York: Berghahn Books.

Deeg, R. and Lütz, S. (2000). 'Internationalization and Financial Federalism: The United States and Germany at the Crossroads?', *Comparative Political Studies*, 33 (3): 374–405.

Deinert, O. (2000). 'Posting of Workers to Germany—Previous Evolutions and New Influences throughout EU Legislation Proposals', *International Journal of Comparative Labour Law and Industrial Relations*, 16 (3): 217–34.

Delarue, M.R. (1995). 'Détachement et dumping social: une approche théorique', in van Regenmortel and Y. Jorens, ibid. 272–83.

Delsen, L. (2002). *Exit Polder Model? Socioeconomic Change in the Netherlands*. Westport, CT: Praeger.

Deneve, C. (1995). 'Le détachement et le droit individuel du travail', in van Regenmortel and Y. Jorens, ibid., 175–94.

Déprez, J. (1995). 'Rattachements rigides et pouvoir d'appréciation du juge dans la détermination de la loi applicable au contrat de travail international', *Droit Sociale*, 4,: 323–8.

Desmazières de Séchelles, A. (1993). 'Free Movement of Workers and Freedom to Provide Services', in H. G. Schermers et al. (eds.) *Free Movement of Persons in Europe*. Den Haag: Marinus Nijhoff, pp. 472–84.

van Dessel, L. (1995). 'Détachement et dumping social: une vision pratique', in van Regenmortel and Y. Jorens, ibid. 286–94.

Dewitte, P. (ed.) (1999). *Immigration et intégration: l'état des savoirs*, [Immigration and Integration: The State of Knowledge]. Paris: Découverte.

Die Welt (July 19, 1995) "Entsenderichtlinie zieht einen Zaun hoch" [Directive on posted workers creates a barrier]

Dimitrova, A. and Steunenberg, B. (2000). 'The Search for Convergence of National Policies in the EU: An Impossible Quest?' *European Union Politics*, 1 (2): 201–26.

Dølvik, J. E. and Martin, A. (1997). 'A spanner in the works and oil on troubled waters: the divergent fates of social pacts in Sweden and Norway', in G. Fajertag, and P. Pochet, (eds.) *Social Pacts in Europe*. Bruxelles: ETUI.

Dølvik, J. E. and Stokke, T. A. (1998). 'Norway: The Revival of Centralizaed Concertation', in A. Ferner and R. Hyman, ibid. 118–45.

Due, J., Madsen, J. S. Petersen, L. K., and Jensen, C. S. (1995). 'Adjusting the Danish Model: Towards Centralized Decentralization', in C. Crouch and F. Traxler, ibid., 121–50.

Dumorthier, J. (1981). *Arbeidsverhoudingen in het internationaal privaatrecht*. Antwerp: Kluwer.

Ebbinghaus, B. and Visser, J. (1994). 'Barrieren und wege "grenzenloser" Solidarität: Gewerkschaften und europäische Union', in W. Streeck (ed.) *Staat und Verbände*, Special Edition of *Politische Vierteljahresschrift*, 25: 223–55.

Ebbinghaus, B. and Visser, J. (2000). *Trade Unions in Western Europe since 1945*. London/New York: Macmillan.

Eckstein, H. (1975). 'Case Study and Theory in Political Science', in F. I. Greenstein and N. W. Polsby (eds.) *Strategies of Inquiry: Handbook of Political Science*. Reading, MA: Addison-Wesley.

Eder, M. (1999). 'Nationale und europäische Lösungsansätze der sozialen Problematik der Entsendung von Arbeitnehmern im Rahmen der Dienstleistungsfreiheit' [National and European Coping Mechanisms regarding the social problems arising with the posting of workers in the framework of the liberalization of service provision], Diploma thesis, Universität Wien, Austria.

Eeckhoff, Johann (1996) "Entsendegesetz – eine Aushöhlung der Wirtschaftsordnung", *Zeitschrift für Wirtschaftspolitik* 45 (1): 17–29

Ehrenberg, R.G. and Smith, R. S. (1997). *Modern Labor Economics: Theory and Public Policy*. Reading, MA: Addison-Wesley.

Eichhorst, W. (1998). *Europäische Sozialpolitik zwischen nationaler und supranationaler Regulierung: Die Entsendung von Arbeitnehmern im Rahmen der Dienstleistungsfreiheit der Europäischen Union* [European Social Policy between National and Supranational Regulation: The Posting of Workers in the Framework of the Liberalization of Services within the European Union], Dissertation, University of Konstanz, Germany.

EIRR – European Industrial Relations Review (1993) "Benelux: Minimum pay setting", May 1993, 232: 34–36

EIRR – European Industrial Relations Review (1994) "Scandinavia: Minimum pay setting", February 1994, 241: 24–27

EIRR – European Industrial Relations Review (1994) "Scandinavia: Minimum pay setting", February 1994, 241: 24–27

EIRR – European Industrial Relations Review (1996) "Current minimum pay rates", March 1996, 232: 16–18

EIRO – European Industrial Relations Observatory (1999), *Travailleurs détachés et mise en oeuvre de la directive*, Dublin: EIRO. September 1999.

EIRO (2002). 'Agreement Reached in Construction after Strike' http://www.eiro.eurofound.eu.int/print/2002/06/feature/de0206204f.html
—— (2003a). 'Thematic Feature: Posted Workers—France' http://www.eiro.eurofound.eu.int/2003/06/tfeature/fr0306108t.html
—— (2003b). 'Thematic feature: posted workers—Germany' http://www.eiro.eurofound.eu.int/2003/06/tfeature/de0306207t.html
—— (2003c). 'Thematic Feature: Posted Workers—the Netherlands'

www.eiro.eurofound.ie/print/2003/06/tfeature/nl0306105t.html

EIRO (2003d). 'Thematic Feature: Posted Workers—Belgium'
www.eiro.eurofound.ie/print/2003/06/tfeature/be0306104t.html

—— (2003e). 'Building Industry Unions Cease Cooperation with Employers' Association'
http://www.eiro.eurofound.eu.int/2003/07/inbrief/dk0307102n.html

—— (2003f). 'Thematic feature: posted workers—Sweden'
http://www.eiro.eurofound.eu.int/2003/06/tfeature/se0306104t.html

—— (2003g). 'Thematic Feature: Posted Workers—Norway'
http://www.eiro.eurofound.eu.int/2003/06/tfeature/no0306104t.html

—— (2003h). 'Thematic Feature: Posted Workers—Finland'
http://www.eiro.eurofound.eu.int/2003/06/tfeature/fi0306204t.html

—— (2003i). 'Thematic Feature: Posted Workers—Austria'
http://www.eiro.eurofound.eu.int/2003/06/tfeature/at0306204t.html

EIRO (2003k) 'Thematic Feature: posted workers – Germany' http://www.eiro.eurofound.eu.int/2003/06/tfeature/de0306207t.html

EIRO (2004) "Trade Union membership 1993–2003" http://www.eiro.eurofound.eu.int/2004/03/update/tn0403105u.html

EIRR (European Industrial Relations Review) (1992). 'Minimum Pay Setting: France', 227, December 1992: 18–19.

—— (1993). 'Five-year Employment Law Adopted', EIRR 239, December 1993: 6.

—— (1994a). 'Five-year Employment Law—Part One', EIRR 242, March 1994: 16–21.

—— (1994b). 'Five-year Employment Law—Part Two', EIRR 243, April 1994: 20–23.

—— (1994c). 'France: Posted Workers Decree', EIRR 247, August 1994.

Elster, J. (1987). 'The Possibility of Rational Politics', Archives Européennes de Sociologie, 28 (1): 67–103.

Esping-Andersen, G. (1990). Three Worlds of Welfare Capitalism. Princeton: Princeton University Press.

Estrin, S. and Holmes, P. (1983). French Planning in Theory and Practice. London: George Allen & Unwin.

Evangelista, M. (1999). Unarmed Forces: The Transnational Movement to End the Cold War. Ithaca, NY: Cornell University Press.

Evans, P., Rueschemeyer, D., and Skocpol, T. (eds.) (1985). Bringing the State Back. Cambridge: Cambridge University Press.

Fajertag, G. and Pochet, P. (eds.) (1997). Social Pacts in Europe. Brussels: European Trade Union Institute.

Falkner, G. (1993). '"Sozialdumping" im EG-Binnenmarkt: Betrachtungen aus politikwissenschaftlicher Sicht', Österreichische Zeitschrift für Politikwissenschaft, 22 (3): 261–76.

—— (1996). 'Sozialpolitik: Zwischen Sparpaketen und Lohndumping' in E. Talos and G. Falkner (eds.) EU-Mitglied Österreich—Gegenwart und Perspektiven: Eine Zwischenbilanz. Wien: Manz, 239–57.

—— (2000). 'How Pervasive are Euro-Politics? Effects of EU Membership on a New Member State', Journal of Common Market Studies, 38 (2): 223–50.

Falkner, G. (2004) with Treib, Oliver; Hartlapp, Miriam; Leiber, Simone (2004). 'Non-Compliance with EU Directives in the Member States: Opposition through the Backdoor?' *West European Politics*, 27 (3): 452–73.

Fassmann, H. and Münz, R. (1992). *Einwanderungsland Österreich?: Gastarbeiter, Flüchtlinge, Immigranten*, 4th edn. Wien: J&V: Edition Wien: Dachs-Verlag.

—— —— (eds.) (1994). *European Migration in the late Twentieth Century: Historical Patterns, Actual Trends, and Social Implications*. Aldershot, Hants, UK; Brookfield, VT: Edgar Elgar.

—— —— (2002). 'EU Enlargement and Future East-West Migration', in F. Laczko, I. Stacher, and A. Klekowski von Koppenfels (eds.) *New Challenges for Migration Policy in Central and Eastern Europe*. The Hague: Asser Press.

FAZ (March 24, 1993). 'Eine verjüngte Hochtief-Mannschaft entdeckt den Bauexport neu' [A younger Hochtief management re-discovers opportunities for export].

FAZ (June 18, 1993). 'In Frankreich wächst der Hang zum Protektionismus' [In France, there is an increasing tendency towards protectionism], p. 15.

FAZ (10 September 1994) 'Leiharbeiter für deutsche Baustellen' [Temporary Workers for German construction sites]

FAZ (September 29, 1993). 'Die Regierung Balladur will die Sozialkosten senken' [The Balladur government want to cut down social expenditures], p. 6.

FAZ (November 25, 1994). 'Holzmann befürchtet schwere Wettbewerbsverzerrungen' [Holzmann fears major disruption of competition].

FAZ (December 6, 1994). 'Am Horizont ein Baugigant' [A major construction colossus on the horizon].

FAZ (22 December 1994) "Einen Streik kann sich die Bauwirtschaft nicht leisten" [The construction sector cannot afford a strike]

FAZ (11 January 1995) "Die Rahmenbedingungen am Bau haben sich verschlechtert" [The conditions in the construction sector have deteriorated]

FAZ (16 January 1995) "Ein Tarifkartell und Europa" [A cartel of prices and Europe]

FAZ (August 23, 1995) "Das Entsendegesetz entzweit die Arbeitnehmerverbände" [Employer association are divided regarding the law no posted workers]

FAZ (15 November 1995) "Ein neuer Anlauf für das Entsendegesetz" [A new attempt at a law on posted workers]

FAZ (December 1, 1995) "Mindestlöhne für ausländische Bauarbeiter" [Minimum wages for foreign construction workers]

FAZ (7 December 1995) "Baugewerbe will einen Mindestlohn von 15 DM" [Construction employers want a minimum wage of 15 DM]

FAZ (16 January 1996) "Die Bauindustrie fürchtet einen Konjunktureinbruch" [Construction sector afraid of economic downturn]

FAZ (January 17, 1996) "Die IG BAU will sich beim Mindestlohn bewegen" [IG BAU wants to compromise regarding the minimum wage]

FAZ (February 10, 1996) "Geschlossen gene das Entsendegesetz" [United against the law on posted workers]

FAZ (15 April 1996) "IG Bau nimmt den Tarifkormpromiss an" [Construction union accept compromise on wages]

FAZ (May 12, 2000). 'Strabag sieht sich bereit für schnellere Verschmelzung' [Strabag prepared for quicker merger].

FAZ (May 19, 1999). 'Holzmann betrachet Umstrukturierung als abgeschlossen' [Holzmann considers to be done with restructuring].

FAZ (29 May 1996) "Im Baugewerbe wird es keine Mindestlöhne geben" [There will be no minimum wages in the construction sector]

FAZ (13 June 1996) "Die Bauindustrie kündigt die BDA-Mitgliedschaft" Construction sector employer quit their BDA membership]

FAZ (16 June 1996) "Bauindustrie fürchtet Welle von Unternehmenszusammenbrüchen" [Construction sector fears waves of bankruptcies]

FAZ (July 5, 1996). 'Das Siechtum von Maculan ist ein Menetekel für die Baubranche' [The slow disintegration of Maculan serves as prediction of disaster for the construction sector].

FAZ (12 July 1999) "Arbeitgeber warnen Riester vor Verfassungsbruch" [Employers warn Riester not infringe upon the constitution]

FAZ (17 July 1997) "Der Mindestlohn in der Bauwirtschaft sinkt" [The minimum wage in the construction sector decreases]

FAZ (15 August 1997) "Bau-Mindestlöhne gelten allgemeinverbindlich" [Minimum wages in the construction sector now universally applicable]

FAZ (24 August 1996) "Letzter Vorstoss für das Entsendegesetz" [Last Ditch Effort for the Law on Posted Workers]

FAZ (8 November 1996) "Blüm: Mindestlöhne bis August 1997 befristen" [Blüm "Limit minimum wages until August 1997]

FAZ (November 23, 1999). 'Rettungsversuch in letzter Minute für den Baukonzern Philipp Holzmann' [Last minute rescue attempt for construction company Philipp Holzmann].

FAZ (April 6, 2000). 'Die IG BAU versucht ein Husarenstück' [The IG BAU is attempting to pull off something outrageous].

Featherstone, K. and Radaelli C. (2003) (eds.). *The Politics of Europeanization*, Oxford: Oxford University Press.

Financial Times (20 August 1993). 'Paris Unveils Five-year Jobs Plan: Taxes on Employers to be Cut—More Flexible Labour Market Sought', p. 2.

Financial Times (6 October 1993). 'France's Job Creation Bill Passes Hurdle', p. 4.

Financial Times (April 6, 1994). 'Balladur Presses Ahead on Jobs', p. 3.

Financial Times (December 1, 1997). 'On Balance, too Good to Throw Away'.

Freyermuth, R. (1995). *Entsenderecht in Frankreich*, unpublished manuscript. Paris.

Garrett, G. (1998). *Partisan Politics in the Global Economy*. Cambridge/New York; Cambridge University Press.

—— and Lange P. (1986). 'Performance in a Hostile World: Economic Growth in Capitalist Democracies, 1974–1982', *World Politics*, 38 (4): 517–45.

—— —— (1989). 'Government Partisanship and Economic Performance: When and How Does "Who Governs" Matter', *The Journal of Politics* 51 (3): 676–93.

L. Gerken, M. Löwisch, V. Rieble (1995) *Der Entwurf eines Arbeitnehmerentsendege-setzes (AentG) in ökonomischer und rechtlicher Hinsicht*, Freiburg: Walter Eucken Institute.

Gerlich, P. (1992). 'A Farewell to Corporatism' in Luther, K. Richard, and W. Mueller (eds.) *Politics in Austria: Still a Case of Consociationalism?* London: Macmillian.

Gerlich, P., Grande, E., and Müller, W. C. (eds.) (1985). *Sozialpartnerschaft in der Krise. Leistungen und Grenzen des Neokorporatismus in Österreich*. Vienna: Signum.

German News (October 11, 1996 edn.). (Internet News Service based on Munich-based Bayerischer Rundfunk).

Geyer, R. (2000) *Exploring European Social Policy*, Cambridge: Polity Press.

Goetschy, J. (1998). 'France: The Limits of Reform', in A. Ferner and R. Hyman (eds.) *Changing Industrial relations in Europe*, 2nd edn. Malden, MA: Blackwell Publishers, pp. 357–95.

Goldstein, J. and R. Keohane (eds.) (1993). *Ideas and Foreign Policy: Beliefs, Institutions, and Political Change*. Ithaca, NY: Cornell University Press.

Goldthorpe, J. H. (ed.) (1984). *Order and Conflict in Contemporary Capitalism*. Oxford: Clarendon Press.

Goodin, R. E. (2003). 'Choose Your Capitalism?' *Comparative European Politics*, 1(2): 203–13.

Gourevitch, P. (1978). 'The Second Image Reversed: The International Sources of Domestic Politics', *International Organization*, 32 (4): 881–911.

Gourevitch, P. (1986) *Politics in Hard Times: Comparative Responses to international economic crises*, Ithaca, N.Y.: Cornell University Press.

Grant, W. (ed.) (1985). *The Political Economy of Corporatism*, London: Macmillian.

Greider, W. (1997). *One World, Ready or Not: The Manic Logic of Global Capitalism*, New York: Simon & Schuster.

Greif, W. (1998). 'Austria', in ETUI, *Handbook of Trade Unions in Europe*. Brussels: European Trade Union Institute, pp. 3–40.

Grote, J. and Schmitter, P. (1997). 'Der korporatistische Sisyphus: Vergangenheit, Gegenwart und Zukunft', *Politische Vierteljahresschrift*, 38 (3): 530–55.

Haas, E. (1968). *The Uniting of Europe*, 2nd edn. Stanford: Stanford University Press.

Hall, P. (1986). *Governing the Economy: The Politics of State Intervention in Britain and France*. Cambridge: Polity Press.

—— (ed.) (1989). *The Political Power of Economic Ideas: Keynesianism Across Nations*. Princeton, NJ: Princeton University Press.

—— and R.C.R. Taylor (1996). 'Political Science and the Three New Institutionalisms', *Political Studies*, 44: 952–73.

—— and Franzese, R. (1998). 'Mixed Signals: Central Bank Independence, Coordinated Wage Bargaining, and European Monetary Union', *International Organization*, 52 (3): 505–35.

—— and Soskice, D. (2001). *Varieties of Capitalism: The Institutional Foundations of Comparative Advantage*. Oxford: Oxford Universtiy Press.

Hammar, Brochmann, T. G. Tamas, K. and Faist, T. (eds.) (1997). *International Migration, Immobility and Development*. Oxford, UK/New York: Berg.

Hanau, P. (1996). 'Das Arbeitnehmer-Entsendegesetz', *Neue Juristische Wochenschrift*, 49 (21): 1369–73.

Hancké, B. (1997). 'Travail, capital et Etat: Relations de travail et ajustement économique en Europe', *Travail et Emploi*, 71 (2): 83–97.

—— (1999). 'Revisiting the French Model: Coordination and Restructuring in French Industry in the 1980s'. Discussion Paper FS 99–301, Berlin: Wissenschaftszentrum Berlin.

—— (2002). *Large Firms and Institutional Change. Industrial Renewal and Economic Restructuring in France*. Oxford: Oxford University Press.

Handelsblatt (11 January 1995) "Schutzzaun für Bausektor gefährdet Aufschwung" [Protective barrier for the construction sector jeopardizes economic recovery]

Handelsblatt (11 May 1995) "Die Weisheit der Weisen im Wandel" [The consensus among the economic advisers is changing]

Handelsblatt (June 28, 1995) "Entwicklung bleibt unterschiedlich" [Economic growth remains inconsistent]

Handelsblatt (July 24, 1995) "SPD will ein unbefristetes Entsendegesetz" [SPd want a temporarily unrestricted law on posted workers]

Handelsblatt (29 May 1996) "Arbeitgeber lehnen Mindestlohn ab" [Employers reject minimum wage]

Handelsblatt (July, 16 1996). 'Branche kämpft mit Überkapazitäten' [Sector struggles with surplus capacities].

Handelsblatt (April, 29 1997). 'Bouygues S.A: Baugruppe kehrt in die Gewinnzone zurück: Servicesparte bleibt Wachstumsmotor' [Bouygues S.A.: Construction company becomes profitable again: service sector remains growth engine].

Hanisch, E. (1994). *Der lange Schatten des Staates: 1890–1990. Österreichische Gesellschaftsgeschichte im 20. Jahrhundert*. Vienna.

Haas, E. B. (1958) *The Uniting of Europe: Political, social and economic forces 1950–1957*, Stanford, CA: Stanford University Press.

Haas, E. B. (1964) *Beyond the Nation-State: Functionalism and International Organization*, Stanford, CA: Stanford University Press.

Hassel, A. (1999). 'The Erosion of the German System of Industrial Relations', *British Journal of Industrial Relations*, 37 (3).

—— and Streeck, W. (2004). 'The Crumbling Pillars of Social Partnership' in H. Kitschelt and W. Streeck (eds.) *Germany: Beyond the Stable State, Special Issue of Western European Politics*, 26 (4): 101–14.

Hay, C. (2004). 'Common Trajectories, Variable Paces, Divergent Outcomes? Models of European Capitalism Under Conditions of Complex Economic Interdependence' *Review of International Political Economy*, 11 (2): 231–62.

Hay, C. and Rosamond, B. (2002). 'Globalisation, European Integration and the Discursive Construction of Economic Imperatives', *Journal of European Public Policy*, 9 (2): 147–67.

Hayward, J. (1973). *The One and Indivisible French Republic*. London: Methuen.

Heinisch, R. (1999). 'Modernization Brokers—Austrian Corporatism in Search for a new Legitimacy', *Current Politics and Economics of Europe* 9 (1): 65–94.

Heinisch, R. (2000). 'Coping with Economic Integration: Corporatist Response Strategies in Germany and Austria in the 1990s', *West European Politics*, 23 (3): 67–96.

Hennion-Moreau, S. (1994). 'Les prestations des services transnationales', *La semaine juridique*, Ed. E, 2: 25–8.

Heritier, A. (1996). 'The Accommodation of Diversity in European Policy-making and its Outcomes: Regulatory Policy as a Patchwork', *Journal of European Public Policy* 3 (2): 149–67.

—— et al. (1996) (eds.). *Ringing the Changes in Europe: Regulatory Competition and the Transformation of the State*. Berlin: DeGruyter.

—— et al. (2001) (eds.). *Differential Europe: European Union Impact on National Policy-Making*. Boulder, CO: Rowman & Littlefield.

Hirsch, J. (1998). *Vom Sicherheitsstaat zum nationalen Wettbewerbsstaat*. Berlin: ID-Verlag.

Hirst, P. and Thompson, G. (1995). *Globalization in Question*. Cambridge, UK: Polity Press.

Hirschman, A. (1970). *Exit, Voice, and Loyalty: Responses to Declines in Firms, Organizations and States*. Cambridge, MA: Harvard University Press.

Hoffmann, A. (1996). 'In Berlin stammen etwa 30,000 Bauarbeiter aus Ländern der EU. Hinzu kommen ebensoviele Illegale. Für die Firmen ist das ein gutes Geschäft, für die deutschen Arbeitnehmer aber nicht' [In Berlin there are about 30,000 construction workers from EU countries. In addition, there are as many illegal workers. For the companies this means good business, but not for the German employees], *Tagesspiegel*, February 1, 1996.

Hollifield, J. F. (1994). 'Immigration and Republicanism in France: The Hidden Consensus', in W. A. Cornelius, P. L. Martin, and J. F. Hollifield (eds.) *Controlling Immigration: A Global Perspective*. Stanford: Stanford University Press, 143–77.

Hollingsworth, J. R. and Boyer, R. (eds.) (1997). *Contemporary Capitalism: The Embeddedness of Institutions*. Cambridge, UK/New York: Cambridge University Press.

Hutton. W. (1995) *The State We're In*, London: Vintage.

Hyman, R. (1996). 'Institutional Transfer: Industrial Relations in Eastern Germany', *Work, Employment and Society*, 10 (4): 601–39.

Ignaz, P. (1997). 'The Extreme Right in Europe: A Survey', in P. Merkl and L. Weinberg (eds.) *The Revival of Right-Wing Extremism in the Nineties*. London: Frank Cass, pp. 47–65.

Immergut, E. (1990). 'Institutions, Veto Points, and Policy Results: A Comparative Analysis of Health Care', *Journal of Public Policy*, 10: 391–416.

—— (1992). *Health Care Politics: Ideas and Institutions in Western Europe*. Cambridge: Cambridge University Press.

—— (1992). 'The Rules of the Game: The Logic of Health Policy-making in France, Switzerland, and Sweden', in: S. Steinmo et al. (eds.), *Structuring Politics: Historical Institutionalism in Comparative Analysis*. Cambridge: Cambridge University Press.

Iversen, T. (1998). 'Wage Bargaining, Central Bank Independence, and the Real Effects of Money', *International Organization*.

Jacobi, O., Keller, B. and Müller-Jentsch, W. (1998). 'Germany: Facing New Challenges', A. Ferner and R. Hyman (eds.) *Changing Industrial Relations in Europe*. Oxford: Blackwell Publishers, pp. 190–239.

Jefferys, S. (1996). 'Down but not out: French Unions After Chirac', *Work, Employment, and Society*, 10 (3): 509–27.

Jordan, A. (2002). *The Europeanization of British Environmental Policy*. Basingstoke: Palgrave.

Karlhofer, F. and Tálos, E. (1996) (eds.). *Sozialpartnerschaft und EU: Integrationsdynamik und Handlungsrahmen der österreichischen Sozialpartnerschaft* [Social Partnership and EU: Dynamics of Integration and Framework of Actions of the Austrian Social Partnership]. Vienna: Signum.

—— (eds.) (1999). *Sozialpartnerschaft: Wandel und Reformfähigkeit*. Wien: Signum-Verlag.

Karlhofer, F. and Sickinger, H. (1999). 'Korporatismus und Sozialpakte im europäischen Vergleich', in F. Karlhofer, and E. Tálos (eds.) *Zukunft der Sozialpartnerschaft: Veränderungsdynamik und Reformbedarf*. Wien: Signum-Verlag, 241–74.

Katzenstein, P. J. (ed.) (1978). *Between Power and Plenty*. Madison: University of Wisconsin Press.

—— (1984). *Corporatism and Change: Austria, Switzerland, and the Politics of Industry*. Ithaca, NY: Cornell University Press.

—— (1985). *Small States in World Markets: Industrial Policy in Europe*. Ithaca, NY: Cornell University Press.

—— (1987). *Policy and Politics in West Germany: The Growth of a Semisovereign State*. Philadelphia: Temple University Press.

Katzenstein, P. (1989). 'Industry in a Changing West Germany', in P. Katzenstein, (ed.), *Industry and Politics in West Germany*. Ithaca, NY: Cornell University Press, pp. 3–29.

—— (ed.) (1996). *The Culture of National Security: Norms and Identity in World Politics*. New York: Columbia University Press.

Kauppinen, T. (1998) *The Impact of EMU on Industrial Relations in the European Union*, Helsinki: Finnish Labour Relations Association

Keeler, J. T. S. (1985). 'Situating France on the Pluralism-Corporatism Continuum', *Comparative Politics*, 17: 229–49.

—— (1987). *The Politics of Neocorporatism in France*. New York/Oxford: Oxford University Press.

—— and Schain, M. A. (eds.) (1996). *Chirac's Challenge: Liberalization, Europeanization, and Malaise in France*. New York: St. Martin's Press.

Keizer, P. K. (2001). 'A Critical Assessment of Recent Trends in Dutch Industrial Relations', in G. Szell (ed.) *European Labour Relations*. Aldershot: Gower, pp. 149–69.

Keohane, R. O. (1984) *After Hegemony*, Princeton, NJ: Princeton University Press.

Keohane, R. and H. Milner (1996) *Internationalization and Domestic Politics*, Cambridge/New York: Cambridge University Press.

Keynes, J. M. (1936). *The General Theory of Employment, Interest, and Money*. New York: Harcourt Brace.

Kirschbaum, Rita-Maria (1995) "Billing-Arbeitskräfte aus EU-Staaten?", *Recht der Arbeit* 6 (45), December: 533–544

Kitschelt, H., Lange, P. Marks, G. and Stephens, J. D. (1999). 'Convergence and Divergence in Advanced Capitalist Democracies', in Kitschelt, Lange, Marks and Stephens (eds.) *Continuity and Change in Contemporary Capitalism*. Cambridge: Cambridge University Press, ch. 15.

—————— (1999) (eds). *Continuity and Change in Contemporary Capitalism*. Cambridge: Cambridge University Press.

Kittel, B. and Talos, E. (1999). 'Interessenvermittlung und politischer Entscheidungsprozeß: Sozialpartnerschaft in den 1990er Jahren', in F. Karlhofer and E. Talos (eds.) *Sozialpartnerschaft: Wandel und Reformfähigkeit*. Wien: Signum-Verlag.

Kjellberg, A. (1998). 'Sweden: Restoring the Model', in A. Ferner and R. Hyman, ibid., 74–118.

Kleine Zeitung (29 August 1995) "EU-Konfliktstoff: Die Löhne am Bau" [EU-induced conflict: Wages in the construction sector]

Knechtel, E. F. (1992). *Die Bauwirtschaft in der EG: Unternehmen im internationalen Vergleich*. Wiesbaden/Berlin: Bau-Verlag.

Knechtel, E. F. (1998). *Auf Dialog gebaut: 50 Jahre Hauptverband der Deutschen Bauindustrie*. Wiesbaden/Berlin: Bau-Verlag.

Knill, C. (2001). *The Europeanisation of National Administrations: Patterns of Institutional Change and Persistence*. Cambridge: Cambridge University Press.

——and Lehmkuhl, D. (1999). 'How Europe Matters: Different Mechanisms of Europeanization', *European Integration Online Papers* (EIOP), 3 (7); available at http://www.eiop.or.at/eiop/texte/1999-007a.htm, internet accessed January, 2 2003.

—————— (2002). 'The National Impact of EU Regulatory Policy: Three Europeanization Mechanisms', *European Journal of Political Research*, 41 (2): 255–80.

——and Lenschow, A. (1998). 'Coping with Europe: The Impact of British and German Administrations on the Implementation of EU Environmental Policy', *Journal of European Public Policy*, 5: 595–614.

Köbele, B. and Leuschner, G. (eds.) (1995). *Dokumentation der Konferenz 'Europäischer Arbeitsmarkt. Grenzenlos mobil? 6.–8. März 1995'* [Documents from the Conference 'European Labor Market: Mobility without limitations?']. Baden-Baden: Nomos.

Koenigs, Folkmar (1997) "Rechtsfragen des Arbeitnehmer-Entsendegesetzes und der EG-Entsenderichtlinie", *Der Betrieb* 4, 1997: 225–231

Kohler-Koch, B. (1999). 'The Evolution and Transformation of European Governance', in B. Kohler-Koch and R. Eising (eds.) *The Transformation of Governance in the European Union*. Routledge: London, pp. 14–35.

Koslowski, T. (1999). 'Migration Flows in the 1990s: Challenges for Entry, Asylum and Integration Policy in Poland', in K. Iglicka and K. Sword (eds.) *The Challenge of East-West Migration for Poland*. London: Macmillan, pp. 45–66.

Krasner, S. D. (ed.) (1983). *International Regimes*. Ithaca, NY: Cornell University Press.

Der Kurier (August 23, 1995). 'Das Bau-Gerüst kippt' [The Construction Sector is falling over].

Labbé, D. (1996). *Syndicats et syndiqués en France depuis 1945*. Paris: L'Harmattan.

Ladrech, R. (1994). 'Europeanization of Domestic Politics and Institutions: The Case of France', *Journal of Common Market Studies*, 32 (1): 69–88.

Le Gales, P. and Aniello, V. (2001). 'Between Large Firms and Marginal Local Economies: The Making of Systems of Local Governance in France', in C. Crouch et al. (eds.), *Local Productive Systems in Europe*. Oxford, UK: Oxford University Press, pp. 147–80.

Lehmbruch, G. (1967). *Proporzdemokratie: Politisches System und politische Kultur in der Schweiz und in Österreich* [Proportional Democracy: Political System and Political Culture in Switzerland and Austria]. Tübingen: Mohr/Siebeck.

—— (1977). 'Liberal Corporatism and Party Government', *Comparative Political Studies*, 10 (1): 91–126.

—— (1982). 'Introduction: Neo-Corporatism in Comparative Perspective', in G. Lehmbruch and P. Schmitter (eds.), *Patterns of Corporatist Policy-Making*. Beverly Hills, CA: Sage, pp. 1–29.

—— (1984). 'Neo-Corporatism in Comparative Perspective', in G. Lehmbruch and P. Schmitter (eds.), ibid, 1–28.

—— and Schmitter, P. C. (eds.) (1982). *Patterns of Corporatist Policy-making*. London/ Beverly Hills, CA: Sage.

Levy, J. (1999) *Tocqueville's Revenge: State, Society, and Economy in Contemporary France*, Cambridge, MA: Harvard University Press.

Lijphart, A. (1968). *The Politics of Accommodation, Pluralism, and Democracy in the Netherlands*. Berkeley: University of California Press.

Lilja, K. (1998). 'Finland: Continuity and Modest Moves towards Company-Level Corporatism', in A. Ferner and R. Hyman (eds.), ibid., 171–89.

Lindberg, L. (1963). *The Political Dynamics of European Integration*. Stanford: Stanford University Press.

Lind, J. and H. Knudsen (1998) "Denmark" in European Trade Union Institute (eds.) Handbook of Trade Unions in Europe, Brussels; ETUI: 1–43

Lind, J., C. Gill and H. Knudsen (1998) "Are there cracks in the Danish model of industrial relations?", *Industrial Relations Journal* 29 (1): 30–41

Lubanski, N. (1999). 'The Impact of Europeanisation on the Construction Industry—A Comparative Analysis of Developments in Germany, Sweden and Denmark', *Industrielle Beziehungen* 6 (3): 268–91.

—— and Sörries, B. (1997). 'Internationalisation of the German Construction Industry—Keener Competition Leads to Pressure on the Collective Bargaining System', *CLR News*, 1: 2–19.

Mahnkopf. B. (1999) "Between the Devil and the Deep Blue Sea: The German Model under the pressure of Globalization", *Socialist Register 1999*: 142–177.

Marin, B. (1985). 'Austria—The Paradigm Case of Liberal Corporatism?', in W. Grant (ed.) *The Political Economy of Corporatism*. London: Macmillian, pp. 89–125.

March, J. G. and Olsen, J. P. (1989). *Rediscovering Institutions: The Organizational basis of Politics*. New York: Free Press; London: Collier Macmillan.

Markovits, A. S. (ed.) (1982). *The Political Economy of West Germany: Modell Deutschland*. New York : Praeger.

Markovits, A. S. (1986). *The Politics of the West German Trade Unions: Strategies of Class and Interest Representation in Growth and Crisis*. Cambridge, UK/New York: Cambridge University Press.

Marks, G. with Hooghe, L. and Blank, K. (1996). 'European Integration and the State: Multi-level vs. State Centric Governance', *Journal of Common Market Studies* 34 (3): 341–78.

——with Hooghe, L. (2003). 'Unraveling the Central State, bot How? Types of Multi-level Governance', *American Political Science Review*, 97 (2): 233–43.

Maromonte, K. R. (1998). *Corporate Strategic Business Sourcing*. Westport, CT.: Quorum Books.

Mekachera, H. (1993). 'La Population active etrangere en France', *Problemes economiques*, 2:356.

van der Meer, M. (2000). 'Less different, more similar to other sectors: Five trends in the Dutch construction industry', paper presented at conference on 'Structural Change in the Building Industry Labour Market', 19–20 October, Gelsenkirchen, Germany.

——and Roosblad, J. (2004). *Overcoming Marginalisation? Gender and Ethnic Segregation in the Dutch Construction, Health, IT and Printing Industries*. Amsterdam: Amsterdam Institute for Advanced Labour Studies, Working Paper, 24.

Mesch, M. (1995) (ed.). *Sozialpartnerschaft und Arbeitsbeziehungen in Europa*. Wien: Manz.

Mény, Y. P. M., and Quermonne, J.-L. (eds.) (1996). *Adjusting to Europe: The Impact of the European Union on National Institutions and Policies*. London/New York: Routledge.

Menz, G. (2001). 'Beyond the *Anwerbestopp?* The German-Polish Labor Treaty', *Journal of European Social Policy*, 11 (3): 253–71.

Millot, L. (2000). 'Tout de même, nous sommes differents', *Libération*, 3 October, p. 15.

MILUMO 1993

Ministerie van Sociale Zaken en Werkgelegenheid (25 September 1991) Letter to the Stichting van de Arbeid (reprinted in Stiching van de Arbeid "Advies inzake de uitvoering van Richtlijn 96/71/EG" [Advice regarding the implementation of EU directive 96/71/EC], Den Haag: Stichting van de Arbeid.

Le Monde (August 5, 1987). 'Dans le Var: le gérant d'une société écroue pour l'introduction illégale de travailleurs portugais en France' [In the Var region: company manager locked up for the illegal import of Portuguese workers to France], p. 22.

Le Monde (August 6, 1987). 'L'enquête: La main-d'oeuvre clandestine en France—Travailleurs sans papiers' [Special: The illegal workforce in France—Workers without documents], p. 1.

Le Monde (December 18, 1987). 'Sur plusieurs chantiers de la région parisienne: Une filière de travailleurs portugais sans papiers' [On several construction sites in the Paris region: A colon of Portuguese workers without working papers].

Le Monde (December 1, 1988). 'Selon l'INSEE 650000 entreprises n'emploient aucun salarie' [According to INSEE, 650,000 companies have no employees].

Le Monde (December 22, 1989). 'Dans l'Allier: Un chef d'entreprise inculpe pour avoir employé des Portugais en situation irrégulière' [In Allier: A company head indicted on charges of having employed Portuguese illegally], p. 9.

Le Monde (March 29, 1990). 'Une décision de la Commission européenne: Les concessionnaires étrangers de Peugeot pourront vendre des voitures en France' [A EU Commission decision: Foreign franchisers of Peugeot may sell cars in France, p. 34.

Le Monde (April 19, 1990). 'Prestation de services ou trafic de main d'œuvre: La délicate circulation des travailleurs portugais' [Provision of service or dealing with human labor: The delicate employment of Portuguese workers], p. 25.

Le Monde (May 16, 1990a). 'Les "placeurs" de main-d'oeuvre nouveaux négriers' [The middlemen of the new illegal workforce], p. 14.

Le Monde (May 16, 1990b). 'Les aléas de la lutte contre le travail clandestine' [The problems of the fight against illegal labor], p. 14.

Le Monde (July 4, 1990). 'Entreprises: Travail précaire pour tous' [Companies: Instable jobs for everybody], p. 2.

Le Monde (January 30, 1991). 'Chantiers européens' [European construction sites], p. 7.

Le Monde (April 24, 1991). 'Le chantier comme modèle: Les grands groupes du BTP multiplient leurs sociétés, mais la dispersion de leurs activités ne saurait tout expliquer' [The construction site as a model: The large construction companies increase their subunits, yet the dispersion of their activities does not account for all of it], p. 5.

Le Monde (June 14, 1991). 'Travail clandestine: Dix-huit chantiers contrôles par la gendarmerie en Ile-de-France' [Illegal work: 18 construction sites controlled by the police in the Ile-de-France (greater Paris region)], p. 38.

Le Monde (October 11, 1991). 'L'examen du projet de loi a l'Assemblée nationale— La fermeté affichée par le gouvernement sur le travail clandestin ne convainc pas l'opposition' [The draft bill in the National Assembly: The government's proclaimed tough stance on illegal labor does not convince the opposition], p. 8.

Le Monde (October 12, 1991). 'A l'Assemblee nationale les députes renforcent la répression du travail clandestin' [At the National assembly the MPs reinforce the suppression of illegal labor], p. 9.

Le Monde (December 12, 1991). 'Près de 100 travailleurs clandestine découverts dans l'Aube' [Almost 100 illegal workers discovered in Aube], p. 24.

Le Monde (June 24, 1992). 'Renforcement de la lutte contre le travail clandestin: Les employeurs devront faire une déclaration préalable d'embauche' [Reinforcement of the fight against illegal labor: Employers have to make a preliminary declaration of hiring workers], p. 20.

Le Monde (November 3, 1992). 'Dossier: La sous-traitance: Les conséquences de cette évolution?' [Special on Subcontracting: What are the consequences of this development?], p. 35.

Le Monde (November 10, 1992). 'A la suite de plusieurs affaires de travail clandestine une enquête est ouverte sur le chantier limousin d'Aussedat-Rey' [Following several incidents of illegal employment an examination is commenced at the construction site of Aussedat-Ray in the Limoges region], p. 16.

Le Monde (November 20, 1992). 'Depuis 1987: La lutte contre le travail clandestin a été nettement renforcée' [Since 1987 the fight against illegal work has been clearly reinforced], p. 18.

Le Monde (November 25, 1992). 'Dossier: Les inspecteurs du travail ont cents' and: l'inspection au quotidien' [Special Section: The labor inspectoriat is a hundred years old: The everyday life of an inspector], p. 29.

Le Monde (December 17, 1992a). 'Point:Les étrangers et l'emploi: L'immigration de travailleurs n'a jamais cesse' [Focus: Foreigners and employment: Labor immigration has never stopped], p. 12.

Le Monde (December 17, 1992b). 'Point: Les Etrangers et l'emploi: Les comptes flous du travail illégal' [Focus: Foreigners and employment: The hazy figures on illegal labor], p. 12.

Le Monde (June 23, 1993). 'Malgré les réserves de l'UDF: L'Assemblee nationale adopte le projet de loi sur l'emploi et l'apprentissage' [Despite the reservations of the UDF: The National Assembly adopts the first draft of the law on labor and education], p. 8.

Le Monde (August 18, 1993). 'La réunion a l'hôtel Matignon de plusieurs ministres autour de M.Balladur—Le gouvernement met la dernière main a l'avant-projet de loi quinquennale sur l'emploi' [Meeting of the ministers at the Matignon building around Mr. Balladur—the government has the final say on the first draft of the five year law on employment], p. 20.

Le Monde (August 24, 1993). 'Les réactions au plan quinquennal pour l'emploi—Le Parti socialiste annonce "une rude bataille" ' [Reactions to the five-year project on employment—the Socialist Party announces a 'tough battle'], p. 8.

Le Monde (September 6, 1993). 'Le CNPF, l'UPA et la CGPME reçues par M. Giraud: Le patronat exprime des réserves face a la loi quinquennale sur l'emploi' [CNPF, UPA and CGPME met by Mr Giraud: The employers express their reservations regarding the Five-Year law on Employment], p. 13.

Le Monde (September 7, 1993). 'Le projet de loi quinquennale sur l'emploi: Les partenaires sociaux attendaient peu de leur rencontre avec M. Balladur' [The Five-Year Law on Employment project: The social partners expect little from their meeting with Mr. Balladur], p. 17.

Le Monde (September 29, 1993). 'Décides a amender le texte du gouvernement les députes jugent insuffisant le projet de loi sur l'emploi' [Having decided to amend the government's draft bill, MPs consider the law on employment to be insufficient], p. 1.

Le Monde (July 6, 1994). 'La mise en œuvre de la loi quinquennale sur l'emploi' [Implementing the Five Year Law on Employment], p. 17.

Le Monde (July 14, 1994). 'Un décret limite la "concurrence déloyale" des entreprises étrangères qui détachent des salaries en France' [A decree limiting the 'unfair competition' of foreign companies which post workers to France], p. 14.

Le Monde (September 24, 1996). 'Les pouvoirs des policiers seront étendus face au travail clandestine' [Police powers concerning illegal employment will be expanded].

Moravcsik, A. (1991). 'Negotiating the Single European Act', in R. O. Keohane and S. Hoffmann (eds.). *The New European Community*. Boulder: Westview Press, pp. 44–84.

Moravcsik, Andrew (1998) *The Choice for Europe. Social Purpose and State Power from Messina to Maastricht*. Ithaca, N.Y.: Cornell University Press.

—— (1993). 'Preferences and Power in the European Community: A Liberal Inter-governmentalist Approach', *Journal of Common Market Studies*, 31 (4): 473–524.

—— (1998). *The Choice for Europe. Social Purpose and State Power from Messina to Maastricht*. Ithaca, NY: Cornell University Press.

Moreau, M.-A. (1995). *'Les problèmes créés par la libre prestation de service dans l'Union européenne'*, unpublished manuscript, University of Aix-en-Provence/Marseille.

Mouriaux, R. (1993). *Les Syndicats dans la société française*. Paris: Fondation Nationale des Sciences Politiques.

—— (1994). *Le Syndicalisme en France depuis 1945*. Paris: La Découverte.

—— (1997). *Le Syndicalisme en France*. Paris: Presses Universitaires de France.

Müller, W. and Wright, V. (1994) (eds.). *Special Issue of West European Politics: The State in Western Europe: Retreat or Redefinition?* 17 (3).

Müller, W. C. (1986). 'Privatization in Austria', *West European Politics*.

Münz, R. W. S. and Ulrich, R. (1999). *Zuwanderung nach Deutschland: Strukturen, Wirkungen, Perspektiven* [Migration to Germany: Structures, Effects, Perspectives], 2nd edn. Frankfurt am Main/New York: Campus.

Neue Kronenzeitung (April 18, 1998). 'Bauwirtschaft: Eine Branche kommt unter den Hammer' [The Construction Industry: A Sector is getting the shaft].

Neue Zürcher Zeitung (September 29, 1998). 'Zwei Schritte vorwärts, eineinhalb zurück' [Two steps forward, one and a half steps back].

Nick, R. and Pelinka, A. (1983). *Bürgerkrieg—Sozialpartnerschaft* [*Civil War—Social Partnership*]. Vienna: Jugend und Volk Verlag.

North, D. (1981). *Structure and Change in Economic History*. New York: W.W. Norton.

North, D. (1984). 'Transaction Costs, Institutions and Economic History', *Journal of Institutional and Theoretical Economics*, 140: 7–17.

—— (1990). *Institutions, Institutional Change, and Economic Performance*. Cambridge: Cambridge University Press.

OECD (1997) *OECD Economic Surveys France 1997*. Paris: OECD.

OECD (1998) *OECD Economic Surveys Germany 1998*. Paris: OECD.

OECD (1999) *OECD Wirtschaftsberichte Österreich 1999*. Paris: OECD.

OECD (2003) *OECD Economic Surveys Austria 2003*. Paris: OECD.

Offe, C. and Wiesenthal, H. (1980) "Two Logics of Collective Action: Theoretical Notes on Social Class and Organizational Form", *Political Power and Social Theory* 1: 67–115.

Ohmae, K. (1990). *The Borderless World. Power and Strategy in the Interlinked Economy*. New York: Harper Business.

Olney, S. L. (1996). *Unions in a Changing World*. Geneva: International Labor Office.

Olsen, J. (2002). 'The Many Faces of Europeanization', *Journal of Common Market Studies*, 40 (5): 921–52.

Olson, M. (1965). *The Logic of Collective Action*. Cambridge, MA: Harvard University Press.

—— (1982). *The Rise and Decline of Nations*. New Haven, CT: Yale University Press.

Ostrom, E. (1990) *Governing the Commons: The Evolution of Institutions for Common Action*, Cambridge/New York: Cambridge University Press.

Pahl, H.-D., Stroink, K., and Syben, G. (1995). *Betriebliche Arbeitskraftprobleme und Produktionskonzepte in der Bauwirtschaft*, Bremen: Forschungsgruppe BAQ Universität Bremen—Abschlußbericht.

Pelinka, A. (1981). *Modellfall Österreich? Möglichkeiten und Grenzen der Sozialpartnerschaft* [Model Austria? Capabilities and Limits of the Social Partnership]. Vienna: Braumüller.

Le Pen, J.-M. (1984). *Les Français d'abord*. Paris: Carrère-Michel Laffon.

Pestoff, V. A. (1995). 'Towards a New Swedish Model of Collective Bargaining and Politics', in C. Crouch and F. Traxler (eds.) *Organized Industrial Relations in Europe: What Future?* Aldershot, UK: Avebury, pp. 151–83.

Peters, B. G. (1999). *Institutional Theory in Political Science: The New Institutionalism*. London/New York: Pinter.

Pierson, P. (1996). 'The Path to European Integration—A Historical Institutionalist Analysis', *Comparative Political Studies*, 29 (2): 123–63.

—— (1997). *Increasing Returns, Path Dependence and the Study of Politics*. Florence: The Robert Schuman Centre at the European University Institute.

Pierson, P. (2000, "Path Dependence, Increasing Returns, and the Study of Politics," *American Political Science Review*, 94 (2), June: 251–67.

Piore, M. J. (1979). *Birds of Passage: Migrant Labor and Industrial Societies*. Cambridge/New York: Cambridge University Press.

Polanyi, K. (1944). *The Great Transformation*. New York: Farrar & Rinehart.

Pollack, M. A. (2003) *The Engines of European Integration: Delegation, Agency and Agenda Setting in the EU*, New York: Oxford University Press.

Pontusson, J. and Golden, M. (1992). *Bargaining for Change: Union Politics in North America and Europe*. Ithaca, NY: Cornell University Press.

Pontusson, J. and Swenson, P. (1996). 'Labor Markets, Production Strategies, and Wage Bargaining Institutions: The Swedish Employer Offensive in Comparative Perspective', *Comparative Political Studies*, 29, 2: 223–50.

Pontusson, J. (1997) "Between neoliberalism and the German model: Swedish Capitalism in Transition" in C. Crouch and W. Streeck (eds.) Political Economy of Modern Capitalism, London: Sage: 77–96.

Powell, W. W. and DiMaggio, P. J. (eds.) (1991). *The New Institutionalism in Organizational Analysis*. Chicago: University of Chicago Press.

Die Presse (2 April 1993) "Vor Wirtschafts-Debatte: Tauziehen um Pleitegesetze – Hesoun sagt Schwarzarbeit neuerlich den Kampf an" [Before the Parliamentary Debates on economic affairs: Conflicts over bankruptcy laws – Hesoun announces measures against illegal forms of employment]

Die Presse (2 June 1993) "Die EG zeigte Verständnis für Wiens Forderungen" [EC accepts Vienna's demands]

Die Presse (September 19, 1995). 'Strabag und Stuag bilden neuen Bau-Riesen' [Strabag and Stuag will from new construction conglomerate].

Die Presse (February 27, 1996). 'Maculan-Gruppe steht vor dem Ende' [Maculan Group is at the end].

Die Presse (January 8, 1996). 'Österreichs Bauwirtschaft kämpft ums Überleben' [Austria's Construction sector in a fight for survival].

Die Presse (January 9, 1996). 'Schon bald 300,000 Arbeitslose? Auch im Sommer hoher "Sockel" ' [300,000 unemployed soon? High levels even in the summer].

Die Presse (6 August 1996). 'Maculan-Konkurs eröffnet' [Bankruptcy process of Maculan commences]

Die Presse (December 2, 1997). 'Konsensdenken—Institutionen prägen Wirtschaftspolitik' [Consensus-style thinking—Institutions shpae economic policy].

Profil (4 September 1995) "Dumpen statt denken" [Dumping instead of thinking]

Przeworski, A. (1985). *Capitalism and Social Democracy*. New York: Cambridge University Press.

—— and Teune, H. (1970). *The Logic of Comparative Social Inquiry*, New York: Wiley-Interscience.

Putnam, R. (1988). 'Diplomacy and Domestic Politics: The Logic of Two-Level Games', *International Organization*, 42 (3): 427–60.

Queneau, H. and Kaisergruber, D. (1997). *Etude sur le marché du travail: France* [A Study of the Labor Market: France], Report commissioned by the European Commission, DG for Employment, Industrial Relations and Social Affairs. Luxembourg: European Communities

Ragin, C. S. and Becker, H. S. (1992). *What is a Case? Exploring the Foundations of Social Inquiry*. Cambridge: Cambridge University Press.

van Regenmortel and Jorens, Y. (1995). *Le détachement international*. Brugge, Belgium: La Charte.

Radaelli, C. M. (2000). 'Whither Europeanization? Concept Stretching and Substantive Change', available at http://eiop.or.at/eiop/texte/2000-008.htm, Internet accessed 15 January 2003.

—— (2003). 'The Europeanization of Public Policy', in K. Featherstone and C. M. Radaelli (eds.) *The Politics of Europanization*, Oxford/New York: Oxford University Press, pp. 27–56.

Regini, M. (1997). 'Still Engaging in Corporatism? Einige Erfahrungen aus jüngsten italienischen Erfahrungen mit der Konzertierung', *Politische Vierteljahresschrift*, 38, (2): 298–317.

—— (2000). 'Between Deregulation and Social Pacts: The Responses of European Economies to Globalization', *Politics & Society*, 28 (1): 5–33.

Reim, U. and Sandbrink, S. (1996). *Die Werkvertragsabkommen als Entsenderegelung für Arbeitnehmer aus den Staaten Mittel-und Osteuropas*. Zentrum für Sozialpolitik, Universität Bremen, Arbeitspapier 12/96.

Reynaud, J.-D. (1978). *Les Syndicats, les patrons et l'Etat—Tendances de la negociation collective en France* [The Unions, the employers, and the State—Tendencies of collective bargaining in France]. Paris: Les Editions Ouvrieres.

Rhodes, M. (1991). 'The Social Dimension of the Single European Market: National versus Transnational Regulation', *European Journal of Political Research*, 19: 245–80.

—— (1997). *Globalisation, Labour Markets and Welfare State: A Future of Competitive Corporatism?* Florence: EUI Robert Schuman Centre, Working Paper 97/36.

Risse-Kappen, T. (1994). 'Ideas Do not Float Freely: Transnational Coalitions, Domestic Structures, and the End of the Cold War', *International Organization*, 48 (2): 185–214.

Ritmeijer, W. S. R. (1994). 'Die Entsendung im Baugewerbe', in B. Köbele, and G. Leuschner, (eds.), ibid., pp. 31–97.

Robin, S. (1994). 'L'application du droit social français aux entreprises prestataires de services établies à l'étranger', *Droit social*, 2: 127–35.

Ross, G. (1982). 'The Perils of Politics: French Unions and the Crisis of the 1970s', in P. Lange, G. Ross, and M. Vanicelli (eds.) *Unions, Change and Crisis: French and Italian Union Strategy and the Political Economy 1945–1980*. London: George Alen & Unwin.

Rojot, J. (1988). 'The Myth of French Exceptionalism', in J. Barbash, and K. Barbash (eds.) *Theories and Concepts in Comparative Industrial Relations*. Columbia, SC: University of South Carolina Press.

Rothery, B. (1995). *The Truth about Outsourcing*. Aldershot, UK/Brookfield, VT: Gower.

Ruggie, J. (1982). 'International Regimes, Transactions and Change: Embedded Liberalism in the Postwar Economic Order', *International Organization*, 36 (2).

Ruggie, J. (1993). 'Territoriality and Beyond: Problematizing Modernity in International Relations', *International Organization*, 47 (1): 139–74.

Russig, V. (1996). 'Bauwirtschaft in Deutschland: Beschleunigter Strukturwandel', *ifo Schnelldienst*, 25–26: 14–29.

—— Deutsch, S. and Spillner, A. (1996). *Branchenbild Bauwirtschaft: Entwicklung und Lage des Baugewerbes sowie Einflußgrößen und Perspektiven der Bautätigkeit in Deutschland*. Berlin: Duncker und Humblot.

Sadowski, D. and Jacobi, O. (eds.) (1991). *Employers' Associations in Europe: Policy and Organization*. Baden-Baden, Germany: Nomos Verlagsgesellschaft.

Salzburger Nachrichten (January 26, 1999). 'Baugewerbe kämpft um Aufträge' [Construction sector is battling for orders].

Sammet, G., Jr. and Kelley, C. G. (1980). *Do's and Don'ts in Subcontract Management*. New York: AMACOM.

Sandholtz, W. and A. Stone Sweet, (eds.) (1998) *European Integration and Supranational Governance*, Oxford/New York; Oxford University Press.

Schain, M. A. (1975). *The French Trade Union Movement: Mass Action, Organization and Politics*. Ann Arbor, MI: University Microfilms.

Schain, M. (1980). 'Corporatism and Industrial Relations in France', in P. G. Cerny and M. A. Schain (eds.) *French Politics and Public Policy*. New York: St. Martin's Press, pp. 191–217.

Schain, M. (1987). 'The National Front in France and the Construction of Political Legitimacy', *West European Politics*, 10 (2): 229–52.

Scharpf, F. W. (1991). *Crisis and Choice in European Social Democracy*. Ithaca, NY: Cornell University Press.

—— (1996). 'Negative and Positive Integration in the Political Economy of European Welfare States', in G. Marks, F. Scharpf, P. Schmitter, and W. Streeck (eds.) *Governance in the European Union*. London: Sage, pp. 15–39.

—— and Schmidt, V. A. (eds.) (2000). *Welfare and Work in the Open Economy*, Vol. I: *From Vulnerability to Competitiveness*; Vol. 2: *Diverse Responsesto Common Challenges*. Oxford: Oxford University Press.

Schemers, H. G., Flinterman, C. Kellermann, A. E. van Haersolio, J. C., and van de Meent, G.-W. A. (1994). *Free Movement of Persons in Europe*. Amsterdam: Martinus Nijhoff Publishers.

Scheuer, S. (1996). 'Denmark: A Less Regulated Model', in A. Ferner and R. Hyman, ibid., pp. 146–89.

Schmidt, M. G. (1982). 'Does Corporatism Matter? Economic Crisis, Politics and Rates of Unemployment in Capitalist Democracies in the 1970s', in G. Lehmbruch and P. Schmitter (eds.) *Patterns of Corporatist Policy-Making*. Beverly Hills, CA: Sage.

Schmidt, V. A. (1996a). *From State to Market? The Transformation of French Business and Government*. Cambridge: Cambridge University Press.

—— (1996b) 'Loosening the Ties that Bind: The Impact of European Integration on French Government and its Relationship to Business', *Journal of Common Market Studies*, 34 (2): 223–54.

—— (2002). *The Futures of European Capitalism*. Oxford: Oxford University Press.

Schmitter, P. C. (1974). 'Still the Century of Corporatism?', *Review of Politics*, 36: 85–131.

—— (1981). 'Interest Intermediation and Regime Governability in Contemporary Western Europe and North America', in S. Berger (ed.) *Organising Interests in Western Europe*. Cambridge: Cambridge University Press, 285–327.

—— (1989). 'Corporatism is Dead! Long Live Corporatism! Reflections on Andrew Shonfield's Modern Capitalism', *Government and Opposition*, 24: 54–73.

Schmitter, P. C. (1974) and G. Lehmbruch (eds.) (1979). *Trends Towards Corporatist Intermediation*. London: Sage.

—— and Grote, J. R. (1997). 'The Corporatist Sisyphus: Past, Present and Future', EUI Working Papers, European University Institute: San Domenico, Italy.

Schwartz, H. (1994). 'Small States in Big Trouble', *World Politics*, 46 (4): 527–55.

Shepsle, K. (1986). 'Institutional Equilibrium and Equilibrium Institutions', in H. Weisberg (ed.) *Political Science: The Science of Politics*. New York: Agathon.

Shepsle, K. (1989). 'Studying Institutions: Lessons from the Rational Choice Approach', *Journal of Theoretical Politics*, 1: 131–47.

Shepsle, K. and Weingast, B. (1995). *Positive Theories of Congressional Institutions*. Ann Arbor, MI: University of Michigan Press.

Shonfield, A. (1965). *Modern Capitalism: The Changing Balance of Public and Private Power*. Oxford/New York: Oxford University Press.

Silverman, M. (1992). *Deconstructing the Nation : Immigration, Racism, and Citizenship in Modern France*. London/New York: Routledge.

Skocpol, T. (1979). *States and Social Revolutions: A Comparative Analysis of France, Russia, and China*. Cambridge: Cambidge University Press.

—— (1992). *Protecting Soldiers and Mothers: The Political Origins of Social Policy in the United States*. Cambridge/New York: Cambridge University Press.

Slomp, H. (1996). *Between Bargaining and Politics: An Introduction to European Labor Relations*. Westport, CT: Praeger.

Snyder, G. H. and Diesing, P. (1977). *Conflict among Nations: Bargaining and Decision-Making in International Crises*. Princeton: Princeton University Press.

Soskice, D. and Schettkat, R. (1993). 'West German Labor Market Institutions and East German Transformation', in L. Ulman, B. Eichengreen, and W. Dickens (eds.) *Labor and an Integrating Europe*. Washington, DC: Brookings.

Soskice, D. and Hall, P. (2001). *Varieties of Capitalism: The Institutional Foundations of Comparative Advantage*. Oxford: Oxford University Press.

SPD 2000 – personal communication to the author by representative of the SPD fraction in the *Bundestag*

Der Standard (November 4, 1992). 'Ausverkauf als Krisenrezept?' [Sell-out as a recipe to master a crisis?].

Der Standard (March 9, 1993). 'Kampf gegen Fremdbestimmung' [Struggle against foreign domination].

Der Standard (28 August 1995) "ÖGB will neues Gesetz gegen EU-Billigarbeiter" [Union wants new law against cheap workers from other EU countries]

Der Standard (29 August 1995) "Haselsteiner beharrt auf Portugiesen" [Haselsteiner insists on using Portuguese posted workers]

Der Standard (28 August 1995) "ÖGB will neues Gesetz gene EU-Billigarbeiter" [Trade unions wants new law against cheap workers from the EU]

Der Standard (30 August 1995) "Nicht nur Bauarbeiter schützen" [Protect not only construction workers]

Der Standard (8 September 1995) "Bessere Dichtung gegen Lohndumping" [Better Insulation against Wage Dumping]

Der Standard (September 25, 1995). 'Bauwirtschaft auf festen Fundamenten' [Construction industry on solid grounds].

Der Standard (4–5 November 1995) "Doch kein Schutz vor Portugiesen" [No protection against "Portuguese" after all]

Der Standard (17 November 1995) "Lange Nächte und kein Ende in Sichtweite" [Long nights and no end in sight]

Die Presse (18 November 1995) "Hochbetrieb bis in die Nachtstunden" [Keeping busy until the wee hours]

Der Standard (22 November 1995) "Haselsteiner stimmt "gegen" Portugiesen" [Haselsteiner votes "against" the Portuguese]

Der Standard (October 28–29, 1995). 'Wifo-Expertin schlägt Konjunkturalarm' [WIFO Expert calls to attention economic development].

Der Standard (April 4, 1996). 'Regierungsoffensive fuer Bauwirtschaft ohne Wirkung' [Government initiatives for construction industry without effects].

Der Standard (October 30, 1996). 'Baukonjunktur vom Kraftakt der Bundesregierung unberührt' [Economic development unaffected by federal government's maneuver].

Der Standard (February 10, 1997). 'Der Konjunkturmotor Bauwirtschaft stottert' [Economic Engine Construction Industry Comes to halt].

Der Standard (November 9, 1997). 'Dinosaurier im Klimawandel' [Dinosaurs in a changing climate].

Der Standard (February 27, 1999). 'Heimische Baubranche fällt zurück' [Domestic construction sector falls back (in competition)].

Der Standard (November 26, 1999). 'Maroder Baukonzern Holzmann erhält Finanzspritze von 30 Milliarden Schilling: Zorn über Schröders Rettungsaktion' [Leaking construction company receives 30 billion AST in aid: anger about Schroeder's intervention].

Steinmo, S. (1993). *Taxation and Democracy: Swedish, British, and American Approaches towards Financing the Modern State*. New Haven: Yale University Press.

—— Thelen, K., and Longstreth, F. (1992). *Structuring Politics: Historical Institutionalism in Comparative Analysis*. Cambridge: Cambridge University Press.

Stone Sweet, A., W. Sandholtz, and N. Fligstein (eds.) (2001) *The Institutionalization of Europe*, Oxford/New York: Oxford University Press

Strange, S. (1996). *The Retreat of the State: The Diffusion of Power in the World Economy*, Cambridge/New York: Cambridge University Press.

Straubhaar, T. (1988). 'International Labor Migration within a Common Market: Some Aspects of the EC Experience', *Journal of Common Market Studies*, 27 (1): 45–62.

Streeck, W. (1991). *From National Corporatism to Transnational Pluralism: European Interest Politics and the Single Market*. Notre Dame, IN: Helen Kellogg Institute for International Studies, University of Notre Dame.

Streeck, W. (1992). *Social Institutions and Economic Performance – Studies of Industrial Relations in Advanced Capitalist Economies*. Newbury Park, CA: Sage.

Streeck, W. (1993). 'The Rise and Decline of Neo-corporatism', in L. Ulman, B. Eichengreen, and W. Dickens (eds.) *Labor and an Integrating Europe*. Washington, DC, pp. 80–99.

—— (1996). *German Capitalism: Does it exist? Can it Survive?* Notre Dame, IN: The Helen Kellogg Institute for International Studies.

—— (1997). 'Le Capitalisme Allemande: Existe-t-il? Peut-il Survivre?' in C. Crouch and W. Streeck, ibid., pp. 33–55.

—— (1998). 'The Internationalization of Industrial Relations in Europe: Prospects and Problems', MPIfG Discussion Paper 98/2. Köln: MPIfG.

Swenson, P. (1989). *Fair Shares: Unions, Pay and Politics in Sweden and West Germany*. Ithaca, NY: Cornell University Press.

—— (1992). 'Union Politics, the Welfare State, and Intraclass Conflict in Sweden and Germany', in Golden and Pontusson, ibid., pp. 45–77.

Sweeney, J. and Weidenholzer, J. (1988). *Austria: A Study in Modern Achievement*. Aldershot, UK: Avebury.

Syndicalisme (February 13, 1992). 'Fausse sous-traitance, travail clandestin'.

Syndicalisme (December 10, 1992). 'Agir préventivement'.

Syndicalisme (February 11, 1993). 'A fond la form'.

Syndicalisme (May 20, 1993). 'Travail clandestin : une convention pour l'action'.

Syndicalisme (June 10, 1993). 'Salaries minima 1993'.

Syndicalisme (August 19, 1993). 'Coups de pouce pour l'emploi et le contractuel'.

Syndicalisme (August 26, 1993). 'Avant-projet de loi quinquennale sur l'emploi'.

Syndicalisme (September 2, 1993). 'Plan quinquennal pour l'emploi et la formation professionnelle'.

Syndicalisme (September 9, 1993). 'Une progression béton'.

Syndicalisme (September 30, 1993). 'La réduction du temps de travail se conjugue avec l'emploi'.

Syndicalisme (November 4, 1993). 'Sortir les irréguliers de la clandestinité'.

Syndicalisme (November 12, 1993). 'Le projet de loi quinquennale au Sénat'.

Syndicalisme (December 2, 1993). 'Les points essentiels'.

Syndicalisme (December 23, 1993). 'À Savoir'.

Syndicalisme (February 24, 1994). 'Loi quinquennale pour l'emploi: Mesures et mises en œuvre'.

Syndicalisme (October 12, 2000). 'L'insoutenable légèreté du patron des bûcherons roumains'.

Tagesspiegel (17 January 1995) "Konzertierte Aktion gegen Billigkräfte" [Concerted action against cheap workers]

Tagesspiegel (September 29, 1995) "Arbeitgeber riskieren den Eklat" [Employers move towards confrontation]

Tagesspiegel, February 1, 1996 "In Berlin stammen etwa 30,000 Bauarbeiter aus Ländern der EU. Hinzu kommen ebensoviele Illegale. Für die Firmen ist das ein gutes Geschäft, für die deutschen Arbeitnehmer aber nicht" [In Berlin there are about 30,000 construction workers from EU countries. In addition, there are just as many illegal workers. For the companies this means good business, but not for the German employees]

Tálos, E. (ed.) (1993). *Sozialpartnerschaft—Kontinuität und Wandel eines Modells.* Wien: Signum-Verlag.

—— and Falkner, G. (eds.) (1996). *EU-Mitglied Österreich—Gegenwart und Perspektiven: Eine Zwischenbilanz.* Wien: Manz.

—— Leichsenring, K., and Zeiner, E. (1993). 'Verbände und politischer Entscheidungsprozeß—am Beispiel der Sozial- und Umweltpolitik', in E. Talos (ed.) *Sozialpartnerschaft: Kontinuität und Wandel eines Modells* [Social Partnership: Continuity and Change of a Model]. Wien: Signum-Verlag, pp. 147–85.

Taquet, F. (1993). 'Détachement, expatriation', *Semaine Sociale Lamy*, 651 (7): D1–D15.

Taylor, A. (1989). *Trade Unions and Politics.* New York: St. Martin's Press.

Taylor, P. (1983). *The Limits of European Integration.* New York: Columbia University Press.

Taz—die tageszeitung (December 4, 1999). 'Lohnverzicht und Mehrarbeit gerettet' [Agreement salvaged on foregoing wages and working longer hours].

Thelen, K. (1991). *Union of Parts: Labor politics in postwar Germany.* Ithaca, NY: Cornell University Press.

Tiroler Tageszeitung (24 August 1995) "Jetzt Wirbel um billige EU-Bauarbeiter" [Controverys surrounding cheap EU construction workers continues]

—— (2001). 'Varieties of Labor Politics in the Developed Democracies', in P. Hall and D. Soskice (eds.). *Varieties of Capitalism: The Institutional Foundations of Comparative Advantage*. Oxford/New York: Oxford University Press: pp. 71–103.

Tomandl, T. and Fuerbock, K. (1986). *Social Partnership—The Austrian System of Industrial Relations and Social Insurance*. Ithaca, NY: Cornell University Press.

Traxler, F. (1995). 'From Demand-Side to Supply-Side Corporatism? Austria's Labour Relations and Public Policy', in C. Crouch and F. Traxler, ibid., pp. 271–87.

—— (1998). 'Austria: Still the Country of Corporatism', in A. Ferner and R. Hyman, ibid., pp. 239–62.

—— (1996). 'Sozialpartnerschaft am Scheideweg: Zwischen korporatistischer Kontinuität und neoliberalem Umbruch', *Wirtschaft und Gesellschaft*, 22 (1): 13–33.

Tsebelis, G. (1990) *Nested Games: Rational Choice in Comparative Politics*, Berkeley, CA: University of California Press.

Tsebelis, G. (1995). 'Decision-Making in Political Systems: Veto Players in Presidentialism, Parliamentarism, Multicameralism and Multipartyism', *British Journal of Political Science*, 25 (3): 289–325.

Ucarer, E. and Puchala, D. J. (eds.) (1997). *Immigration into Western Societies: Problems and Policies*. London/Washington: Pinter.

Ulman, L., Eichengreen, B., and Dickens, W. T. (eds.) (1993). *Labor and an Integrated Europe*. Washington, DC: Brookings Institution.

Unger, B. (1999). 'Österreichs Wirtschaftspolitik: Vom Austro-Keynesianismus zum Austro-Neoliberalismus?' in F. Karlhofer and E. Talos (eds.) ibid., pp. 165–90.

Unger, B. and van Waarden, F. (1993). *A Comparison of the Construction Industry in Europe*. Wirtschaftsuniversität Wien, Working Paper 18. Vienna: Wirtschaftsuniversität Wien.

Visser, J. (1994). 'Afschaffen van de algemene verbindend verklaring: Lichtzinnige flinkheid?', *Tijdschrift voor Arbeidsverhoudingen/Zeggenschap*, 5 (3): 6–11.

—— (1998). 'The Netherlands: The return of responsive corporatism', in A. Ferner and R. Hyman (eds.) *Changing Industrial Relations in Europe*. Oxford: Blackwell, pp. 283–315.

—— and Hemerijck, A. (1998). *Ein holländisches Wunder? Reform des Sozialstaates und Beschäftigungswachstum in den Niederlanden*. Frankfurt: Campus.

van Waarden, F. (1995). 'Employers Associations', in C. Crouch and F. Traxler (eds.) *Organized Industrial Relations in Europe: What Future?* Aldershot, UK: Avebury, pp. 45–97.

Wallace, H. (1994). 'Rescue or Retreat? The Nation State in Western Europe 1945–1993', *Political Studies*, 42: 52–76.

Wallace, H. (2000). 'Europeanisation and Globalisation', *New Political Economy* 5 (3): 369–82.

Watson, M. (2003). 'Ricardian Political Economy and the "Varieties of Capitalism" Approach: Specialization, Trade, and Comparative Institutional Advantage', *Comparative European Politics*, 1 (2) 227–40.

Weber, S. (ed.) (2001). *Globalization and the European Political Economy.* New York: Columbia University Press.

Weir, M. and Skocpol, T. (1985). 'State Structures and the Possibilities for "Keynesian" Responses to the Great Depression in Sweden, Britain, and the United States', in P. Evans, D. Rueschemeyer, and T. Skocpol (eds.) *Bringing the State Back In.* Cambridge: Cambridge University Press, pp. 107–63.

Weiss, L. (ed.) (2002). *States in the Global Economy: Bringing Domestic Institutions Back In.* Cambridge: Cambridge University Press.

Werner, H. (1996). 'Befristete Zuwanderung von ausländischen Arbeitnehmern', *Mitteilungen aus der Arbeitsmarkt- und Berufsforschung,* 1: 36–53.

Werner, H. (1990). 'Free Movement of Labour in the Single European Market', *Intereconomics* 25 (2): 77–81.

Williamson, P. J. (1989). *Corporatism in Perspective.* Newbury Park, CA: Sage.

Wilson, F. L. (1987). *Interest-Group Politics in France.* Cambridge, UK: Cambridge University Press.

Wirtschaftsblatt (28 October 1995) "Wer hat Angst vor Ausländern?" [Who is afraid of foreigners?]

Wirtschaftsblatt (December 11, 1997). 'Bauindustrie wird auch '98 stagnieren' [Construction sector will stagnate in '98 as well].

Worthmann, G. (1998). *Der Bauarbeitsmarkt unter Veränderungsdruck. Kontrolldefizit in Folge der Transnationalisierung? [The Construction Services Sector Under Pressure to Adapt. A Regulatory Deficit as a Result of Transnationalization?].* Wuppertal, Germany: Wuppertaler Institut für Klimaforschung.

Yamamura, K. and Streeck, W. (2001) (eds.). *The Origins of Nonliberal Capitalism: Germany and Japan in Comparison.* Ithaca, NY: Cornell University Press.

Yamamura, K. and Streeck, W. (2003) (eds.). *The End of Diversity? Prospects for German and Japanese Capitalism.* Ithaca, NY: Cornell University Press.

Yerochewski, C. (1997). 'Le travail illegal dans le collimateur', *Alternatives Economiques,* 145: 26–9.

Zeuner, B. (November 13, 1996). 'Von der Konzertierten Aktion zum Bündnis für Arbeit—Neun Thesen zu einem ökonomischen und politischen Lehrstück', *Frankfurter Rundschau,* p. 5.

Zysman, J. (1977). *Political Strategies for Industrial Order: State, Market, and Industry in France.* Berkeley: University of California Press.

Zysman, J. (1983). *Governments, Markets, and Growth: Financial Systems and the Politics of Industrial Change.* Ithaca, NY: Cornell University Press.

Index